TIMELINES OF NATIVE AMERICAN HISTORY

The bitterness of yesterdays
The painful expectancy of
tomorrows
and yet, another tomorrow.
Blessed by the ~~presence~~ of the
Creator. A present, a gift, to
be sure!
But, today is today.
Rachel L. Murphy
7 Hilda Rd.
Bedford, MA. 01730
275-6824
Purchased May 6, 1999

TIMELINES OF NATIVE AMERICAN HISTORY

THROUGH THE CENTURIES WITH MOTHER EARTH AND FATHER SKY

SUSAN HAZEN-HAMMOND

A PERIGEE BOOK

A Perigee Book
Published by The Berkley Publishing Group
200 Madison Avenue
New York, NY 10016

Copyright © 1997 by Susan Hazen-Hammond
Book design and interior art by Irving Perkins Associates
Map © 1997 by Mark Stein
Cover design and collage by Wendy Bass Design
Cover photographs courtesy of UPI/Corbis-Bettman and Corbis-
Bettman

First edition: July 1997

Published simultaneously in Canada.

The Putnam Berkley World Wide Web site address is
http://www.berkley.com

Library of Congress Cataloging-in-Publication Data

Hazen-Hammond, Susan.
    Timelines of Native American history : through the centuries with
Mother Earth and Father Sky / Susan Hazen-Hammond. — 1st ed.
        p.   cm.
    "A Perigee book."
    ISBN 0-399-52307-3
    1. Indians of North America—History—Chronology.   I. Title.
E77.E395   1997
970.004′97′00202—dc20   96-36559
                                                         CIP

Printed in the United States of America

10 9 8 7 6 5 4 3 2 1

CONTENTS

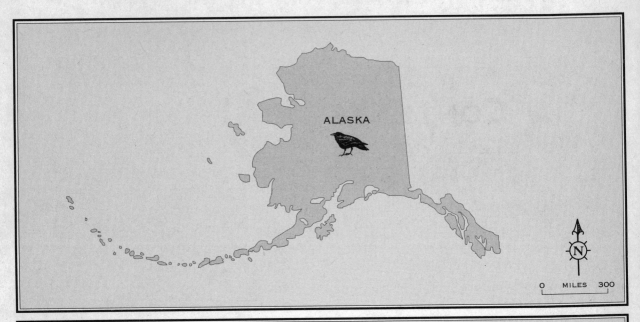

ALASKA

N

0 MILES 300

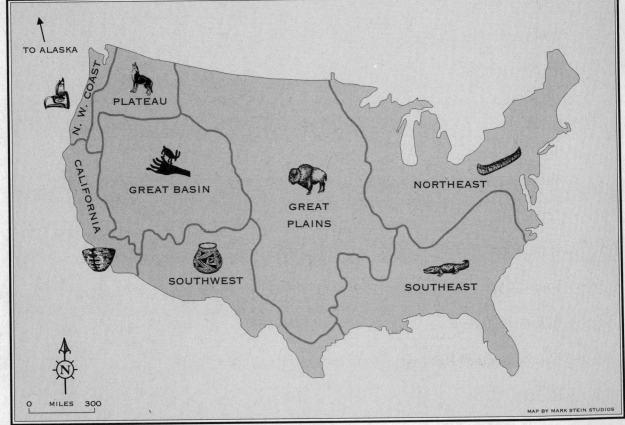

TO ALASKA

N. W. COAST

PLATEAU

CALIFORNIA

GREAT BASIN

GREAT
PLAINS

NORTHEAST

SOUTHWEST

SOUTHEAST

N

0 MILES 300

MAP BY MARK STEIN STUDIOS

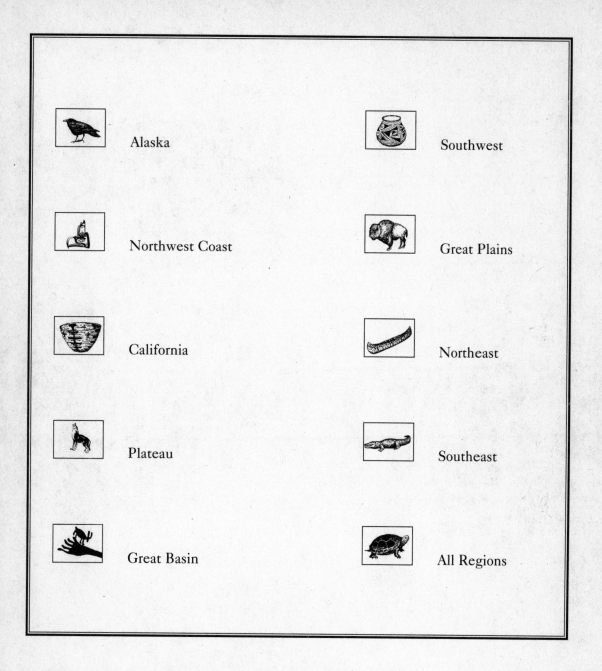

Alaska

Southwest

Northwest Coast

Great Plains

California

Northeast

Plateau

Southeast

Great Basin

All Regions

The symbols above appear throughout this book to indicate which region or regions of the country each of the events occurred in.

INTRODUCTION

—◇—

Today Native Americans in the United States are divided into more than five hundred tribes. They speak two hundred languages. Their traditional lands are broken down into nine geographic regions. They and their ancestors have lived in what is now the United States for probably at least 22,000 years, perhaps many, many thousand years more. What is known of their lives before 1492 forms a long, flowing tapestry full of migrations and settlements, cultural blossoming and cultural decay, peace and warfare, illness and health, life and death, Mother Earth and Father Sky. What is known of their lives since 1492 forms an even more vivid tapestry, one filled with darkness, upheaval, and grief, but with intermittent images of hope, peace, and light.

Although those whose names we don't know and lives we can't see are more numerous than seashells or stars, the story of Native Americans is the story of individual people, operating collectively and independently. It is the story of how the lives of individuals, together and alone, intersect with the forces of history and chance.

In my own family in about the 1830s, my grandfather's great-grandfather was a white New Englander who traced his origins in the United States back to the *Mayflower.* He earned a living as a trapper. He spent his days wandering along the rivers and streams of upper New England, among the birch, pine, and maple trees. Where animals came to the water to drink, he set traps. He skinned otters, foxes, beavers, and other animals. He carried the pelts out of the woods, traded them for food and supplies, and visited family members in Nottingham, New Hampshire. Then he slipped back into the forest. There his only human companions were the Abenaki Indians, whose ancestors had once lived across northern New England, from the Atlantic to Lake Champlain.

One day the trapper met a young Abenaki woman. They fell in love and married in an Abenaki ceremony. Following Abenaki tradition, he settled among her people, where he learned to fish with stone bait greased with moose tallow, eat from dishes of wood and bark, and consider himself, as his wife's people did, one of the Children of the Dawn Country.

Although the details of their life together have vanished, the young couple would have lived in the summer in a pyramid-shaped home made of portable poles and birch-bark sheets and in the winter in a log cabin. While he was out trapping, she wove baskets, made winter moccasins from moose hide, and used spruce roots to attach maple hoops to the rims of her birch-bark containers. During festivities, she may have helped the trapper don a ceremonial moose-skin coat and deer-scalp mask. When someone in the family fell ill, she consulted a shaman. Both listened to storytellers recount how, eons ago, the wife of Kloskurbeh, the Great Teacher, was transformed into the people's first corn.

I like to think that, in spite of the cultural differences between them, they loved each other very much.

Babies born among the Abenaki in the worst part of winter usually died, so probably some of the babies born to the trapper and his Abenaki wife died, but four children survived. Then the trapper's wife became pregnant again.

This time, although the shaman tried to save them, both she and the baby died.

During his marriage to his Abenaki wife, the trapper had had no contact with his parents and siblings. As far as they knew, he was dead. But after his wife's death he gave up trapping, packed up his pelts and some supplies, and began walking toward Nottingham, his half-Abenaki children in tow. With four children to care for, he moved to Boston, where he opened a shop.

It must have been a hard adjustment for the children, who spoke little English and knew only Abenaki ways. At first, they must have missed their mother terribly, and their Abenaki relatives. But gradually they adjusted, and they grew up into conventional New Englanders, steeped in New England values and tastes.

One of those children was my grandfather's grandmother. Although I have searched through family albums and keepsakes, I have not found a photograph or portrait of her. The single item of information that has survived about her in family tradition is that she never reconciled the two sides of herself, the Abenaki and the white New Englander. She never returned to visit her Abenaki relatives, but she always felt torn between her two worlds. She looked at her brown skin and knew she was different, knew there was more to life than white frame houses and city streets. She also knew that her non-Indian neighbors and relatives didn't consider her one of them. So, most of her adult life, she seldom went out, staying home and shunning contact with people beyond her immediate family.

When she died, the memory of the Abenaki stories and traditions she had learned as a child died with her. The only obvious legacy she left was genetic: my grandfather and his sister inherited her high cheekbones and her large build.

My heart breaks to think of this half-Abenaki woman, my ancestor, passing an entire lifetime feeling as if she didn't belong. But beyond that, and the general information available on Abenaki history and culture, I know nothing about her, or about her father and mother and brothers and sisters.

Their faces are gone. Their Indian names are gone. Their likes, dislikes, and idiosyncrasies have all vanished with them. After more than a century and a half, their blood has grown so diluted that there is nothing in my face or hair or skin that hints at their existence. But there is something in me that still connects to those Indian men and women, back in the shadows of my family's past, and to the other Native Americans rumored to be hidden, far back, in the foliage of other branches of my family tree.

This book is dedicated to their memory and to all Native Americans who have lived in what is now the United States over the last 20,000 years or more. It is dedicated to the triumph of human spirit and human will, and to the surviving power of culture, language, and custom, through centuries of upheaval, disaster, and unease.

NOTE TO THE READER

◇

With more than 20,000 years of history and many hundred distinct peoples, it would take a thousand volumes of a thousand pages each to cover all that deserves to be said about Native Americans, present and past. In a short work such as this one, all that can be done is to hint at the range of what has happened and the people and cultures who have lived and died. When you read about one discovery, or one cultural change, in the years before 1492, know that this one example stands for tens of thousands of discoveries and changes. When you read about one brutality in the years after 1492, know that this one cruelty stands for uncountable thousands more. There were times, writing this book, when I spent the whole day weeping.

But know, too, that when you read of one triumph of the spirit, that triumph stands for thousands more.

TIMELINES OF NATIVE AMERICAN HISTORY

Before 20,000 B.C.

 The ancestors of today's Native Americans begin arriving from Asia and spread across the Americas. They come with fire, dogs, a love of beauty, and a deep spirituality. In the New World, they eat mammoths, camels, and other large animals and move frequently from hunting camp to hunting camp.

About 14,000 B.C.

 People move into the Meadowcroft Rockshelter, a sandstone shelter near present-day Pittsburgh. They hunt animals and gather walnuts, black cherries, berries, and other wild fruits. For the next 14,000 years, they leave behind bone, wood, fiber, and other artifacts that tantalize twentieth-century archaeologists.

About 12,500 B.C.

 Hunters leave a projectile point and a blade in a cave in southern Idaho.

About 11,000 B.C.

 Hunters leave projectile points and a hide scraper in a cave in Oregon.

About 10,000 B.C.

 On the Olympic Peninsula of Washington State, hunters leave artifacts behind as they track and kill mastodons in order to feed their families.

THE FIRST NATIVE AMERICANS

 For decades, scholars believed that the first human beings reached North America from Asia no earlier than 10,000 B.C. But archaeologists have pushed that date back. Some say chipped bones and stones prove that people lived here as early as 400,000 years ago. More modest proposals suggest 20,000 to 70,000 B.C. Today many scholars agree that a few humans reached the Americas by 20,000 B.C.

Who were the people who left home and why? Studies of more recent immigration patterns suggest they were probably more adventurous and restless than the people they left behind. They may also have been more desperate. They were probably highly intelligent and may have felt a strong desire to provide a better life for their children and descendants than their ancestors had.

Whoever they were, they may have followed a northern route, walking across a land bridge in the Bering Strait. However, numerous tribal legends of watery origins and floating on water suggest that some traveled by raft across the Pacific. A few writers theorize that others came from Europe or the Middle East. Some Latin American scholars believe that human life began in the Americas and spread from here to other continents.

Dogs

 The first dogs in the Americas are believed to have crossed the land bridge from Asia with the ancestors of today's Native Americans. They were probably wild dogs, and when they reached the Americas, at first they continued to live in packs in the wild.

IN THE BEGINNING

 For centuries, story-tellers among the Bison Path People, the Arapaho of the Great Plains, have told their children and grandchildren an ancient tribal tale of creation.

A very long time ago, only water existed. There was no land anywhere. An Arapaho man floated on the water, all alone except for Seicha, his sacred Flat-Pipe.

The man grew lonely and wailed in his misery.

The ducks heard him crying and flew to him. Then Seicha, who was also the Earthmaker, the Creator, ordered the birds to dive into the water and bring up land.

Again and again, the ducks dove, but they failed to reach the earth at the bottom of the sea. Finally a turtle swam deeper, deeper, deeper into the sea and returned with clay in his mouth.

From that piece of earth, Seicha, the Earthmaker, created the world and everything that lives in it.

 In Florida, hunters kill tortoises by driving wooden stakes into their shells.

About 9500 B.C.

 Clovis culture extends across the continent. Clovis people live in small bands related by family ties and hunt cooperatively in groups. They make tools from antlers, bones, and stones. They chip their spearpoints in a distinctive fluting style.

A talented inventor develops a sophisticated spear thrower, the atlatl, which increases the safety, accuracy, and ease of hunting. Hunters use the atlatl to kill mammoths, mastodons, camels, horses, dire wolves, tigers, and other large game animals.

 In western Missouri, mastodon hunters leave artifacts behind.

About 9300 B.C.

 In south-central Arizona, people hunt horses, tapirs, and ground sloths. They make choppers, knives, and scrapers from coarse-grained basalt.

HOW THE WORLD BEGAN

 Pima (Akimel O'odham) storytellers in Arizona relate how the world began:

In the beginning, there was only water and darkness. In some places, the darkness was thicker than in others; it bunched together and spread apart. One time, at a place where the darkness was thick, a man emerged.

For a long time, the man walked through darkness, until he began to think. He realized that he was a human being and that he had some reason to exist.

He rested his hand across his heart, and a large greasewood stick emerged. It guided him as he wandered in the darkness. He leaned on it when he grew tired.

Then from out of his body, he created ants. From the ants and the greasewood resin, he formed a round ball. He stood on the ball, rolling it under his feet, and sang the song of creation.

As he sang, the ball grew and grew until by the end of his song, the earth was formed.

From within himself, the man pulled out a rock and broke it into pieces. From these, he made the stars, the Milky Way, and the moon. But still he could not see well enough in the darkness. So he made two large bowls. He filled the first bowl with water and covered it with the second bowl.

The water in the bowl turned into the sun.

Four times the man threw the sun into the sky: once to the east, once to the north, once to the west, once to the south. But each time, the sun stayed where it was, unmoving in the sky.

Finally the man threw the sun once more into the east. This time it bounced and started on a journey across the sky. Since then, the sun has moved every day, bouncing every morning out of the east.

About 9000 B.C.

 People live along the shores of Healy Lake in Alaska in a settlement that will be continuously occupied for the next 11,000 years.

Long ago, moose were so tall they grazed on treetops and killed people with their hooves. One day, the Great Spirit sent Kloskurbeh, the Great Teacher, to talk to the moose.

Kloskurbeh took a length of birch bark, rolled it into a horn, and used it to call the moose. At first, the sound of the moose was far in the distance. The next time, it came closer. Finally a moose arrived, with its head high in the trees.

"Bend down," said Kloskurbeh. "I need to make you smaller so that you won't ever hurt people again."

The moose lowered his head, and Kloskurbeh placed his hands between the animal's horns. The Great Teacher pushed and pushed until the moose had shrunk from the height of the treetop to the height of the lower branches. Then Kloskurbeh said, "From now on, never come until you are called." And that is why hunters today use a horn of birch bark to call a moose.

After 9000 B.C.

 Mammoths, mastodons, camels, horses, saber-toothed tigers, dire wolves, and more than two dozen other species of large mammals decline suddenly. Weather changes or overhunting may be responsible. To make up for the food shortage, hunters from Florida to Washington State turn to bison.

Clovis culture begins to fade.

  Folsom culture develops in a broad band from Montana to south Texas. These nomads camp on slopes or crests of hills downwind from watering holes of the animals they hunt: coyotes, antelope, buffalo, and others.

A Folsom inventor studies an eyeless needle made of bone and realizes sewing would be easier if the needle had an eye in it.

About 8800 B.C.

 People living in the Delaware River Valley of Pennsylvania eat seeds, roots, hackberries, wild plums, ground cherries, grapes, blackberries, and other wild foods.

 Bands of hunters from the north and south converge periodically in northern Colorado, leaving behind flint-knapping debris and the bones of antelope, bison, wolves, foxes, and other animals.

HOW THE BIG DIPPER CAME TO BE

 Kiowa storytellers say that once, long ago, a boy and his seven sisters were playing outdoors. Suddenly the boy could not speak. His body trembled, and he fell on all fours. Fur sprouted from his skin, and his toes and his fingers changed to claws. The boy had become a bear.

In terror the seven sisters raced away from this bear who had been their beloved brother. The bear no longer knew his sisters. He chased them, longing to kill them.

The girls reached the stump of what had once been an enormous tree. "Climb me," the stump commanded.

They did, and the tree rose into the air.

At that moment, the bear caught up with them, but the girls were already out of reach. Angrily the bear lashed at the tree trunk and scratched through the bark.

The tree continued to rise until the seven sisters reached the night sky and were transformed into stars.

Once more the boy-bear changed form and became a vast monolith of black rock towering toward the stars.

Today you can see the monolith which in Kiowa is called Tsoai, Rock Tree, rising 1,200 feet above the Belle Fourche River in the Black Hills of Wyoming. And you can see the seven sisters in the seven stars of the Big Dipper.

About 8300 B.C.

  Hunters develop methods for trapping bison by driving whole herds over cliffs or forcing them into box canyons, corrals, and ravines. The techniques survive for nearly 10,000 years, until the 1800s A.D.

About 8000 B.C.

The population of the continent reaches the maximum density that is readily sustainable by a hunting-and-gathering lifestyle.

Across the continent, tribes living hundreds of miles apart develop a trade network for flint, jasper, and chalcedony, which they use to manufacture spearpoints and tools. Another important trade stone is the razor-sharp obsidian.

  East of the Mississippi, Archaic cultures emerge. They stop relying so much on large game. They fish, collect plant foods, or hunt small animals like turtles, turkeys, and squirrels. They use bone, copper, stone, asphalt, clay, and other materials to make items of everyday life. They develop elaborate rituals for burying their dead and sometimes honor domesticated dogs with burial rites. Their lifestyle begins to change in the direction of permanent settlements. For nearly 4,000 years, the old and the new continue side by side, until the new way wins out about 4000 B.C.

   People living in the Great Plains, the Great Basin, and the Plateau begin to use stone tools, the *mano* and *metate*, to grind seeds into flour.

 In eastern Colorado, a single hunting party typically consists of about 150 people from several bands who gather to hunt bison. A shaman performs rituals to help hunters kill bison. On one hunt, they kill 190 bison and collect about 70,000 pounds of meat. The rituals survive for 11,000 years, until buffalo vanish from the Plains in the last half of the 1800s A.D.

 The last ice age ends, raising sea levels worldwide. Water covers the ancient land bridge to Asia across the Bering Strait and creates the Aleutian Islands. Future migrants to the Americas will have to arrive by sea.

The Man Who Scolded the Manitous

Storytellers from the Fox people say that once, long before the white man arrived on the earth, a young man married a beautiful woman. She gave him a son, whom he loved with all his heart. But one day the son fell ill and died. Then the man's beloved wife died, too.

"The Manitous [spiritual powers or supernatural beings] could not possibly have created us," the young man wailed, and he set out to wander the earth. To everything he saw, he gave an offering, to the water, the rocks, the trees, saying, "I give this tobacco to you because I do not know what will become of me." And every night he wailed, "Why, O Manitous, do you create human beings if they are going to die?"

For four years, the young man fasted and wailed and argued with the Manitous.

Finally a Manitou said to him, "You have loved your son and your wife very much. When you finish grieving and lamenting, I will bless you and stay with you as long as the earth remains."

The man stopped mourning, and the Manitou blessed him all the days of his life.

About 7700 B.C.

In the northeastern Great Basin, people make baskets of twine. They collect, store, and cook seeds in the baskets.

About 7000 B.C.

Across the continent, the few remaining mastodons and other large mammals die out; more than thirty species have become extinct.

Along the Colorado River in California and Arizona, Native peoples long ago rearranged earth and stones to create more than 120 figures on the desert floor. Known as geoglyphs, they depict animals, human beings, spirits, gods, and geometric designs.

Of the nearly sixty human figures, the largest measures fifty-two by forty meters; the smallest is lifesize. Animal geoglyphs represent serpents, mountain lions, thunderbirds, and quail.

One geoglyph, which anthropologists call the Fisherman, shows a man holding a spear near a wavy line. Fish swim beneath the line.

Anthropologists estimate that the earliest figures were created about 8,000 years ago, and the most recent in the past 500 years. Native peoples along the Colorado River today relate the geoglyphs to ancient legends. They perform sacred ceremonies ranging from coming-of-age rituals to healing rites at the geoglyph sites.

 In eastern Washington, hunters kill bison, elk, pronghorn antelope, and deer. People also eat freshwater mussels, rabbits, and beavers.

About 6000 B.C.

    The ancestors of the Navajos and Apaches of the Southwest and of the Athabaskan peoples of Alaska, California, and the Northwest Coast move to North America from Asia and settle in the Far North.

 People living in the desert along the Colorado River discover that by moving stones on the desert floor, they can create giant, cameo-like figures of animals, humans, and gods. Twentieth-century anthropologists call these figures geoglyphs.

 Along the Atlantic coast, an inventor develops the toggling harpoon. The swiveling head makes it easier to hunt marine animals.

 In the Great Basin, bison provide 40 percent of the meat. People also eat deer, rabbits, pronghorn antelope, rodents, and wild sheep.

 Plateau peoples move into the Northwest Coast, where they intermingle with peoples who have migrated south from the Arctic. The newcomers fish for salmon, collect shellfish, and hunt for wapiti, seals, and deer.

 Cut off from the mainland, the oceangoing people of the Aleutian Islands develop a separate

THE MOJAVE STORY OF CREATION

 For generations, storytellers among the Mojave Indians of the Colorado River area have told the story of creation:

Long ago, people lived underground, until they had eaten all the food there was. Finally they sent a humming-bird to search for more. It flew into the sky and found a hole that led from the underworld to the upper world. There, in the new world, grew foods of all kinds.

A grapevine connected the world below with the world above. The people who lived underground climbed the vine and moved happily into the new world.

One day, water rose from the underworld into the upper world. It filled canyons and covered hills. It climbed toward the highest mountaintops. No one could stop it. Finally the people chose a beautiful young woman and lay her in a boat built from a hollow tree. They put fruits and blankets in with her and set her afloat on the flood.

Eventually the waters receded, but when the woman climbed out, she was the only person left on earth. Before sunrise, she went to the mountaintops and lay on the earth. The sun warmed her, and water dripped from the rocks, making her pregnant with a daughter. When her daughter grew up, the woman took her back to the same spot, and the sun gave the daughter a son. In this way the world was repopulated.

culture from their cousins on the mainland. They hunt sea mammals using barb-headed harpoons, and they develop their own styles of making scrapers, adzes, knives, and other tools and weapons.

About 5800 B.C.

  Salmon provide a basic food source for the migratory peoples of the Plateau and the Northwest Coast.

NARRAGANSETT

In the beginning, the creator, Cautantowwit, made the first man and first woman from stone. Unhappy with them, he created another man and woman from a tree, and the second couple became the mother and father of all human beings.

Much time passed. The Narragansetts became a people and wandered toward the south and east until they arrived at what is now southeastern New England, where they settled along the coast. They made snares and trapped lynx and deer. They built boats large enough for ten people and caught fish and lobsters. They wove baskets and made mats with bark. They made elegant bows and arrows and shot ducks and other birds. But they didn't shoot crows, because crows had brought the Narragansetts the first corn and beans from Cautantowwit's garden.

Both men and women could be sachems, or rulers, and often two sachems ruled together. When the first white men arrived, Narragansett sachems also governed the Shawomet, Pawtuxet, Coweset, and Niantic peoples. Giovanni da Verrazano, the first European known to have met the Narragansett, reported in 1524, "These people are the most beautiful and have the most civil customs that we have found. . . . Their manner is sweet and gentle."

In the early 1600s, there were approximately 30,000 Narragansett. Smallpox and other diseases killed many. So did conflicts with whites. By 1880, only 324 Narragansetts survived. Except for place-names around Rhode Island and words like "papoose," "powwow," "squaw", and "wigwam," the Narragansett language had died, and much of the culture had been lost. In that year, in a legal process known as detribalization, the Narragansetts lost their identity as a tribe. In 1934, they retribalized unilaterally, and in 1983, the U.S. government again recognized the Narragansett people as a tribe.

Today the 2,400-member tribe owns a little more than 2,000 acres in Rhode Island.

About 5600 B.C.

 In southern Illinois, people begin building permanent homes, using wooden posts, logs, and clay. They eat marsh elder seeds, hickory nuts, fish, mussels, and other foods.

About 5500 B.C.

 Along the southern California coast, people begin to hunt large game less and eat more fish and seeds.

Before 5000 B.C.

 Peoples across the continent begin making baskets to use in gathering, processing, and storing fruits, nuts, and seeds.

 In the Illinois Valley, hunter-gatherers establish permanent communities.

About 5000 B.C.

 Across the continent, the Altithermal, a period of warm, dry weather, begins. It lasts for at least 2,000 years.

 In the Great Basin, lakes recede, leaving food-rich salt marshes.

 In parts of Arizona, residents abandon their arid homeland; it remains unoccupied for 2,000 years.

Thirst and lack of food diminish bison herds. Many animals die; others retreat from the central plains into the stream valleys and foothills.

About 4000 B.C.

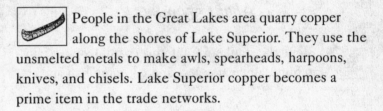 People in the Great Lakes area quarry copper along the shores of Lake Superior. They use the unsmelted metals to make awls, spearheads, harpoons, knives, and chisels. Lake Superior copper becomes a prime item in the trade networks.

In the Plateau region, people spend their winters in pit houses, semisubterranean dwellings that are well insulated from the cold. In the northern Plateau, they camp along riverbanks in the summer and catch salmon. In the spring and fall, they scatter across the hills gathering food.

In the southern end of the Plateau, in the Surprise Valley of northeastern California, people live year-round in earth-covered pit houses. They eat deer, mountain sheep, bison, and antelope and use mortars and pestles to grind nuts.

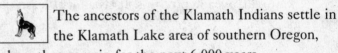 The ancestors of the Klamath Indians settle in the Klamath Lake area of southern Oregon, where they remain for the next 6,000 years.

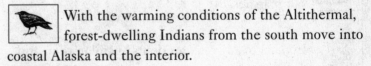 With the warming conditions of the Altithermal, forest-dwelling Indians from the south move into coastal Alaska and the interior.

 In California, hunter-gatherers begin to live in permanent villages.

After 4000 B.C.

 Cultures east of the Mississippi undergo a population explosion as they settle into semipermanent villages and increase their food-gathering activities. Trading with other tribes increases, and burial practices become more elaborate. Life expectancy for women is only thirty, because so many women die in childbirth. About one man in five lives to be over sixty.

About 3500 B.C.

 Domesticated corn arrives in the Southwest from Mexico but remains a curiosity.

About 3000 B.C.

 Along the Snake River of eastern Washington, people grind stones and attach them to their fishing nets for sinkers.

 Residents of the Santa Barbara area hunt bears, deer, elks, seals, and other land and sea animals. They weave baskets and use stone mortars and pestles to grind nuts.

The peoples of central California make fishing spearheads from antlers. They grind stones into long slender objects sometimes shaped like spindles, sometimes like phalluses. They hang these charmstones from branches, probably to provide or symbolize supernatural powers.

QUAPAW

 Eons ago, the Quapaw Nation, the Downstream People, came into existence in the froth of the sea. The sky's breath blew them ashore. For centuries, they wandered, until they settled in villages along the shores of the Mississippi and Arkansas Rivers.

They lived in rectangular homes with elevated beds, wore beads in their noses and ears, and feasted on dog meat before going to war. They shaped clay into pots and incised the pots with designs that represented the movement of the waves in which the People were born. When a man and woman married, the wife presented her husband with an ear of corn; he offered her the leg of a deer.

In the late 1600s, the Downstream People numbered an estimated 20,000. In 1800, only 1,000 survived. By the 1970s, only 5 full-blooded Quapaws remained. Today the tribe lives on in historical documents, legends, place-names, and the memories and genes of more than 2,000 mixed-blood descendants.

Before 2500 B.C.

 The peoples of the Northwest Coast develop techniques for grinding and polishing slate and other stones.

By 2500 B.C.

 Domesticated chile peppers arrive in the Southwest from Mexico. Ancestors of Pueblo Indians decide the culinary volcanoes are too hot to eat.

 Domesticated peppers don't make it into the trade routes, but residents along the Gulf coast eat tiny wild peppers called chiltepíns.

 Domesticated pumpkins, squashes, and gourds reach Missouri and Kentucky.

About 2500 B.C.

 In western Kentucky, men use axes and incisors to do woodwork. They fish. They work leather. Women engrave stones and prepare food. Both men and women use atlatls. Both use the spiritual tools of the shaman, including turtleshell rattles and bone flutes. The Kentuckians import copper from the Great Lakes area and marine seashells from the Florida coast. They bury their dead in a five-foot-deep mound that eventually covers two acres and includes 1,100 people.

Along the North Atlantic coast, fishermen trap fish in weirs made by pounding thousands of stakes into tidal flats and river mouths. At high tide, fish wash inland, over the stakes. At low tide, the fish are stranded and captured.

CROW

 Apsaalooke, the Crow people call themselves: Children of the Large-Beaked Bird.

Centuries ago, a vision instructed an ancestral leader named No Vitals to lead the Apsaalooke farther west to search for a sacred tobacco plant. By the 1600s, the Crow were living in southern Montana and northern Wyoming along the Musselshell, Yellowstone, and Powder Rivers and their tributaries. They farmed and lived in homes of earth and brush. When horses reached the northern Plains, about the 1750s, the Apsaalooke gave up most farming, except for the sacred tobacco, planted by members of the Tobacco Society. The people became migratory, living in tepees and hunting buffalo. At this time, they were probably about 10,000 strong. But the white man's disease, smallpox, arrived soon after the horse. In the first part of the 1800s, the oozing pustules killed approximately half of the population.

Although the Crow received 38 million acres of land in the Fort Laramie Treaty of 1851, settlers and gold seekers invaded Crow territory, and by 1905, the Children of the Large-Beaked Bird had only 2.3 million acres. Subsequently, non-Indians took possession of a million more acres of Crow land.

Today there are approximately 8,500 people enrolled in the Crow Nation; their base is a reservation in south-central Montana.

The Apsaalooke preserve many ancient traditions, including a clan system based on the mother's family ties. From the father's clan come the *aassahke,* or godparents, who give children their sacred Indian names and perform spiritual and sacred functions. Traditional healers using medicine bundles and prayers supplement contemporary Western medicine. The Tobacco Society remains strong, and the Sun Dance has been revived.

Along the coast, people spend summers fishing and move inland during the winter. In southeastern Massachusetts, they live in circular, multifamily homes thirty to forty feet in diameter, built of posts and covered with bark or hides. A larger, similar building measuring sixty-six feet in diameter provides space for community ceremonies and rituals.

In central New York, people build rectangular homes about sixteen feet by thirteen feet and live in semipermanent villages of as many as 150 to 200 people. They fight battles with neighboring groups and sometimes practice ritualistic cannibalism, perhaps of their captives.

In the western Great Basin, people live in caves and brush shelters. They eat tubers, seeds, and roots. They collect shellfish and fish from marshes and use cording and twining techniques to make baskets from rushes. They use the baskets to gather and store seeds. They also weave jugs and trays from the rushes. They make clothes from shredded bark and blankets from rabbit fur. They carry on an elaborate trade with the Pacific Coast and leave behind figurines made of clay, stone, and wood. The figurines depict people, grasshoppers, fish, bears, wolves, and imaginary animals.

At the southern end of the Plateau, in northeastern California, people abandon their old pit houses in favor of less durable domed homes made of brush. This changes the society. In the pit houses, extended families lived together, but the brush wickiups are only large enough to house a single, nuclear family.

As the 2,000-year period of warmer, drier climate ends across the continent, the forest and forest-dwelling peoples of Alaska retreat southward, and the ancestors of today's Eskimos arrive from Asia. Some stay in

Alaska; others migrate eastward across the uninhabited tundra. Those in Alaska separate into two groups and develop separate languages. On the mainland, they speak Inuit. On the Aleutian Islands, the Aleut language develops. People living along the coast dig square pit houses to survive the winters; they live on caribou, salmon, and other fish.

 As the 2,000-year period of drought ends in the Great Plains, grasslands return, and with them the bison. Human population of the Plains grows. People fish, forage, live in rock shelters, and hunt bison.

Before 2000 B.C.

 In Alabama, Georgia, and the Carolinas, people begin making cooking vessels from steatite, a soft stone. Over the following centuries, the new cooking fashion spreads to the Northeast.

In Illinois, people begin to smoke tobacco, using stone pipes.

By 2000 B.C.

 Along the Pacific coast, people live in semipermanent villages. They fish, gather berries, and make tools from bone, wood, and stone.

About 2000 B.C.

In the Northeast, people begin making pottery. They use grass and fiber roots for tempering.

ARAPAHO

Since time began, storytellers say, the Arapaho have called themselves Hinóno'éno', the Sky People, or the Roaming People.

Three thousand years ago, the Sky People lived in year-round villages on the shores of the Great Lakes. But then something—perhaps climate changes, pressures from other tribes, or a longing for the healthier, happier wandering life of their ancestors—caused them to give up their villages and become drifters again. They wandered out into the Great Plains and spread across southeastern Wyoming, southwestern Nebraska, eastern Colorado, and northwestern Kansas. Eventually they split into two related groups, the Northern Sky People and the Southern Sky People.

During the upheavals of the 1800s, as whites moved westward, the Sky People lost their traditional lands. The Southern Arapaho had to move to Oklahoma with the Cheyennes, and the Northern Arapaho went to live with the Eastern Shoshone on the Wind River Reservation in Wyoming.

After losing 4 million acres of reservation land, 3,000 surviving Southern Sky People live scattered across Oklahoma, and 3,500 Northern Sky People share the Wind River Reservation with the Shoshones. Both groups pass ancient traditions on to new generations.

The Price of Becoming Farmers

 In the Southeast, when hunter-gatherers made the transition to farming many hundreds of years ago, their life expectancy decreased. This may have been partly because their diet became less diverse. Moreover, dependence on cultivated crops made them more vulnerable to famine.

 The Indians of California begin using beads made from seashells as currency.

About 1700 B.C.

 In the Northeast, more and more people become farmers. They plant gourds, tobacco, and edible seeds, but they also continue to hunt wild game and collect wild plant foods.

About 1500 B.C.

 A fishing community develops at what is now Cape Alava on the coast of Washington State and remains continuously occupied for 3,000 years, until a mud slide buries it.

People in Michigan, Ohio, and Indiana bury their dead at the summits of hills made from glacial gravel.

About 1200 B.C.

At Poverty Point, Louisiana, people build an elaborate complex of earthen mounds. The largest rises seventy feet high and measures six hundred feet across. Builders also construct six concentric embankments that require 3 million hours of labor. Mound building is so labor-intensive that subsequent generations revert to pre–mound building cultural patterns. Future mound-building practices in the Southwest will come from other sources.

 People living near the shores of the Great Salt Lake move away because the water level has risen, ruining the food-rich marshes.

By 1000 B.C.

 The Indians of the Southeast have made the transition from hunter-gatherers to seminomadic farmers. They cultivate squash, gourds, sunflowers, maygrass, marsh elder, goosefoot, knotweed, and other plants. They grind and polish stones to make tools and ornaments.

On Long Island, people of the Orient culture bury the cremated remains of their loved ones in collective and individual graves at the crest of sand hills. They place spearpoints, steatite utensils, and other objects of everyday life in the graves.

About 1000 B.C.

Domesticated beans arrive in the Southwest from Mexico.

An early geneticist develops a new cultivar of corn that grows well in both the cool highlands of the Southwest and the arid lowlands, and corn becomes an important part of the diet.

 The ancestors of the Arapaho begin migrating away from the Great Lakes out into the Great Plains. They give up their sedentary lifestyle and become nomadic buffalo hunters. Eventually they split into two groups of culturally related peoples, the Northern and Southern Arapaho.

About 900 B.C.

The ancestors of the Mohawk, Oneida, Seneca, Cayuga, and Onondaga peoples become allies in the earliest version of what becomes known as the Iroquois Confederacy.

Musical Instruments

 No matter where they lived or what cultural heritage they followed, Native Americans used musical instruments to accompany their chants and songs. From animal hides and hollowed logs they made drums. From gourds they made rattles. From bird bones they made whistles and flutes.

Ancient Violence

 Between 1000 B.C. and A.D. 500, 10 percent of the population of California died violent deaths, probably as a result of intertribal warfare.

About 500 B.C.

 In the central Ohio Valley, the Adena people hunt and gather wild plants. They live in round, multifamily homes and focus communal energy on constructing elaborate earthen burial mounds. Trade networks extend as far west as Yellowstone and all the way south to the Gulf Coast.

 The peoples of the Northwest Coast begin to evaluate themselves in terms of social status.

 Plateau peoples along the rivers of eastern Washington live in pit houses up to forty feet in diameter and keep domesticated dogs. The customs and culture they have developed will remain stable until the 1800s A.D.

About 300 B.C.

People in the Ohio and Illinois Valleys begin to grow corn, but it remains an incidental crop for another 1,000 years.

In the Gila River Valley of southern Arizona, a new agricultural culture, the Hohokam, emerges. People build canals to irrigate their fields and harvest two crops of corn, beans, and squash a year. They also eat mesquite pods, cactus fruits, and other desert bounty. They make figures from clay, carve stones in the shapes of animals, and make pottery. They live in square houses and cover the pole roofs with brush.

MOUND BUILDERS

  In the central Ohio Valley mound-building practices developed about 500 B.C. and eventually spread across the Northeast and Southeast, but they may have evolved from the earlier custom of burying the dead at the summits of hills. Many of the hundreds of mounds known to exist contain burials. Early mounds in the Adena era were also typically placed inside or near a sacred enclosure in the form of a circle, square, or pentagram. A sacred circle averaged three hundred feet in diameter and may have been used for ceremonial activities.

One notable mound that does not contain a burial is the Serpent Mound of Ohio. The enormous earthen mound is 1,254 feet long and about 5 feet above ground level. It depicts a giant snake with an undulating body and a tightly coiled tail. The snake appears on the verge of devouring an oval object, perhaps a frog or an egg.

The Grave Creek Mound in West Virginia is among the largest of the early mounds: 240 feet in diameter, it rose 70 feet high. One basketful at a time, workers piled up 72,000 tons of earth to create the mound.

The dead were typically buried in the center of the mound, lying on their backs. To accompany the deceased, mourners placed practical items close to the corpses: drills, scrapers, spearpoints, or copper armor. But they also left decorative and symbolic objects, such as shell necklaces, copper bracelets, and trophy skulls. Sometimes they placed carved effigies or engraved tablets with the dead.

When the Hopewell culture replaced the Adena culture about 100 B.C., mound building took on an even larger scale. Some Hopewellian mounds included half a million cubic feet of earth and took 200,000 hours of labor to build. Sites covered as much as four square miles and included elaborate groupings of earthen circles, squares, and octagons.

Burials also became grander, with richer grave goods. In one case, a young woman was buried with thousands of pearl beads and copper-covered buttons made from wood and stone. Three hundred pounds of obsidian chips accompanied one man in death, and another man traveled to eternity surrounded by 3,000 sheets of mica.

About 250 B.C.

Along the river valleys of the Plains, people settle into villages. They cultivate crops and collect wild foods. Culturally they are linked to the peoples of the eastern woodlands.

People of the Plains learn to make pottery from the peoples of the Northeast. Across the northeastern and central Plains, people also adopt the practice of building burial mounds. The largest are about thirteen feet high and one hundred feet in diameter.

About 100 B.C.

The Adena culture of the Ohio Valley gives way to the Hopewell culture. Hopewell peoples continue Adena mound-building practices. Hopewell culture and mound-building practice spread across the Northeast and Southeast.

About A.D. 1

The peoples of western Alaska acquire their first iron tools through trade with Asia.

Twelve centuries after construction of the mounds at Poverty Point, Louisiana, the peoples of the Southeast again build mounds, this time through the influence of the Hopewell culture of the Northeast.

The peoples of the San Francisco Bay area use bone whistles and wear bone pendants. They battle with their enemies and bury shells, coyote teeth, and bear claws with the dead.

By A.D. 100

 Across the Southwest, people from many different backgrounds evolve into a loosely related cultural group known today as the Basket Makers because of their fine baskets.

About A.D. 250

 Influenced by their Hohokam neighbors, hunter-gatherers in southwestern New Mexico and southeastern Arizona settle into communities and create the Mogollon culture. They dig pit houses four feet into the ground and cover the roofs with branches. Each village has a large pit house, the forerunner of kivas, for use in ceremonies. Villagers make pottery and develop distinctive styles of decorating the shaped clay.

The basketmaking peoples in the northern part of the Southwest, the ancestors of the Anasazi, make the transition to village life.

After A.D. 400

 The Hopewell culture declines in the Northeast but continues to flourish in the Southeast.

About A.D. 450

 The early Anasazi domesticate turkeys. Children are assigned the job of herding the birds.

 In the lower Mississippi Valley people modify mound-building practices. No longer used for burials, the new mounds are conical or flat-topped.

TRADE

 Across North America in the centuries before Europeans arrived, Native Americans walked, ran, or traveled by canoe to visit and trade with distant tribes. These tribes in turn traded with others, still more distant, so that items traveled many hundreds of miles from their source.

In the centuries just before and after Christ, the Indians of what is now Wisconsin possessed conch shells from the Gulf of Mexico. Residents of Illinois owned shark's teeth, and one inhabitant of western Michigan owned a pipe shaped like an alligator. In Ohio, people treasured obsidian and grizzly-bear teeth from the Far West.

 In Alaska, trade routes by land and sea ran south to the Northwest Coast, west to Asia, and east to central Canada.

Tall Men

Among the Hopewell people of Illinois, tall men automatically received higher social status than short men. This gave them the right to perform two high-status activities: throwing spears and diving for mussels.

War Clubs

In pre-European days, one of the most popular weapons among warring tribes was the war club. Made of a stone head attached to a short wooden handle, it could break bones and split skulls. As iron became available, warriors switched to short-handled battle-axes.

Birth Rituals

During the final stages of labor, an Athabaskan woman of Alaska would squat or kneel while another woman pressed down on her abdomen to help push the baby out. The newborn's umbilical cord was tied with sinew, cut, and rubbed with soot. A piece of the cord was placed in a medicine bag to prevent harm, and the afterbirth was wrapped in skins and hung in a tree. Following the birth, both mother and father could eat only cold foods, and the father was not allowed to hunt for a month.

About A.D. 500

In the southeastern Great Basin, hunter-gatherers from the Fremont culture live in pit houses and aboveground homes made of stone and adobe. From the Anasazi or Mogollon, they learn to make pottery and grow corn. They and their cultural relatives farther north make unfired clay figurines depicting humans. On rock walls, they paint pictographs that depict larger-than-life figures resembling humans.

The peoples of central California weave elaborate baskets. They heat pieces of baked clay to use in place of stones to make water boil. They begin hunting with bows and arrows and cremating their dead.

About A.D. 550

The Hohokam people of southern Arizona expand from the river valleys into the desert. They exchange trade items and cultural patterns with the peoples living farther south. They make mounds reminiscent of Mexican pyramids and build ball courts two hundred feet long.

After A.D. 600

The peoples of the Great Basin begin hunting with bows and arrows. The new weapons allow them to hunt so much more efficiently that they quickly deplete game supplies.

About A.D. 700

 Perhaps because of the influence of the Hohokam, the Anasazi begin moving from pit houses into aboveground homes of stone, mud, and brush. The ancient pit house survives as a ceremonial structure, the kiva, with sacred and social functions. From the Mogollon, the Anasazi borrow the custom of cultivating cotton and weaving.

Hunters give up the ancient atlatl and dart for the bow and arrow.

From the Mogollon culture, the Anasazi borrow the custom of flattening infants' heads with cradleboards.

 Villages along the Mississippi, Tennessee, Cumberland, and lower Ohio Rivers have a uniform layout. Around a central plaza, temples and residences of the socially elite are built on top of platform-shaped mounds. Less elaborate homes surround the platforms.

After A.D. 800

 An enterprising tinkerer develops a new, cold-hardy cultivar of corn, and Indians of the Northeast begin cultivating it as a major crop.

About A.D. 900

 The Anasazi population expands suddenly, causing a building boom. The largest collection of communities goes up in Chaco Canyon, with eight towns clustered together in the canyon and four more on the nearby mesas. The largest community, Pueblo Bonito, contains eight hundred rooms and is built in a curve

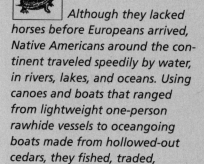

Faster Than Horses

Although they lacked horses before Europeans arrived, Native Americans around the continent traveled speedily by water, in rivers, lakes, and oceans. Using canoes and boats that ranged from lightweight one-person rawhide vessels to oceangoing boats made from hollowed-out cedars, they fished, traded, hunted, and fought wars.

In Virginia, Indians used seashells to scrape out logs and shape them into canoes. Among some tribes along the Atlantic coast, hunters drove animals into the water, where they were attacked by other hunters in canoes.

Chaco Canyon

 Between A.D. 900 and 1100, about 10,000 people are believed to have lived in Chaco Canyon. However, no cemetery has ever been found, causing anthropologists to wonder if the elaborate villages in the canyon were only part-time homes, or served as some kind of administrative center.

Metamorphosis

 In shamanistic cultures like the Athabaskans of Alaska, certain animals, including bears, wolves, lynx, and wolverines, were believed to have the power to change easily into humans and back into animals. Wolves were called grandfathers and bears brothers. When one of these animals was killed, special rituals and ceremonies had to be performed.

around a central plaza. For roof beams, builders bring logs from as far as fifty miles away. The Chaco complex develops a system of seventy outlying communities linked by broad, straight roads.

In Mesa Verde in southwestern Colorado, the Anasazi construct lookout towers and move from the vulnerable mesa top to the more easily defended canyon walls.

Anasazi trade connections extend into Mexico, where the northerners exchange turquoise beads for Mexican macaws and copper bells.

 Athabaskan-speaking Tolowa and Hupa peoples move down from western Canada and settle along the coast of northern California. Meanwhile, the Wiyot and Yurok peoples move in from the east. The easterners ascribe special powers to albino deer skins and the scalps of scarlet woodpeckers.

 The Eskimos (Inuit) of mainland Alaska split into two groups and develop divergent laguages, Inupik in the north and Yupik in southwestern Alaska.

  Farmers from the Northeast migrate into the Great Plains and settle in villages overlooking stream valleys from the Dakotas all the way to Texas. They live in multifamily homes made of earth-covered timber. They hunt with bows and arrows, make pottery, and farm with hoes made from the shoulder blades of bison.

About A.D. 1000

 Along the Northwest Coast, complex societies produce elaborate artwork that is connected to the custom of ranking themselves according to inherited status. Three broad social groups are slaves, commoners, and nobles. The artwork displays the inherited symbols of status and rank in the form of animal figures carved into totem poles.

 In the years before non-Indians arrived, the Iroquois and other peoples of the Northeast defended themselves from attack by outsiders by building a tight fence of stakes all around the village.

The Mimbres culture emerges from the Mogollon tradition of southwestern New Mexico and southeastern Arizona and expands rapidly. Mimbres art reaches its peak with black-on-white pottery. Artists paint the pottery with geometric and representational designs that depict humans and animals. Before burying a piece of pottery with a corpse, the dish is symbolically "killed" by punching a hole through it.

The Hohokam culture stretches across 10,000 square miles. An elaborate system of canals brings water to the desert. Artists use vinegar made from saguaro juice to etch shells acquired in trade from coastal peoples. Burial rituals include cremating the dead.

The Inupik-speaking peoples of Alaska migrate eastward and spread across northern Canada all the way to Greenland, displacing earlier residents, their distant relatives. Some stay behind in Alaska.

People across the northern woodlands live in villages and farm corn and other crops. They also hunt deer and make clothing from the hides.

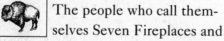 The people who call themselves Seven Fireplaces and eventually become known as the Sioux move into Minnesota and Wisconsin from the Southeast and settle there.

LOVE SONGS

 Across the continent for thousands of years, Native Americans have chanted ancient songs to the beat of a drum. Some songs relate to death and grieving, others to war, healing, and the mysteries of nature. Some speak of love.

CHIPPEWA LOVE SONG

A loon I thought it was.
But it was
My love's
Splashing oar.

MAKAH LOVE SONG

No matter how hard I try
to forget you,
you always
come back to my mind,
and when you hear me singing
you may know
I am weeping for you.

ABENAKI SONG OF LONELINESS

Look oft up the river, look oft and oft.
In spring at the breaking of the ice, look oft;
You may see me coming down in my canoe.
Look oft up the river, look anew, anew.

About A.D. 1050

 In Cahokia, Illinois, mound builders construct about one hundred small mounds and create the largest mound in North America. The terraced earthwork rises 110 feet, covers sixteen acres, and contains more than 21 million cubic feet of earth. The community surrounding the master temple covers five square miles and houses an estimated 40,000 people.

About A.D. 1150

 The climate of the Colorado Plateau grows cooler and drier. The growing season shortens and farming becomes more difficult. The pattern continues throughout the 1200s.

By A.D. 1200

 The ancestors of the Apaches and Navajos migrate southward from western Canada. When they reach the land of the Anasazi, they encounter a stark volcanic formation and name it Tsébida'hi, the sacred Rock with Wings. In the twentieth century, Navajo storytellers will recount that the People flew to the Southwest on the back of Tsebida'hi from the land beyond the setting summer sun.

About A.D. 1200

 The Ponca and Omaha peoples migrate westward from the eastern woodlands into the Great Plains and settle in Nebraska.

RELIGION

 A strong sense of the spiritual and a connection with the divine have pervaded the worldview of the peoples of the Americas for millennia. Most people's lives were rich in rituals.

 In the traditional Bladder Festival of the Inuit of the Bering Strait and elsewhere, the bladders of all the animals that died to feed the people during the previous year dangled from the roof of the communal lodge. After ritual songs and dances, hunters followed a torch made of wild celery stalk through the darkness until they reached a hole that had been cut in the ice. They tore open the bladders and used a kayak paddle to push them, one by one, into the water. As the bladders disappeared in a trail of bubbles, the life-forms that the bladders represented began a symbolic journey of transformation and return from death to life.

 Thousands of miles away, the Carolina village of Secotan performed religious dances that acted out the rituals of mating and warfare. In one dance, warriors and women danced around a circle of poles whose tops were carved in the shape of human heads. Three virgins stood in the center of the circle.

 Before 1492, the peoples of the Americas had developed thousands of ceremonies and rituals, each reflecting the worldview and religious concepts of the people who performed them. Today many of the ceremonies, rituals, and beliefs of the ancient inhabitants of the Americas survive, at least in fragments.

Nowhere are they better preserved than in the Southwest, where Navajo medicine people still perform elaborate ceremonies that typically last four days, and Pueblo Indians still reenact the cycles of the ceremonial year with dances, songs, rituals, and prayers. Among the ancient beliefs that survive at Zuni Pueblo is the tradition that animals, who understand the world better than human beings do, serve as intermediaries between humans and the gods.

 New religious traditions that arose following the European invasion of the Americas ranged from the Handsome Lake religion of the Iroquois at the end of the 1700s to the Native American Church, incorporated in 1918.

About A.D. 1230

 Building activity peaks at Mesa Verde. About 7,000 people live in 1,000 cliff houses. But already, across the Southwest, the Anasazi are beginning to abandon their stone homes.

About A.D. 1250

 The Mississippian community at Cahokia, Illinois, declines. Beside the Black Warrior River in Alabama, another major mound-building town emerges, with about twenty platform mounds and 2,000 inhabitants. Other similar communities develop at the same time in Georgia and eastern Oklahoma.

 A religious cult spreads across the Southeast. Its followers worship the sun and honor sacred fire. Its priests use tools and objects that craftspeople make especially for them. These include axes, in which both the shaft and the blade are carved from a single piece of stone, copper pendants ornamented with depictions of weeping eyes, and shell neck pieces decorated with images of spiders, woodpeckers, rattlesnakes, and fighting cocks. The priests eat from copper plates and drink from cups made of engraved shells.

About A.D. 1275

 Colonists from the Mississippi area settle in southern Missouri and set up a temple town and fortified communities.

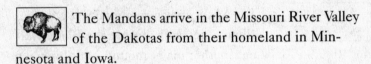

The stone homes of the Anasazi survive in ruins today at Chaco Culture National Historical Park, Mesa Verde National Park, and thousands of other excavated and unexcavated sites. Because Anasazi is a Navajo word meaning Enemy Ancestors, the Anasazi's descendants hope to replace the name with the term Puebloan Peoples.

A.D. 1276

A severe drought destroys crops in the Colorado Plateau and contributes to the growing exodus of the Anasazi from their stone villages. The drought lasts until 1299.

Before A.D. 1300

The Mandans arrive in the Missouri River Valley of the Dakotas from their homeland in Minnesota and Iowa.

About A.D. 1300

Speakers of Numic languages—Monos, Paiutes, Panamints, Shoshone, Kawaiisu, and Utes—migrate out of southeastern California and spread northward and eastward across the Great Basin. They push out the Fremont culture peoples, who vanish, leaving behind elaborate rock art.

The Chumash of California fish in plank canoes and build circular homes from poles and reed mats. They perform rituals in partly buried sweat lodges and carve bowls from steatite and sandstone. Their artwork includes steatite sculptures depicting whales, canoes, and other important elements of Chumash life.

The Iroquoian peoples live in longhouses in clans traced through their mothers.

ART

 Across North America, art was an important part of life in pre-Columbian days.

 In California, people wove intricate designs into baskets. They created temporary art by painting their skin or using colored sands to form sandpaintings. They sculpted stones into the shapes of animals and birds. They painted designs on pottery, clay figurines, and rocks. They used bits of shell to form intricate patterns on wood.

 In the Southeast, Native American artists embossed copper plates. They engraved shells with images of snakes, people, eagles, falcons, and pumas. Sometimes they drew fantastic creatures they had seen in visions or dreams.

 In Alaska, the Inuit used the raw material at hand—driftwood—to carve some of the most elaborate and inventive masks the world has ever seen.

The cultural upheavals that followed the arrival of Europeans produced a decline in Native art traditions, but in the twentieth century they have revived. Today Native American artisans sell their arts and crafts at festivals, open-air markets, powwows, shops, and galleries to buyers from around the world. Some of the finest artists painting and sculpting in the U.S. today are Native Americans.

SLAVERY

 Across the continent, people from one cultural group sometimes captured and enslaved members of other groups.

 In the Southwest, Navajos or Pueblo Indians sometimes had Plains Indian slaves.

 In Alaska, Athabaskan Indians like the Tanaina sometimes captured Inuit (Eskimos) for slaves. Such slaves could be traded to other tribes, or traded back to their own people and freed.

 Along the Northwest Coast, when a new longhouse was built, a slave was sacrificed by being crushed under a house post. Slaves were also killed when a visiting chief arrived by canoe: the slave served as a "roller" for the canoe as it came ashore. Special stone clubs carved in the shape of animals were also used to kill slaves.

About A.D. 1325

 Mississippian colonists in Missouri abandon the colony. They pack their possessions, burn down their homes, and leave.

About A.D. 1350

 Keresan-speaking Pueblo peoples arrive in the Rio Grande region and settle along the river among Tanoan-speaking Pueblo people.

LANGUAGES

 Before 1492, the inhabitants of the Americas spoke an estimated 2,000 different languages, as well as numerous dialects of the same language. About 250 of these languages are still spoken in the United States and Canada. Linguists group them into loosely related clusters called language families, such as Athabaskan, Iroquoian, Siouan, and Uto-Aztecan. Even so, scholars use the great diversity in language as confirmation of the theory that there is not one single common ancestry or one single common history for the country's early inhabitants, but many.

Rich and complex, full of metaphor, symbolism, and nuance, Native American languages often distinguish carefully between animate and inanimate. They make precise distinctions among those parts of the world to which a person is connected: between relationships one is involved in by definition—with family, for instance—and relationships that are random or incidental, such as one's connection to possessions like hide scrapers or knives. They add prefixes and suffixes to show location, such as above, below, within, or beside. They duplicate nouns and verbs to express nuances in meanings: for instance, in the Washoe language of the Great Basin, *gusu* refers to buffalo; *gususu* means "buffalo here and there."

Like languages everywhere, the Native American languages reflected and molded their speakers' worldviews. When the culture changed, the meanings of words changed. For instance, when Navajos moved from Alaska and Canada to the Southwest, they used an old word for snowflakes in a new meaning: seeds for planting. And when Navajo "code talkers" devised a code to mystify the Japanese during World War II, they used traditional Navajo words in completely new ways.

 Similarities in languages suggest cultural connections between tribes living thousands of miles apart. The Yurok and Wiyot of California spoke languages related to the Algonquian languages of the Northeast.

 In the Plateau region as in other parts of the continent, languages united widely scattered tribes and separated close neighbors. The Yakima, Umatilla, Tenino, and Nez Perce Indians spoke Sehaptin languages. Some Indians of the Columbia River Valley spoke Chinookan, related to languages in California and the Northwest Coast. The Kalispel, Flathead, and Wenatchi Indians spoke Salishan languages.

 Among the Pueblo Indians of the Rio Grande in New Mexico, the two northernmost villages, Taos and Picurís, and the two southernmost villages, Sandía and Isleta, speak Tiwa. San Juan, Santa Clara, San Ildefonso, Pojoaque, Nambe, and Tesuque speak a related language, Tewa. The Jemez people speak another related language, Towa. But Cochiti, Santo Domingo, San Felipe, Zia, Laguna, and Acoma speak Keresan, a completely unrelated tongue. And only the Zuni people speak the Zuni language.

Before A.D. 1400

After centuries of constructing apartment-building villages, the Anasazi have completely abandoned Chaco Canyon, Mesa Verde, and other sites around the Southwest. Twentieth-century anthropologists say many Anasazi moved to Hopi and Zuni territory to the Rio Grande and its tributaries in New Mexico, where they became known as Pueblo Indians. Apaches say the Anasazi left the earth and moved to the Big Dipper. Navajos say the Anasazi learned the secret of life and were destroyed.

About A.D. 1400

The Wiyot, Yurok, Karok, Hupa, and Tolowa peoples of the northern coast of California live in plank houses and emphasize prestige and riches like the peoples of the Northwest Coast.

Farmers from southwestern Minnesota and northwestern Iowa move to the Dakotas and develop a culture known as Middle Missouri. They live in rectangu-

According to oral history, sometime in the early 1400s, a pregnant young Huron woman received omens that she should kill her baby, because otherwise great harm would befall her people. When her son was born, she and her mother broke a hole in the ice and tried to drown the infant. Three times they tried. Three times he survived. So they let him live. His name was Dekanawida.

As a young man, Dekanawida earned a reputation for his wisdom and his supernatural powers. When he reached adulthood, he left home and joined the Iroquois. Among them, he became known as a lawgiver and prophet. With Hiawatha, Dekanawida helped to reform and strengthen the Iroquois Confederacy.

Later, when the reinvigorated Iroquois League crushed the Hurons, the prophecy that Dekanawida's mother had tried to avoid came true.

lar houses up to sixty-five feet long, war with surrounding peoples, and scalp their enemies.

About A.D. 1450

Hiawatha, an Onondaga chief, strengthens the ancient League of Five Iroquois Nations, or League of the Five Great Fires, which unites the Cayuga, Seneca, Onondaga, Oneida, and Mohawk Tribes.

1492

Before Columbus arrives, an estimated 2 to 8 million people inhabit what will eventually become the United States. Separated by language, customs, and religion into hundreds of distinct groups, frequently with relatively little in common, Native Americans often call their own cultural group, simply, People. Dineh, for instance, the Navajo word for Navajos, means "the People." Kiowa means "Principal People." Cherokees call themselves *ani yun wiya*, "Real Human Beings." Delawares name themselves Lenni Lenape, meaning "True People."

Approximately 40 million bison roam the open spaces of the continent.

In boats made of driftwood frames and walrus hides, the ancestors of today's Iñupiat (Inuit or Eskimos) hunt walrus and whales with a toggle harpoon. They use tools of bone and antlers to cut blocks of snow with which to build winter houses or insulate wooden summer houses for winter use. Here they spend the long, sunless winter. When light returns after winter's darkness, the people connect several of these houses to form one large ceremonial space. They sing, dance, and celebrate the mysteries of light and dark, life and death, human and divine.

Meanwhile, their non-Iñupiat neighbors, the Athabaskan Indians in the Far North, fish with weirs. They hunt with snares or bows and arrows. They make clothes from animal hides. Using birch-bark or caribou-skin canoes while on water, and sleds while on land, they travel across vast, empty spaces in shifting bands connected by kinship. As children, they go on solitary vision quests in which a spirit guide appears and gives them sacred gifts of song and dance.

More than 100,000 people live along the Northwest Coast, making it one of the most densely populated parts of what is now the United States. They live in multifamily cedar houses that are typically sixty-five feet long and thirty-five feet wide. They possess steel adzes and steel knives, perhaps scavenged from wrecks of Asian ships. They raid other tribes and capture slaves. They build cedar canoes forty-five feet long and six feet wide and hunt each spring in the open ocean for whales and fur seals, sometimes in heavy fog. Whole villages move seasonally to freshwater fishing stations when the salmon swim upstream to spawn; the pink flesh of the salmon, fresh or dried, feeds families year-round. People define social status partly through the ability to amass and then give away material wealth in rituals known as potlatches. Superb artists, the people carve masks, rattles, drums, and spirit figures from the wood of the forests all around them. Shamans perform curing ceremonies for the ill, whose sicknesses are believed to come from soul loss, or spirit loss.

While the peoples of the Northwest Coast enjoy a mild climate year-round, their neighbors in the interior, between the Cascade and Rocky Mountains, live in a climate that ranges from more than 100 degrees Fahrenheit in the summer to below 20 degrees in the winter. In some areas, only eleven inches of rain fall a year.

Menstrual Huts

In some cultures, a girl had to move into a specially constructed hut when she experienced her first menstruation.

 Among Athabaskan groups of Alaska, she could eat only cold foods, had to wear a special hood and mittens, and had to drink water through a tube made from bone. In some villages, the hut was attached to the main house, and the girl stayed secluded for only a few weeks. In others, the hut lay half a mile from the village, and the girl lived in solitude for a full year. Typically other women brought the girl food and trained her in domestic duties and arts. When the puberty rituals ended, a girl returned to her family and married.

NATCHEZ CULTURE

The Natchez people of the lower Mississippi Valley lived in an elaborately hierarchical society. A supreme chief, the Great Sun, ruled, along with his younger brother, the Tattooed Serpent. The Great Sun's other relatives were called Suns; only they could become subrulers. Below the Suns were Nobles, below them Honored People, and at the bottom were Commoners.

An unusual feature of this rigid hierarchy was that the upper classes were required to marry Commoners. The children of high-class women retained their mother's social status, but the children of high-class men became members of the class one step below their father's. Commoners could also improve their social status during warfare.

The Great Sun's feet never touched the earth. He either walked on mats or was carried in a litter. Only he and a few priests could enter the temple where the sacred fire burned. The Great Sun's people paid their taxes in food that fed the Great Sun. When the Great Sun died, his wives were sacrificed and buried with him.

During the winter, people live in villages in the valleys, beside rivers and lakes. When they leave their homes to hunt, collect wild foods, or fish, they camp in caves and natural shelters created by rocks, or they build temporary shelters of poles and mats. Unlike the peoples of the coast, they acquire or create only those possessions that they need in daily life: quivers made of animal skins, in which to keep their arrows; baskets for collecting and storing food; mats made from cattails; flaking kits for making arrowheads; canoes for fishing and transportation; tools made of elk antlers. Year-round, men and women clean themselves physically and spiritually by taking sweat baths. During the winter, they celebrate religious ceremonies, to which they invite people from other villages. Both women and men may become shamans, and throughout life, each person receives assistance from a guardian spirit, who first appears during a solitary spirit quest before puberty.

 Mandans, Hidatsa, Pawnees, Omahas, and others live along streams and rivers. They grow corn, squash, tobacco, beans, sunflowers, and other crops. Lacking horses, they hunt buffalo and other animals on foot. Many live in large villages, with houses built close together to discourage enemies from trying to steal the food they have preserved and stored. To protect themselves from other enemies—summer's heat, winter's cold, and the howling wind—they build log homes covered with earth. From buffalo hides, they make small boats so light a person can carry one on his or her back. Like other peoples across the continent, they are deeply spiritual and have rituals that pertain to every part of life. One, the Okeepa ceremony of the Mandans, takes place at midsummer, for four days. A stranger, Lone Man, arrives and tells the listening crowd all the stories of the People. Dancers dress as buffalo, grizzly bears, vultures, wolves, swans, and rattlesnakes, and young men undergo tortures in order to be admitted to the sacred Buffalo Bull Society.

 The Shoshone people live scattered across the sparsely populated Great Basin from western Wyoming to the eastern fringes of California. The land they inhabit is dramatic but austere, and they must work constantly to survive. They migrate from one hunting or food-gathering camp to another and use their creative energies for practical tasks like making snowshoes and weaving baskets. In spring, they trap groundhogs, ground squirrels, and sage grouse. In late summer, they gather berries. In fall, they harvest piñon nuts and hunt pronghorn antelope, stalking the animals on foot and driving them into concealed corrals. When other foods grow scarce, they eat ants, rattlesnakes, crickets, and horned lizards.

The Shoshones' neighbors in the Great Basin, the Utes and Paiutes, also develop inventive ways of using the sparse gifts of nature. They tan deer hides with animal brains. They create duck decoys to lure birds within range. They build irrigation canals to water crops that grow wild.

 More than two dozen Indian nations fill the deserts, mountain valleys, and coastal regions of what is now California. Divided into clans, moieties, and lineages, they are tribes in a social and cultural sense more than a political sense. They speak sixty languages and use shell beads as money. Among sedentary cultures, villages average about one hundred residents, and hereditary chiefs are responsible for arranging trade meetings, ceremonial feasts, and alliances with neighbors. Although they grow no food crops, the hunter-gatherers of California cultivate tobacco.

The Luiseños, a coastal-dwelling people in the south, fish and gather acorns, which they store in elevated granaries made of branches and grass. Food is plentiful, and women

Sweat Lodges

 Across the continent, many cultural groups used sweat lodges for physical and spiritual purification.

 Among the Athabaskan people of the Alaska Plateau, for instance, the sweat lodge consisted of a small, skin-covered shelter. Water was thrown on heated stones, producing steam. The moist air cleaned the body, drove away mosquitoes and blackflies in summer, and moistened the skin and lungs during winter's aridity.

War Shields

Across the Great Plains, many warriors carried circular shields made of buffalo hide. Typically a warrior would bring an unpainted shield to a medicine man or woman, who would seek visions of an animal that would protect the warrior. Then the medicine person would paint the animal on the shield and return it to the warrior.

BUFFALO

If bread was the staff of life to Europeans, buffalo was the life-giver to the Indians of the Great Plains. The meat was the single most frequent item on their menu, year-round. The hide provided robes and coverings for tepees. It also served like money in trading with other tribes and with non-Indians. People who lived near waterways made one-person boats from the hides. Shaped like tubs, the boats were light enough to carry.

The animal's stomach and intestines became containers used in storing, transporting, and cooking. The bones became tools. Where other fuels were scarce, buffalo dung kept campfires burning.

Among the seven divisions of Sioux, hunters belonging to the Buffalo Society performed rituals to ensure that the buffalo would arrive and the hunts would go well.

When buffalo robes became fashionable in the East, white hunters swarmed across the Great Plains and began exterminating the sacred animal. Between 1871 and 1881, they killed more than 10 million, leaving the carcasses of the shaggy, humped life-givers to rot. By the time the white marauders had finished, the buffalo was nearly extinct.

use their spare time on comfort-oriented tasks like repeatedly rinsing acorn pulp to remove the bitter taste. But life is not soft. In order to teach courage and the ability to endure great pain, the Luiseños subject their young people to intense rites of passage. In one, a teenage boy must lie motionless and silent in a pit while ants crawl across him and bite him.

Farther north, around present-day Santa Barbara, the Chumash people make oceangoing canoes, from which they harpoon otters, sea lions, and seals. At this moment in history, the culture of the Chumash is at its peak. They perform elaborate spiritual rituals honoring swordfish, barracudas, bears, and other creatures of the earth, sea, and sky. They weave fine baskets, carve soapstone into bowls and figurines, and decorate cooking utensils with mother-of-pearl inlay.

For two centuries before 1492, what is now the Southwest has seen great upheaval and change. Village-dwelling Pueblo peoples have abandoned Mesa Verde, Chaco Canyon, and other spiritual and secular centers and have moved into communities along the Rio Grande and its tributaries and onto the Hopi mesas. They weave, coil clay into fine pottery, perform elaborate ceremonial rituals, and live in communities divided into Summer People and Winter People. They grow corn, beans, squash, cotton, and tobacco.

Meanwhile, Athabaskan-speaking peoples from Alaska and Canada, the ancestors of today's Navajos and Apaches, have become well-established in their new homeland. Navajos live in the region bounded by four sacred mountains: Blanca Peak, Mount Taylor, the San Francisco Peaks, and La Plata Mountains. In a rich storytelling tradition, they recount the lives of the Holy People and assign spiritual meanings to the lava flows, volcanic cones, mesas, valleys, and mountains around them.

Other peoples of the Southwest grow cotton, harvest the fruits of the desert, and walk hundreds of miles each year on yucca-fiber sandals along the Gila, Verde, Hassayampa, and Colorado Rivers.

As in other parts of the continent, the environment determines many aspects of the lives of the peoples of the rivers and woodlands of the Northeast. In the winter, they walk on snowshoes, fish through the ice, stalk deer, and repeat the stories of their ancestors around the fire. In the spring, those who live near birch trees peel the thick spring bark and use it to make canoes with which they can travel quickly across lakes and on rivers. As the weather warms, they plant corn, squash, beans, and other crops.

RULES OF WARFARE

Native Americans in each region of the country followed different customs of warfare.

In northern Florida in the 1500s, warring tribes customarily stopped fighting at nightfall. To torch stockaded villages, archers attached moss to their arrows, set it on fire, and aimed at their enemy's rooftops. To declare war, they decorated arrows with locks of hair and planted them outside an enemy's village. When a warrior died, his widow cut her hair and scattered it across his grave; she would not remarry until her hair grew out again.

In the Southwest, Chiricahua Apaches allowed young boys to come along as apprentices during raids on white travelers and settlements. The boys had to learn a special war language and follow taboos and traditions closely. In order to drink water, they had to use a hollow reed; if they itched, they had to use a special scratching stick painted with lightning designs.

Among the Indians of the northern Plains, one rule of battle was to give the enemy a chance for an equal fight. In one recorded fight between a Mandan leader on foot and a Cheyenne chief on horseback, the Cheyenne dismounted. The Mandan fought with a tomahawk, the Cheyenne with a knife. After they had repeatedly wounded each other, the Mandan saw that his opponent was beaten and allowed him to escape.

For many warrior tribes, behind the rules and rituals of warfare lay the sentiment found in a Blackfeet song:

It is bad to live to be old
Better to die young
Fighting bravely in battle.

Algonquian-speaking peoples of New England devise a popular dish of mixed vegetables which, five hundred years later, will still carry its Algonquian name: succotash.

Periodically people burn the meadows and the underbrush so that grass will sprout and attract deer. Those in the eastern part of this vast, varied territory also burn their fields and hoe the ashes back into the earth. Often men clear the land, and women farm. Many people live in matrilineal communities, in which the rights to farming land are passed down through the mother, and the oldest woman living in a communal longhouse rules as Clan Mother. Some villages hold as many as 2,000 residents, but in general, even heavily populated areas contain only an average of five people per square mile, while inhospitable areas support only five people per ten square miles.

 Across the Southeast, many people live among the ruins of the Mississippian Society, which centered around fortified towns and ceremonial sites and showed heavy influence from Mexico. The Muskogean-speaking peoples still erect ceremonial buildings on low mounds and still burn sacred fires in ceremonial plazas. In the Natchez communities of the lower Mississippi, people still live in a complex society composed of four classes. Members of the three higher classes must still marry into a lower class. Children inherit the class of their mother, but men rule. When a ruler dies, his wives must die with him, and leadership passes not to his son, but to his sister's son.

Farther east, in Florida, agriculturists in the north share the peninsula with hunters and gatherers in the south, and both live in complex societies. A single chief rules as many as fifty villages, and public works include mounds, platforms, and walkways decorated elaborately with shells.

 In order to approach a deer, hunters in Florida would sometimes don a deer skin, complete with head and antlers, and creep on all fours to a water hole. His scent and form hidden by the animal skin, the hunter could shoot a deer at close range with bow and arrow.

Men's Work, Women's Work

 Among the Tanana of the Alaska Plateau, men did the cooking. They roasted meat directly over flames or dropped hot stones into birch-bark containers to boil food. When food was scarce, they made soup by boiling broken bones. Meanwhile, Tanana women were in charge of hauling heavy loads by sled.

By 1500

  Residents of mound-building communities in Illinois, Georgia, and eastern Oklahoma abandon their homes and resettle in scattered small villages.

1500s

 Pushed out by larger tribes from the north and the east, the Tsitsista (Cheyenne) people move slowly southward and westward from what is now Minnesota.

About 1500

 The Mandans of the Dakotas reach the height of their cultural powers.

1513

 Florida Indians befriend Spanish explorer Juan Ponce de León when he lands in Florida and searches for the Fountain of Youth.

1521

 After too many brutal encounters with Europeans, Florida Indians attack their former friend, Spanish explorer Ponce de León, who dies of complications from an arrow wound.

1522

 Chicora, a Carolina or Yamassee Indian, is kidnapped by the Spanish and taken the next year to Spain. His accounts of native lifeways are preserved for posterity.

1524

 Indians along the Atlantic coast observe the arrival of an outsider, Giovanni da Verrazano, an Italian sailing for the King of France. As the stranger works his way up the coast from what is now Wilmington, North Carolina, some tribes welcome him, but others flee or warn him away with a shower of arrows.

1528

 Tribes across Texas and southern New Mexico encounter their first non-Indians in the form of four shipwreck survivors walking on a random, zigzag journey that eventually takes them to Mexico.

1534

 Iroquois Indians meet their first non-Indian, French explorer Jacques Cartier.

1539

 Unhappy at being bullied, the Zuni people execute Estevanico, a black traveling with a party of Spanish explorers.

Medicine Bundles

 People from many different tribes carried a leather pouch that came to be known to non-Indians as a medicine bundle or medicine bag. A typical medicine bundle contained objects that represented or embodied power: eagle feathers, a bear's claw, a swatch of fur. Among the Potawatomi of the Great Lakes region, a thunder medicine bundle gave the owner the strength contained in thunder, a power so strong it carried messages between heaven and earth.

Hairstyles

 Among the Tanaina of southern Alaska, men wore their long hair loose, tied back in knots, or in a long braid which they greased and covered with feathers and down. Women wore their hair loose or braided it into two strands.

1540–42

 Many Native peoples of the Southeast meet Europeans for the first time as Hernando de Soto travels from Florida to the Mississippi and into Arkansas and Oklahoma. Alternately making treaties and fighting, he leaves a legacy of anxiety and mistrust.

  The Native peoples of Arizona, New Mexico, Texas, and Kansas meet large numbers of non-Indians for the first time as Francisco Vázquez de Coronado and three hundred Spanish men and women search for the fabled Seven Cities of Gold. Pueblo peoples protest when they discover the outsiders expect to be allowed to rape Native women. The Tiquex people fight the Spanish and are destroyed.

1542

 Indian peoples along the coast of California and Oregon encounter their first non-Indian in the form of explorer Juan Cabrillo.

1550

At Ozette on the Pacific coast of Washington, a mud slide seals a Makah village intact. Wooden boxes, harpoons, art objects, baskets full of food, and entire longhouses made of cedar planks disappear into the mud.

1560s

 King Outina, ruler of forty Indian villages in Florida, allies with French newcomers to fight his ancestral enemies, including Indians under Chief

WA-HUN-SEN-A-CAWH

Wa-hun-sen-a-cawh grew up in what is now Virginia as the son of an exceptional leader: an Indian from Florida or the West Indies who emigrated to Virginia, joined an Algonquian tribe, and persuaded the Algonquian tribes to unite, sometime around the year 1600. At his father's death, Wa-hun-sen-a-cawh expanded the confederacy to include two hundred villages.

Once a year Wa-hun-sen-a-cawh visited each village in the confederacy in person. It is said that on these visits, he wore a deer skin robe, to which seashells were sewn in intricate designs. Non-Indian observers said later that he had the power of life and death over every person in the thirty-two tribes under his rule.

When English settlers founded Jamestown in 1607, they renamed Wa-hun-sen-a-cawh Powhatan and called the Algonquian confederacy the Powhatan Confederacy. Famous among non-Indians as much for being the father of Pocahontas as for his leadership of the Algonquians, Wa-hun-sen-a-cawh, at Pocahontas's request, allowed colonial leader John Smith to live. But he was not simply an indulgent father. He wanted to live in peace with the white newcomers.

Even so, Algonquians and Virginia settlers skirmished repeatedly over the years. But again and again, when Wa-hun-sen-a-cawh could have attacked and destroyed the tiny English settlement at Jamestown, which numbered only 150 in 1610, he didn't. After whites took Pocahontas hostage in 1613, Wa-hun-sen-a-cawh agreed to her marriage to John Rolfe to help preserve the peace.

Potanou. Then Indians in Florida watch Europeans battling each other as the Spanish wipe out a French outpost and establish St. Augustine.

1585

The Indians of Virginia welcome a newcomer, Sir Richard Grenville, as he and a band of explorers

The Spaniards Meet the Hopi

 "The [Hopi] people are very healthy. The men cover their privy parts with a piece of cloth similar to a hand towel, figured with tassels. When they feel cold, they wear cotton blankets. The women are always well dressed and have their hair done up in puffs. Their houses are of stone and mud, small, which is due to the lack of lumber. . . . The greatest handicap in this land is the lack of water . . . which the inhabitants obtain from very deep wells."
—Spanish explorer Diego Pérez de Luxán, among the Hopi in what is now northeast Arizona, April 1583

press inland. But the Indians learn the true nature of the outsiders when one Indian takes a silver cup belonging to Grenville, and the explorer burns and plunders an entire village.

Indians of North Carolina watch uneasily as the English try to establish a permanent colony on Roanoke Island.

1598

 The life of the Pueblo Indians of New Mexico changes permanently when Don Juan de Oñate and a group of Spanish colonists move into northern New Mexico. The newcomers introduce new crops, including wheat, melons, apples, peaches, apricots, chile peppers, and pears. Used to luxury and comforts back home, the colonists require Indians to work for little or no pay as servants. Franciscan missionaries disrupt traditional religious practices in their zeal to convert the Pueblo peoples to Christianity.

1599

 In a brutal, uneven battle, the people of Acoma Pueblo are defeated by Spanish soldiers. Acoma prisoners are maimed and sentenced to twenty years of slavery. Pueblo tribes talk among themselves about uniting to throw the Spanish out.

Throughout the 1600s, 1700s, and 1800s

 From the 1600s on, as Native peoples across the continent find themselves forced to deal with the intrusions of non-Indians, they are required to participate in the ritual of making treaties, sometimes willingly, more often unwillingly. Nation after nation learns to its grief that white people honor treaties only when they feel like

WARNING AT JAMESTOWN

 In 1609, Wa-hun-sen-a-cawh, leader of the Powhatan Confederacy, spoke with Captain John Smith of Jamestown:

"I wish . . . that your love to us might not be less than ours to you.

"Why should you take by force that from us which you can have by love? Why should you destroy us, who have provided you with food? What can you get by war? We can hide our provisions, and fly into the woods; and then you must consequently famish by wronging your friends. What is the cause of your jealousy? You see us unarmed, and willing to supply your wants, if you will come in a friendly manner, and not with swords and guns, as to invade an enemy.

"I am not so simple, as not to know it is better to eat good meat, lie well, and sleep quietly with my women and children; to laugh and be merry with the English; and, being their friend, to have copper, hatchets, and whatever else I want, than to fly from all, to lie cold in the woods, feed upon acorns, roots . . . and to be so hunted, that I cannot rest, eat, or sleep. In such circumstances, my men must watch, and if a twig should but break, all would cry out, 'Here comes Captain Smith'; and so, in this miserable manner, to end my miserable life; and, Captain Smith, this might be soon your fate too, through your rashness and unadvisedness.

"I, therefore, exhort you to peaceable councils; and, above all, I insist that the guns and swords, the cause of all our jealousy and uneasiness, be removed and sent away."

it. White people consider themselves superior to Native peoples. Whites see Native peoples either as an obstacle to be eliminated or as a workforce to be exploited. And whites consistently demand that Indians accept the white man's God and worship the white man's way.

POCAHONTAS

 As a child, the daughter of Wa-hun-sen-a-cawh (Powhatan) acquired the name Pocahontas, an Algonquian word meaning "frisky." Soon after the 1607 founding of Jamestown, the first permanent English settlement in the Americas, Pocahontas entered history in scenes replayed repeatedly in literature, history books, and films. When her father's bodyguards were about to kill John Smith, a Jamestown leader who was their prisoner, the thirteen-year-old girl threw herself forward and protected him with her body. Her father released Smith, who called the beautiful Indian teenager "the instrument to preserve this colony from death, famine and utter confusion."

In 1613, the governor of Virginia held her hostage, hoping to barter her for English prisoners held by her father. Colonists renamed her Lady Rebecca and baptized her a Christian, but she remained frisky. She took off the scratchy English clothes and turned handsprings naked in the streets of Jamestown.

Instead of being traded back to her people, she married colonist John Rolfe. From her tribespeople, her husband learned how to cultivate tobacco, and he became a leader in the Virginia tobacco industry. In 1616, he took her to London to present her to the King. She died there the next spring, at the age of twenty-one. Her son, Thomas Rolfe, moved back to Virginia as an adult and became a leading citizen.

About 1600

 Five Algonquian tribes band together in what is now Virginia to form the kernel of what becomes known as the Powhatan Confederacy.

1607

 At the moment when non-Indian outsiders are about to establish the first permanent British colony in what will become the United States, the Algonquian alliance, called the Powhatan Confederacy, numbers 10,000 people in thirty-two tribes. The Powhatan Confederacy and the newcomers at Jamestown agree to live together in peace.

About 1608

 Pocahontas, the teenage daughter of Algonquian leader Wa-hun-sen-a-cawh (Powhatan), saves the life of Jamestown colonial leader John Smith.

1609

 The Native peoples living along the Hudson River and New York Bay encounter explorer Henry Hudson, who introduces them to firearms and alcohol.

1610

Pueblo Indians continue to work unwillingly as servants for the Spanish as the center of Spanish colonization in the Southwest shifts to Santa Fe.

1613

Algonquian beauty Pocahontas is kidnapped by Virginia colonial leaders Samuel Argall, Thomas Dale, and others to use as a pawn in negotiating with her father for return of English prisoners.

1613–17

 European diseases, including smallpox and measles, ravage the Timucua people of Georgia and Florida.

Death Rituals

 Every tribe or cultural group had its own beliefs and rituals related to death.

In order to scare off evil spirits, the Tanaina of Alaska made loud noises when someone was dying. After death, the corpse was removed through a window, never a door, then burned.

APACHE

 Apaches, like their cultural and linguistic cousins, the Navajos, arrived in the Southwest from the Far North sometime after A.D. 1000.

Before Spanish colonists arrived in the Southwest in 1598, Apaches had already gained a reputation among Pueblo Indians as cunning raiders and enemies to be feared.

During the centuries of Spanish rule, Apaches developed into superb guerrilla warriors. They traveled light and moved quickly. They could endure extreme thirst and survive on a diet of insects and lizards. They faced death with laughter, and they studied the enemy for weeks or months before attacking. Spanish Viceroy Bernardo de Gálvez said of the Apaches, "They are the most feared because of their knowledge, cunning, and warlike customs—acquired in the necessity of robbing in order to live—and their number."

When Americans began settling and mining in traditional Apache territory, Apaches fought back more fiercely and more successfully than any other indigenous group had ever done. Whole generations of Apache children grew up believing that the only cause of death was battle wounds. Only with Geronimo's surrender in 1886 did the era of Apache warfare end.

During the late 1800s, agents of the federal government tried to reduce the traditional power of women in Apache life. They jailed grandmothers whose granddaughters didn't attend school, and they punished men for the actions of female relatives. But the role of women remains strong.

According to traditional Apache beliefs, White Painted Woman was the first human being. She had two sons, Child of Water and Enemy Slayer, who made the world safe for humans to live in. During the puberty ceremonies for young women each summer, Mountain Spirit dancers still perform at night around bonfires, and Apaches celebrate the continuing influence of White Painted Woman in their lives.

Other traditions that flourish today include the Bear Dance, to heal illnesses and ensure long life, and the commemoration of an ancient race between the moon and the sun. In that ceremony, one group represents the moon and plants; another represents the sun and animals.

Today the Apaches live in nine tribal areas in Oklahoma, New Mexico, and Arizona. The two largest tribes, San Carlos and White Mountain, own 3.5 million acres of land in Arizona. Among reservation Apaches, 75 percent still speak the Apache language.

1614

 The Indians of New York find their lives changing as Dutch traders and colonists move in.

1615–20

 A five-year epidemic of smallpox, plague, and other diseases brought to the Americas by Europeans kills between 75 and 90 percent of the men, women, and children of the Massachusetts, Wampanoag, and Pawtucket peoples.

1616

 Oneida Indians in New York are attacked by French under Champlain, beginning centuries of conflicts with outsiders.

Pocahontas sails to England with her English husband John Rolfe. There she meets the King.

1617

 Nearly ready to return home to America, Pocahontas dies of smallpox and is buried in the town of Gravesend under the name Rebecca Rolfe.

DISEASE: THE ULTIMATE WEAPON

 Many anthropologists now believe that the number-one reason the Native peoples of the Americas could not fight off the European invaders was not the imbalance in weapons, but the imbalance in their immune systems. Native Americans had no antibodies to Old World diseases like smallpox and measles. In Central and South America, in the first seventy-five years following contact with Europeans, 90 percent of the Native population died.

In what is now the United States, it was common for 50 to 80 percent of a tribe to die in a single smallpox epidemic. Sometimes the effects were even worse.

 In 1750, the Mandans were a mighty people on the Great Plains, numbering 9,000. In the 1800s, disease so depleted the Mandans that today they are considered extinct, although some mixed-blood Mandans live among the Hidatsa and Arikara.

1618

 The Algonquian leader Wa-hun-sen-a-cawh (Powhatan) dies. His brother, Opechancanough, chief of the Chickahominy branch of Algonquians, becomes leader of the Algonquian Confederacy. Unlike Powhatan, Opechancanough wants to drive the colonists out of Virginia.

1619

 Opechancanough invites the British to raid traditional Algonquian enemies to the west.

1620

 The Wampanoag and other peoples watch as English newcomers settle at Plymouth, Massachusetts.

1621

 Indians try to befriend the English in the new settlement at Plymouth. Samoset, an Indian from Maine who has learned English from traders, arrives in Plymouth. So do Massasoit, chief of the Wampanoag, and Tisquantum, a Wampanoag who has survived being kidnapped and taken to England. Tisquantum, whom the settlers nickname Squanto, arranges for peace between settlers and the Wampanoag.

The Narragansett tribe sends the colonists at Plymouth a bundle of arrows tied in a rattlesnake skin to remind the colonists of the tribe's fighting power. The colonists return the skin filled with shot and powder to remind the Narragansett of theirs.

1622

 In March, Nemattanow, an Algonquian, is wrongly accused of having killed an English settler. Before Nemattanow can be brought to trial, the settlers kill him. His murder makes Opechancanough decide to begin his long-planned attack on the colonists of Virginia and Maryland. In a surprise attack in March 1622, Opechancanough and his warriors kill 347 colonists and destroy seventy-four plantations. Settlers retaliate by inviting Indian leaders to a peace council and massacring most of them. Opechancanough escapes. Opechancanough's attack prompts the English to adopt a policy of extermination, and fighting continues intermittently for ten more years.

1623

 Witawamet, chief of the Massachusetts Indians, is lured into a peace conference by Captain Miles Standish, then killed, along with all his companions. The Pilgrims mount Witawamet's head on the wall of the fort at Plymouth to warn other Indians of their possible fate.

1624

 Mohawks and Mahicans battle each other.

 "The sun shines brightly, and it is a good day to die!"
—Ancient battle cry of the Tsitsista (Cheyenne) people

CHEROKEE

  Before Europeans arrived, Cherokees lived in a 40,000-square-mile area that covered parts of the Carolinas, the Virginias, Kentucky, Tennessee, Georgia, and Alabama. By the early 1800s, they had been forced to turn over all of their land except a mountainous region that included parts of North Carolina, Tennessee, Georgia, and Alabama. In the 1830s, they lost even that and began the enforced move to northeastern Oklahoma, 1,000 miles away, along the Trail of Tears. Thousands died. Others fled and returned to their mountainous home, where federal agents harassed them for years. Ultimately these people became the Eastern Band of Cherokees.

Those who reached Oklahoma formed the Cherokee Nation of Oklahoma. They adopted a constitution, started businesses, and published Oklahoma's first newspaper. They also established 144 elementary schools and 2 high schools. More Cherokees could read and write than whites living in the same region.

After the Civil War, the Cherokees lost much of their land in Oklahoma, and Congress reduced the Cherokee Nation's power to function as a separate government in 1907.

In spite of these and other adversities, Cherokees continue to thrive. Among the Eastern Band of Cherokees, artisans still make traditional baskets from split cane and white oak. In Oklahoma, 13,000 people still speak the Cherokee language, and various groups, including the separate United Keetoowah Band, preserve ancient religious traditions.

To be eligible to enroll as an Eastern Cherokee, a person must have one-thirty-second Cherokee blood and be able to trace Cherokee heritage through someone registered as a Cherokee in 1924. To become a member of the Cherokee Nation of Oklahoma, a person must be able to trace descent from someone enrolled in 1906, but there is no specific requirement for a percentage of Cherokee blood. The United Keetoowah Band requires one-quarter Cherokee blood in order to become a member.

Approximately 140,000 people are officially registered as Cherokees, but in the 1990 U.S. census, a total of 308,000 identified themselves as Cherokee, making the Cherokee people the largest group of Native Americans in the United States.

1626

Algonquian-speaking Manhattan Indians of the Wappinger Confederacy, for whom the European concept of landownership is totally foreign, enter into a transaction with the Dutch in which the Dutch believe they have bought Manhattan Island from the Indians. However, the Indians believe they have simply agreed to share.

1630

Approximately 40,000 to 60,000 Pueblo Indians occupy ninety villages in New Mexico and eastern Arizona. The largest, Pecos Pueblo, holds 2,000, the smallest 50. In the fields around their homes, they grow corn, beans, gourds, cotton, and tobacco. Although Spanish laws protect the Indians, Spanish colonial governors continue to require them to work in a variety of jobs for little or no pay. Any Indian child whom the Spanish perceive as an orphan can be seized and required to work as a servant until reaching adulthood. Spanish officials sometimes encourage, sometimes punish, the Pueblo Indians for performing ancient rituals and dances.

1630–1730

In the generations following the arrival of Europeans, diseases unknown earlier in the Americas kill an estimated 80 percent of Native Americans throughout New England.

1631

A flotilla of canoes swarms into Massachusetts Bay by night. At dawn, warriors disembark, sack colonial settlements, and flee by sea.

For centuries before the Tanana Indians of the Alaska Plateau encountered white people personally, they knew of the presence of whites farther away because of the intertribal grapevine. Old people told the young, "Someday strangers will arrive. They will have yellow hair and pale skin. They will try to kill us and take away our hunting grounds."

When Russian traders from the west and English traders from the east finally arrived in the interior of Alaska in the early 1800s, the cultural effects were complex and insidious, but profoundly devastating. The prophecy proved right.

1634

 The Winnebago (Hochungra and Wonkshiek) peoples of Wisconsin encounter their first non-Indian but cannot know the upheavals that lie ahead.

1634–36

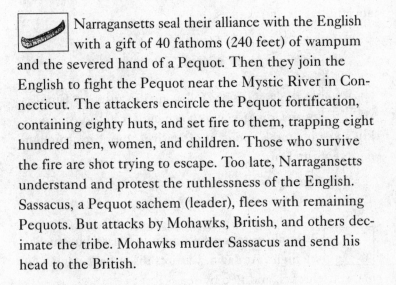 As more and more Europeans arrive in the Northeast, Pequot chief Tatobam of the Connecticut Valley is kidnapped by a European trader. Pequots pay ransom but receive their chief back dead.

Narragansett leaders Canonicus and Miantonomo offer to pay reparations for the murder of an English trader, but innocent Narragansetts and Pequots die in a retaliatory raid.

As war begins, Narragansetts under Miantonomo ally with the English against the Pequots. Pequots warn the Narragansett that the English will turn on them, too.

1637

Narragansetts seal their alliance with the English with a gift of 40 fathoms (240 feet) of wampum and the severed hand of a Pequot. Then they join the English to fight the Pequot near the Mystic River in Connecticut. The attackers encircle the Pequot fortification, containing eighty huts, and set fire to them, trapping eight hundred men, women, and children. Those who survive the fire are shot trying to escape. Too late, Narragansetts understand and protest the ruthlessness of the English. Sassacus, a Pequot sachem (leader), flees with remaining Pequots. But attacks by Mohawks, British, and others decimate the tribe. Mohawks murder Sassacus and send his head to the British.

"It was a fearful sight to see them thus frying in the fire, and the streams of blood quenching the same, and horrible was the stink and scent of hair."
—Governor William Bradford of Plymouth Colony, regarding the massacre of Pequots in Connecticut in 1637

1638

The Pequot War ends with the Treaty of Hartford, by which the few surviving Pequots are divided as prisoners among tribes allied with the British. Miantonomo and his band of Narragansetts receive eighty, while Uncas and his band of Mohegans receive another eighty. Ninigret and his band of Niantics are given twenty. Pequots are required by treaty to assume the cultural identity of their captors and are forbidden from returning to their traditional lands.

1641

The Potawatomi people of Michigan find their lives rearranged when French settle among them. Potawatomi migrate into Winnebago territory, but the Winnebago resent them and try to drive them back.

"Brothers, we must be as one, as the English are, or we shall all be destroyed."
—A Narragansett, speaking to the traditional enemies of his people, 1642

1642–44

Eighty Wappinger men, women, and children flee their Mohawk pursuers by seeking sanctuary on Dutch-controlled Staten Island. Although the Wappingers and the Dutch are at peace, the governor of New Amsterdam orders the refugees slaughtered. The Dutch women of New Amsterdam use the severed heads of the Wappingers for a macabre game of kickball. Other captives are tortured. For the next two years, Wappingers and other area Indians war against Dutch settlers.

1643

Uncas, Mohegan leader, kills Miantonomo, Narragansett leader, under instructions from English authorities. Narragansetts protest, in vain.

1644

After years of planning revenge against the English, Opechancanough leads the Powhatan Confederacy and their allies against the newcomers again. Now so old he must be carried into battle on a litter, he and his warriors kill about four hundred settlers, then vanish into the forest. He fights for two more years before the British capture and kill him. For generations afterwards, he endures in memory as a symbol of the power of persistence and determination.

1646

"Bore out your ears with sticks."
—Saying among the Sioux, used when someone isn't listening well enough

Necotowance, Opechancanough's successor, agrees to peace with the British in Virginia. In theory, the British now recognize the Algonquians' right to their own land for the first time since their arrival. In practice, the colonists continue to harass and arbitrarily murder their Indian neighbors.

1647

 Canonicus, Narragansett sachem, dies at about age eighty-two.

1648–49

The Iroquois Indians nearly annihilate the Huron Indians, who have already been decimated by European diseases, as the two groups fight over fur supplies and trade relations with the French. For the next two hundred years, non-Indian market demands for furs continue to disrupt traditional lifeways and cause conflicts among tribes across the United States and Canada.

1650

Indians in New York discover that unscrupulous white settlers and traders have been importing imitation wampum from Europe. The Dutch outlaw the counterfeits, but the practice continues.

1650–51

Hoping to force the Swedes from the Delaware Bay area, the Dutch use Mohawk and Susque-

DEATH SONGS

 In many tribes, it was common to sing a death song while dying.

 In 1643, an Indian captive of the Dutch in New Amsterdam sang his death chant while his captors skinned him alive and castrated him. His song ended only when soldiers bashed his brains out.

 In 1871, Satank, a Kiowa leader in custody for murder, sang his death song to show that he knew what was coming next. Then he ripped off his handcuffs and died as he tried to escape from soldiers guarding him.

COCOPAH

 For centuries, the Cocopah Indians lived along the Colorado River of southern Arizona and northern Mexico. They traveled the river on rafts made from reeds. They ate fish, hunted the animals that came to the river to drink, and made flour from the pods of mesquite and other desert trees. Women made skirts from willow bark, and both men and women decorated their bodies and faces with paint. In the summer, people lived under ramadas, open-air shelters consisting of posts and a brush roof that protected them from the sun. In the winter, they lived in homes made of posts, sticks, brush, and mud. Fine potters, they stored food in pots that hung from the ceiling, out of the reach of rodents.

Traditionally the Cocopah considered it dishonorable to collect material possessions. When people died, their possessions went with them to the spirit world in a great ceremonial fire.

The Cocopah developed elaborate rituals of war that included vision quests and fasting. They allied themselves with the Pimas and Maricopas and were enemies of the Quechan and Mojaves.

In the 1600s, there were approximately 5,000 Cocopah. Today their descendants number only about 1,000, but they continue to speak their ancestral language and follow ancient traditions. These include elaborate funeral ceremonies, long storytelling cycles, and puberty ceremonies. Most Cocopah in the United States live in the Somerton area near Yuma, Arizona.

---

hannock Indians as pawns. They arm Mohawks and persuade them to attack the Swedes' allies, the Susquehannock. This policy is destructive to both groups, but other tribes have learned to protect themselves by playing Europeans against each other. The English respect Iroquois land claims in order to prevent their siding with the French. The French respect Iroquois land claims so the Indians won't ally with the British.

1655

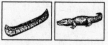 Hopi Indian Juan Cuna is accused of idolatry by a priest and whipped until he bleeds. The priest then smears burning turpentine on Cuna and burns him to death.

1656

Tottopotomoi, King of the Pamunkeys, agrees to help the British peacefully evict Indians who are not part of the Powhatan Confederacy from the James River area of Virginia. When the British murder five Indian rulers who have come to a peace parley, a battle begins, and Tottopotomoi dies.

The Virginia assembly makes it legal to kill without questions any Indian construed to be trespassing on colonists' land.

1660

Delaware Indians grieve when Dutch kidnap their children as a way to force the Delawares to submit to the Dutch.

1661

Chief Massasoit of the Wampanoags, longtime friend of the Pilgrims, dies of old age. His son Wamsutta (Alexander), ordered to Plymouth to pledge his loyalty to the English, dies on the way home. Some say the English have poisoned him. Wamsutta's brother, Metacomet, becomes ruler of the Wampanoags, and the English christen him King Philip.

THE FIRST POTLATCH

  From Alaska to Oregon, Native Americans have celebrated elaborate gift-giving ceremonies called potlatches for centuries. Rituals vary from tribe to tribe, but typically the host or hostess gives lavish gifts to guests. The more they give, the more their guests and others respect them.

Storytellers from the Quileute Tribe of Washington State explain the origin of the potlatch custom this way:

Once a beautiful bird with feathers of many colors flew above the ocean near the village. All the hunters tried to shoot it but failed.

Then Golden Eagle boasted to Blue Jay, "My daughters can shoot that bird."

Blue Jay laughed. "Girls couldn't do that."

But the daughters of Golden Eagle went into the forest and made themselves arrows, something no woman ever did. Then they disguised themselves and paddled out across the ocean to a spot near the bird of many colors. They shot one arrow. Two. Three. The bird fell.

The girls returned and asked their father to invite all the birds in the world to his lodge.

When the guests arrived, Golden Eagle announced, "My daughters have a present for you."

To each bird, the girls presented feathers of different colors. Robin got red and brown. Finch got yellow and black. Meadowlark received yellow and brown. And so on, until all the feathers were gone.

From then on, each bird has grown feathers of a certain color. And ever since that day, people have presented potlatches, giving gifts to all who come.

Mid-1660s

  Indian bows, arrows, and tomahawks fall further behind in the uneven contest of weapons as colonial importers introduce a new weapon, the flintlock.

1666

 Cheeshatemauck, a Wampanoag, dies of a white man's disease, tuberculosis, a year after becoming the first Native American to graduate from Harvard.

After centuries of considering themselves one people, Pequots in Connecticut are forced by whites to divide into two groups. One branch receives a grant of land at Mashantucket and becomes known as the Mashantucket Pequots. The other group, known as the Paucatuck or Eastern Pequots, must wait another seventeen years before receiving land in North Stonington.

Mohawks are attacked by French soldiers in New York.

The Unkechaug people, also called Possepatuck, enter a peace treaty with white invaders in exchange for the guarantee to be allowed to live on a fifty-two-acre portion of their ancestral land on Long Island. The agreement goes on to become one of the few that are still honored three centuries later.

 A severe, years-long drought hits the Southwest. Indians hardest hit are Pueblo farmers.

 "What's the matter [with] your medicine? You got polecat medicine!"
—Saying among the Comanches when a medicine person's predictions fail

1669

 Mohawks and Mahicans battle in New York; Mohawks win.

1670s

 Sioux and Chippewa Indians of Michigan and Minnesota begin trading with the French.

CREEK

  Before Europeans arrived, the Creek people lived spread widely across the flatlands of Georgia and Alabama. Women farmed corn, squash, and beans. Men hunted. They built rectangular homes out of mud and wood and lived in villages called *etvlwas* surrounding a central plaza, or stomp ground. Each midsummer, they performed the Green Corn ceremony on the plaza in honor of the first fruits of the harvest.

In the 1700s, as white settlers began invading their territory, and Native peoples displaced from other areas began moving in, the Creeks banded together to form the Creek Confederacy. It included Muskogee-speaking Creeks and related Indians: Hitchiti, Apalachee, Mikasuki, Alabama, and Koasati. Some Shawnees, Natchez, Timucua, and Yuchi also joined them. Intermarried whites and runaway black slaves lived among them, too.

When the Creeks were forcibly removed to Indian Territory in the 1820s and 1830s, they reestablished themselves in new *etvlwas* built around new stomp grounds. There they performed traditional rituals.

Century-old differences between two factions, the Lower Creeks and the Upper Creeks, moved to Oklahoma with them and survive to this day.

In Alabama, a few Creeks escaped removal to Indian Territory; today they are known as the Poarch Band of Creeks. Ironically, staying in their homeland surrounded by whites ultimately meant they lost more of their traditional culture than did the Creeks who endured removal.

Creeks in Oklahoma still perform the Green Corn ceremony of their ancestors.

1671

 After four years of extreme drought, an epidemic of mysterious origins attacks Pueblo Indians, Spanish settlers, and livestock in New Mexico, killing many people and animals and increasing tension between Indians and non-Indians.

1671

 Awashonks, a woman sachem (leader) of a band of Narragansetts, gives in to British pressure and agrees to the resettlement of her people in a new location in Massachusetts.

"The Indians, our neighbors, are absolutely subjected, so that there is no fear of them."
—Governor William Berkeley of Virginia, 1671

1672

 In sixty-five years of interactions with British colonists, the Algonquian population of Virginia colony has declined from 10,000 to about 3,000. The British, whom the Algonquians saved from starvation and extinction, now number 40,000.

Apaches and Navajos attack Pueblo Indian and Spanish settlements in New Mexico, destroying homes and carrying off sheep and cattle.

1675

John Sassamon, a Native American educated at Harvard, is found dead in a frozen pond near Plymouth. Although his injuries are consistent with a fall on the ice, three innocent Wampanoags are tried, convicted, and executed by the English. In despair, Wampanoag ruler Metacomet, known to the English as King Philip, prepares the Wampanoags for war. When the colonists kill a fourth Wampanoag, Metacomet attacks, and King Philip's War begins. In Massachusetts and Connecticut, Indians from

ASSINIBOINE

The Assiniboine peoples once lived around the Great Lakes and were part of a larger culture that included the Yanktonai Sioux. In the 1600s, under pressure from French and British fur traders, they split from the Yanktonai and moved out into the Great Plains in search of buffalo hides. Known to others as Those Who Cook with Stones, the Assiniboine moved into Montana and southern Canada.

In 1780, there were 10,000 Assiniboine. A century of cultural upheavals and smallpox epidemics reduced the U.S. Assiniboine population to under 2,000 by 1890.

Today most reservation Assiniboine live in Montana on the Fort Peck and Fort Belknap Reservations. After a century of decline, the Assiniboine language, a dialect of Dakota Sioux, has been revived, along with traditional spiritual activities. These include handgames, spirit lodges, naming ceremonies, and dances. The peace pipe remains an important part of Assiniboine ritual: the pipe is an instrument in offering prayers.

Contemporary Assiniboine women are noted for their fine handmade quilts, which feature star motifs. The ancient motifs and the quilts on which they appear have aesthetic, spiritual, and social meanings. People seeking a vision wrap themselves in a star quilt. People wishing to honor a friend give a star quilt as a gift.

many different tribes join the fighting. Narragansetts side with the colonists until they, too, are attacked.

"A white settlement is like a spot of raccoon grease on a new blanket. When you first see the tiny stain, you don't realize how wide and how fast it will spread."
—Saying among the Northeast tribes, as whites began spreading west from the coast

Cockacoeske, a Pamunkey woman known to whites as Queen Anne, becomes leader of the Pamunkey.

Pueblo Indians of New Mexico suddenly find themselves punishable by death for practicing their ancient rituals. Forty-seven Pueblo medicine men are charged with sorcery and witchcraft. Some are sentenced to death; others are sold as slaves. Enraged, the Pueblos unite and send a delegation of seventy to offer gifts and plead for their tribesmen. Those not already sold or hanged are released, but tensions between Indians and Spanish increase.

1675–76

A chief of Maryland's Nanticoke Indians is killed by British during a peace parley. In the ensuing battle, British kill fourteen of their own allies, the Susquehannocks. When the Susquehannocks fight back, the British invite five Susquehannock chiefs to a peace conference, then murder them. As war escalates, the British fight among themselves, and Occaneechi, Manakin, Pamunkey, and other peaceful Indians are murdered before peace is restored.

1676

Metacomet (King Philip) of the Wampanoags moves his base to New York, but Mohawks ally with the English and drive him back to New England. After Metacomet's wife and nine-year-old son are captured and sold into slavery in Europe by the English, he returns brokenhearted to his old Wampanoag homeland on the side of Mount Hope, a peninsula in Narragansett Bay. Another Wampanoag informs the English, who attack with

IROQUOIS

 Not long before the first Europeans arrived, a visionary prophet named Dekanawida urged the Iroquois-speaking Mohawks, Oneidas, Onondagas, Cayugas, and Senecas to strengthen ancient alliances in what has become known as the Iroquois Confederacy. In the 1700s, the five tribes added a sixth, the Tuscaroras, and became known as the League of Six Iroquois Nations.

Politically the confederacy was ruled by a hereditary council of fifty sachems, who were appointed by leading women from the tribes, known as clan mothers. Decisions were based on consensus. A central rite among the Iroquois, carried over from pre-European days, involved elaborate funeral customs known as the Condolence.

Wars between Europeans contributed to the weakening of the Iroquois League and its ancient traditions. In 1777, the Iroquois council fire died when Iroquois leaders could not reach a consensus about whether to side with the British or the Americans.

In the twentieth century, descendants of the original Iroquois Confederacy have worked as activists. They have fought against the 1924 Indian Citizenship Act, the 1934 Indian Reorganization Act, the construction of highways across traditional Iroquois land, and the desecration of ancient burial grounds and other sacred sites.

their Indian allies. Metacomet dies in the fighting, ending King Philip's War. His sister-in-law Wetamoo, a sachem, tries to swim to safety but drowns. Surviving Wampanoags are deported and sold as slaves in the West Indies and Spain for thirty shillings each.

Mugg, a Native American who has learned the art of privateering from the English, attacks towns and ships along the coast of New England. He sacks a settlement at Black Point, Maine, and seizes a thirty-ton English ketch. It becomes the lead ship in his small navy, which includes two

THE PUEBLO REVOLT

In 1680, eighty-two years after Spanish colonists settled in northern New Mexico, the Pueblo Indians revolted. Led by Popé, from San Juan Pueblo, the Indians attacked at dawn on August 10. Over the next several days, they killed four hundred settlers.

On August 15, the warriors converged on Santa Fe, where 1,000 colonists—men, women, and children—had crowded into the Palace of the Governors for protection. The Indians cut off the water supply. While they waited for the Spanish to surrender, they sang, "The God of the Christians is dead, but our God, which is the sun, will never die."

The Spanish surprised them with a counterattack, and the Indians pulled back. But on August 21, the Spanish abandoned Santa Fe and began the long walk south toward El Paso. Indians watched from the hilltops and mesas but didn't attack again.

For the next twelve years, the Pueblo Indians ruled themselves. They turned the government buildings in Santa Fe into a Pueblo village and transformed the Chapel of Our Lady of Light into a ceremonial kiva. They stopped speaking Spanish and stopped planting wheat and other crops introduced by the Spanish. But year after year, the summer rains didn't come. The corn crops failed. Apaches attacked. And Popé and other leaders ruled ruthlessly.

When Spanish soldiers returned briefly in 1692, the Pueblo Indians agreed to accept Spanish rule again. By 1693, when the colonists returned, the Indians had changed their minds. But it was too late. Some Pueblos surrendered. Others fought.

By 1697, the Pueblos had stopped resisting and did not rebel again for 150 years, until the Taos Revolt of 1847. The Pueblo Revolt lives on in memory as the most successful attempt by Indians to drive out European invaders in the history of the United States.

Namachkani: Taking the Enemy's Gun

 During the battle-filled 1600s, 1700s, and 1800s, most tribes considered it more noble to kill an enemy by any means other than a gun. But taking a musket from an enemy was considered an act of particular valor.

 The Blackfeet of the northern Great Plains had a word for it, namachkani.

heavily armed eighty-man ships. His plan to blockade and burn Boston and control the coast fails when he dies in a skirmish, but his followers continue to capture British ships, making off with thirteen ketches in the Salem area alone.

More than 2,000 Narragansetts die in a battle with English soldiers. Another 400 are sold as slaves.

1677

 The Pamunkey and Mattaponi Indians of Virginia sign a treaty with the British that guarantees them local autonomy. Unlike many other Native groups, the Mattaponi are able to maintain local autonomy for the next three hundred years.

1680s

 The Indians of southern Arizona find their ancient lifeways disrupted when the first in a long series of Jesuit missionaries settles among them.

About 1680

 The Ottawa (Odawa) people of Canada migrate from Ontario into the Lower Peninsula of Michigan, which becomes known as the Odawa homeland.

1680

 In fifty years of disease, enforced servitude, and cultural disruption, the Pueblo Indian population has dropped by 50 percent. The Pueblo Revolt begins in August when Popé, a spiritual leader from San Juan Pueblo in northern New Mexico, sends out messengers to other Pueblos. The runners carry a yucca cord tied with knots to indicate which day the revolt is to start. Within two weeks, the allied Pueblo people push Spanish colonists out of New Mexico and reclaim their ancient territories.

1682

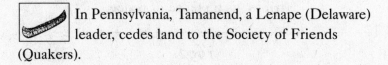 Following the Pueblo Revolt, refugees from Isleta Pueblo settle at Ysleta del Sur on the site of present-day El Paso. Joined by people from other Pueblo and non-Pueblo groups, the Ysletans merge over the decades into a new tribe.

1683

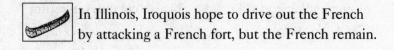 In Pennsylvania, Tamanend, a Lenape (Delaware) leader, cedes land to the Society of Friends (Quakers).

1684

In Illinois, Iroquois hope to drive out the French by attacking a French fort, but the French remain.

1687

After the Iroquois have harvested and stored the fall crops, the Marquis de Denonville destroys more than 1 million bushels of their corn.

1688

The Abenakis of Maine ally themselves with a French trader married to the daughter of an Abenaki chief. After the English governor of New York plunders the Frenchman's home, and English settlers capture Abenakis, the Indians retaliate by seizing settlers. Bands of Pannacook, Ossippee, Pigwacket, and other Indians plunder settlements in Maine and New Hampshire. These hostilities begin seven decades of intermittent warfare, in which Indians fight beside French and British soldiers.

1691

 The Caddo people of Louisiana are struck by smallpox. Many die.

 "We will bury the tomahawk in the earth."
—**Saying among the Sac and other tribes, as a pledge of peace**

1692

 The Pueblo Indians allow Spanish soldiers under Don Diego de Vargas to enter Santa Fe without fighting and agree to allow the Spanish colonists to return to New Mexico.

1693

 Pueblo Indians of New Mexico decide they don't want the Spanish to return, but Spanish colonists take Santa Fe back. Pueblos and Spanish battle intermittently for another three years.

1694

 At Jemez Pueblo, eighty-four people die and nearly four hundred are taken prisoner in an attack by Spanish soldiers. In order to obtain the release of the prisoners, Jemez people are forced to pledge to help the Spanish subdue other Pueblos.

 While traveling under a truce flag, Abenaki leader Bomazeen is captured and imprisoned by the British.

1696

 Lorenzo Tupatu, a leader of the Pueblo Revolt, leads a new attempt to drive the Spanish out, but it fails.

Early 1700s

 The Lummi Indians migrate into the Nooksack River region of Washington State, driving out the Indians who already live there.

 The Sauk (Sac) and Mesquaki (Fox) peoples in the Great Lakes region join forces to fight for their survival as cultural upheavals farther east push new tribes into their traditional territory.

1700

 Approximately 14,000 Pueblo Indians live near the Rio Grande and its tributaries.

Hopis opposed to Christianity kill Hopis who have converted. It is the only time in Hopi history that Hopis kill one another.

SUBARCTIC FASHIONS

 In the harsh landscape of the Alaska Plateau, caribou, moose, and other animals provided the basic material for clothing. For winter clothing, the animal's hair was allowed to remain on the hide, and the garment was often worn with the hair inside for added warmth. Winter trousers had moccasins attached. Socks, mittens, and parkas helped block out the cold. For summer clothing, the animal hair was removed before tanning. People tanned and softened the tough hides with a paste made from animal brains.

Both men and women wore fringed shirts, secured by belts. Sometimes the edges of men's shirts were V-shaped, front and back; usually women wore longer shirts, with straight edges.

Maternity clothing included a soft strap of tanned moose or caribou which a woman wore below her belly for support.

Porcupine quills, shells, plant seeds, and paint decorated the clothing and indicated the wealth and social standing of the wearer.

Typically a set of clothes lasted only a season or two.

PLAYING THE SYSTEM

 In the 1700s, the Navajo people cooperated with the Spanish colonists and priests only when it suited them. They refused to convert to Christianity themselves, saying they had grown up wild and free and would remain that way. Sometimes they allowed priests to baptize their children, but only because the priests gave the parents of baptized children picks and hoes. The parents then continued to instruct their children in traditional Navajo ways.

The Navajos saw Spanish farms as an excellent source of horses, sheep, and goats, and they sometimes appropriated thousands of head of sheep and horses in a single season of raiding. In the spring, when Navajos were ready to plant crops, they offered the settlers peace. Once the crops were harvested, they resumed raiding. When pressed by Spanish soldiers, they would retreat into the safety of the wild canyons and mesas, which only they knew.

1702–13

 Major tribes in the Southeast—including the Alabama, Chickasaw, Creek, and Yazoo—are attacked again and again by British soldiers. The attacks are so brutal and so disrupt the Indians' lives that in order to survive they agree to unfavorable peace treaties.

1702

 In a battle between Chickasaws and Choctaws, more than 2,300 Choctaws are killed or captured. Prisoners are sold as slaves.

1704

 A party of two hundred Abenaki and Caughnawaga warriors, along with fifty French soldiers, attack the sleeping village of Deerfield, Massachusetts, killing fifty settlers and taking more than one hundred prisoners.

1706

 Following his unjust imprisonment by the British, Abenaki leader Bomazeen leads attacks on Massachusetts settlers in Chelmsford and Sudbury.

1707

  Fourteen hundred Indians in South Carolina colony are officially listed as slaves out of a total census of 9,580 free whites, white servants, black slaves, and Indian slaves. This continues a century-long pattern of formally enslaving Indians in the British colonies. Indians typically become slaves in one of three ways: (1) as punishment, (2) as prisoners of war, or (3) as captives of other tribes.

1710

Four Mohawk leaders travel to England to seek Queen Anne's support for a joint Mohawk-English attack on French Canadians. In England, the Mohawks entertain and are entertained by aristocrats and the Queen. She promises to send more soldiers to America.

The Tuscarora Indians of North Carolina, fed up with rough treatment at the hands of traders and colonists, and fearful of being made slaves, petition colonial authorities in Pennsylvania to allow them to migrate there. But the North Carolina government refuses to recommend them, and the Pennsylvanians turn them down.

1711

Tuscarora Indians living at the confluence of the Neuse and Trent Rivers are startled when a group of Swiss settlers arrive and insist they own title to the Indians' land. When the Swiss try to force the Tuscaroras to move, the Indians attack coastal settlements. In the attacks and counterattacks that follow, colonists capture the chief of an allied tribe and roast him alive.

1712

The Tuscaroras agree to peace, but it is broken immediately when an Irish soldier kidnaps a group of Tuscaroras and sells them as slaves.

Horses and Gender Roles

When the Plains Indians acquired horses in the 1700s, it dramatically altered basic patterns of society. Among the Dakota Sioux and Cheyenne, for instance, women had held an honored position in society because they were the farmers. But when the People acquired horses, the two groups gave up farming to become nomadic, and the status of women dropped. Some tribes, like the Arikara, shifted from a mother-focused culture to a father-focused one.

War Belts

 Throughout the Northeast, strings of wampum known as war belts served as encoded messages. One tribe could ask another to ally with it by sending a war belt. In 1758, when a French officer wanted Delaware chiefs allied with the British to join the French, he sent the Delawares a war belt. They refused to accept it. When the Frenchman threw it to them, the Delawares kicked it back and forth with their feet, then tossed it away.

1713

The Tuscaroras are defeated by a force of white and Indian troops. Several hundred Tuscaroras are killed. Four hundred more are sold into slavery, at ten pounds each. Survivors retreat northward and join the Iroquois Confederacy as the Sixth Fire.

1715

The Yamassee of South Carolina rebel against white settlers and trappers. When the militia defeats them, the Yamassee flee into northern Florida, where they are joined by Creeks and other Indians and by runaway slaves. From this amalgam, the Seminole Tribe emerges, named for the Creek word *simanoli*, runaway. The Yamassees' former homeland becomes the new colony of Georgia.

Cherokees ally with Carolina settlers to counterbalance the power of the Creeks and ensure peace.

1721–25

 Abenakis skirmish with white settlers and soldiers who have appropriated Native lands in Maine. Fighting spreads to New Hampshire and Massachusetts and continues for four years, until the Abenakis are forced to agree to submit to English rule again.

1729

 After a decade of enduring attacks by the French, the Natchez of the Mississippi Valley, the last of the mound-building Indians, strike back. They successfully attack Fort Rosalie (present-day Natchez, Missis-

ALUTIIQ

Although related to the Inuit (Eskimos) of mainland Alaska, the Alutiiq people of the Aleutian Islands and the coastal areas of Alaska prefer not to be called Eskimos. Sometimes they are called Aleuts, like the indigenous peoples of the Aleutian Islands. The Alutiit (plural of Alutiiq) probably numbered about 20,000 people at the time of first contact with Europeans in 1728. There were sixty-five Alutiiq villages on Kodiak Island alone. The Alutiit had no centralized government and chose local leaders on the basis of talents and skills. They crafted skin-covered boats to hunt seals, sea otters, whales, and sea lions. During the long, cold winter nights, they danced, told tales of their ancestors, and carved figures in wood.

When the United States bought Alaska from Russia in 1867, the Alutiit lost citizenship rights, but they retained many customs acquired from the Russians, including Russian foods, Russian surnames, the Russian Orthodox Church, and the Russian language.

Disease and cultural upheaval decimated the Alutiit as it did other tribes. Today there are about 5,000 Alutiiq people, living in fifteen villages and five urban enclaves.

sippi), but the French retaliate and destroy the Natchez Nation. Survivors flee to the Chickasaws and Creeks.

About 1730

Horses reach the Plateau area, changing the lives of the people there. Now they can travel more quickly, hunt buffalo more easily, and trade more frequently with people from the Great Plains.

1730

Cherokee chiefs travel to London, where they agree to form an alliance with the British.

COOSAPONAKEESA (CREEK MARY)

 During the 1740s, Coosaponakeesa, a Creek woman who spoke both English and Creek, worked as an interpreter for Governor James Oglethorpe, the founder of the colony of Georgia. Her skills impressed him. He made her his negotiator with the Creeks and paid her $500 a year, an excellent salary for the era. But she considered herself first and last a Creek. By the early 1750s, she had proclaimed herself "Empress of the Creek Nation." She demanded that white settlers return stolen land to her people, but colonists ignored her. Finally she sent a message to Oglethorpe that she was coming to claim the land in person. She raised an army of Creeks and led them to Savannah.

There the British forced the Creeks to turn over their weapons. Then they negotiated with Coosaponakeesa and other leaders for several days. Meanwhile, her warriors seized back their weapons, but before a battle could begin, the British arrested Coosaponakeesa and put her in prison.

Although she didn't succeed in reclaiming her people's land, she did bring early attention to the plight of Native nations throughout the Northeast and Southeast, as they lost tract after tract of ancestral land to white newcomers.

Coosaponakeesa died in 1763, in her early sixties.

1741

The lives of Alaska Natives change forever when Vitus Bering, a Russian explorer, arrives in Alaska, followed over the next decades by fur hunters and traders.

1750–1837

In the space of four generations, smallpox epidemics strike the Mandan Sioux three times, reducing them from a powerful group of 9,000 men, women, and children to a band of under 200.

1752

The Schaghticoke people of Connecticut receive a promise that they will be allowed to live undisturbed on four hundred acres of their traditional lands. As the decades and centuries pass, and cultural disruptions proliferate, the land becomes the one firm connection with their ancestors and their past.

1754

Half-King, a leader of the Mingo tribe, joins George Washington to attack the French in Pennsylvania. Decades of intermittent fighting between the English and French and their respective Indian allies intensify into the French and Indian War of 1754–1763.

1755

In a battle typical of the era, Mohawks ally with the British while other Indians ally with the French at Crown Point.

The Akwesasne Mohawk community is founded at St. Regis along the U.S.-Canada border. It goes on to become the oldest permanent settlement in northern New York.

Delawares split into factions. One group, led by Teedyuscung, opposes the English and fights to preserve Indian lands from white settlement.

1758

  Little Carpenter, Cherokee leader, agrees to fight with the British against the French, as does Chief Outacite. Delawares, Shawnees, Mingos, and others question the intentions of the British, but agree to peace.

1759

 Cherokee warriors returning home after fighting side by side with English soldiers are killed by English colonists. Feeling betrayed, the Cherokees of Virginia, Georgia, and the Carolinas counterattack. Cherokees and English battle for two more years before Cherokees are forced to agree to a harsh treaty.

1762

Neolin, a prophet from the Delaware Tribe, predicts that if Indians would return to the ways of their ancestors, they could drive whites away. He suggests giving up European clothes and returning to animal-skin clothing. He urges his followers to stop drinking the white man's liquor and "drive off your land those dogs clothed in red who will do you nothing but harm." His teachings spread across the Northeast and help set the mood for Pontiac's War.

PONTIAC'S WAR

When the French turned over forts in the Great Lakes area to the British in 1760, at the end of the French and Indian War, the British acted as if the Indians on whose land the forts sat had become their servants, or as if the Indians didn't exist. Pontiac, Ottawa chief, agreed to ally with the King of England and to call him uncle, but he warned the British that if they mistreated the Indians of the region, he would block their access to the interior.

As they grew increasingly unhappy with the British, Senecas, Delawares, Potawatomis, Miamis, Shawnees, Ottawas, and other tribes talked of throwing the British out. Pontiac emerged as their leader. Echoing the words of Neolin, the Delaware prophet, he announced that Wolf, the Master of Life, had said of the British, "Send them back to the country which I made for them! There let them remain."

In May 1763, the allied Indians began attacking forts throughout the Great Lakes area. Fort Sandusky, on the shore of Lake Erie, fell first. Then a British fort among the Miami Indians of Indiana, near present-day Fort Wayne. Then Fort Ouiatenon and Fort Michilimackinac. In Pennsylvania, two more forts fell.

All told, Pontiac and his allies attacked twelve forts, capturing nine. The British abandoned a tenth.

(continued)

1763

Teedyuscung, Delaware leader, dies when his cabin burns down on April 19. It is rumored that leaders of the Six Nations, jealous of his power among the Delawares, have had him murdered and then burned. Others blame the British, who are said to have killed him for refusing to let whites steal Indian lands.

War belts pass among the Miamis, Shawnees, Potawatomis, Senecas, Ottawas, Delawares, and other tribes. They resent the imperious attitudes and incursions of the English who have taken over French forts and settlements in the Indians' territory. Pontiac, an Algonquian chief of the Ottawa Tribe of the Great Lakes region, emerges as leader of tribes from Lake Erie to the Mississippi as they try to drive out the British. Pontiac and his allies attack twelve forts, capturing nine and forcing a tenth to be abandoned before agreeing to peace. In response to Pontiac's War, King George proclaims lands west of the Appalachians closed to white settlers.

A mob of colonial ruffians attacks a Conestoga Indian village in Pennsylvania. The marauders hack four villagers to death and shoot others. Survivors seek protection in the Lancaster jailhouse, but the mob strikes again, killing all. Benjamin Franklin convinces the villains to stop their rampage and writes an enraged call for justice, but nothing happens.

1766

Two thousand Indian leaders meet with British peace negotiators at Fort Niagara. The plight of the Native peoples is symbolized in the hunger and exhaustion of those who represent them.

1768

Tecumseh is born near present-day Dayton, Ohio, among the Shawnees, who have settled in the area after being pushed out of their ancestral lands by Virginia settlers, Iroquois Indians, and Creeks.

1769

In Cahokia, Illinois, a Peoria Indian shoots Pontiac in the back as they leave a store. The assassin flees to an English fort for protection, and Pontiac dies.

Indians living near the future site of San Diego experience disruption of their cultures and religions as the first of twenty-one missions is founded in California. During the mission period, which continues until 1835, disease and cultural upheavals reduce the population of coastal Indians from about 70,000 to under 15,000.

Early 1770s

In spite of the English King's promise to keep colonists out of Indian country, colonists establish settlements in Kentucky.

Seven Indian communities, including members of the Narragansetts, Pequots, Montauks, and Mohegans, join to create the Brotherton (Brothertown) tribe and move to upstate New York to land provided by the Oneidas.

At Fort Pitt, the British resorted to biological warfare. Pretending to give the Indians gifts, they sent out blankets infected with smallpox, a disease to which the Indians had no resistance. Among the Delawares, hundreds of Indians died.

In October, Pontiac agreed to peace, and the British agreed to prohibit colonists from moving into Indian territory west of the Appalachians. Three years later, a peace treaty formally ended the rebellion.

THE GREAT SPIRIT SPEAKS

 On April 27, 1763, shortly before the war that bears his name broke out, Pontiac, Ottawa leader, spoke to a council of thirty chiefs and five hundred warriors. In his speech, he described an encounter with the Great Spirit, who said:

"I am the Maker of heaven and earth, the trees, lakes, rivers, and all things else. I am the Maker of mankind; and because I love you, you must do my will. The land on which you live I have made for you, and not for others. Why do you suffer the white men to dwell among you? My children, you have forgotten the customs and traditions of your forefathers. Why do you not clothe yourselves in skins, as they did, and use the bows and arrows, and the stone-pointed lances, which they used? You have bought guns, knives, kettles, and blankets from the white men, until you can no longer do without them; and, what is worse, you have drunk the poison fire-water, which turns you into fools. Fling all these things away; live as your wise forefathers lived before you. And as for these English—these dogs dressed in red, who have come to rob you of your hunting grounds, and drive away the game—you must lift the hatchet against them. Wipe them from the face of the earth, and then you will win my favor back again, and once more be happy and prosperous."

A SHAWNEE CAPTIVE

In 1758, Shawnee Indians living at the juncture of the Ohio and Shenanjee Rivers captured fifteen-year-old Mary Jemison. Sixty-four years later, Jemison published this account of her early years with the Indians.

They seemed to rejoice over me as over a long-lost child. I was made welcome amongst them as a sister to the two squaws . . . and was called Dickewamis; which being interpreted, signifies a pretty girl, a handsome girl, or a pleasant, good thing. That is the name by which I have ever since been called by the Indians. . . .

Being now settled and provided with a home, I was employed in nursing the children, and doing light work about the house. Occasionally I was sent out with the Indian hunters, when they went but a short distance, to help them carry their game. My situation was easy; I had no particular hardships to endure. But still, the recollection of my parents, my brothers and sisters, my home, and my own captivity, destroyed my happiness, and made me constantly solitary, lonesome and gloomy. . . .

Not long after the Delawares came to live with us [early in her captivity], my sisters told me that I must go and live with one of them, whose name was Sheninjee. Not daring to cross them, or disobey their commands, with a great degree of reluctance I went; and Sheninjee and I were married according to Indian custom.

Sheninjee was a noble man; large in stature; elegant in his appearance; generous in his conduct; courageous in war; a friend to peace, and a great lover of justice. He supported a degree of dignity far above his rank, and merited and received the confidence and friendship of all the tribes with whom he was acquainted. Yet, Sheninjee was an Indian. The idea of spending my days with him at first seemed perfectly irreconcilable to my feelings: but his good nature, generosity, tenderness, and friendship towards me, soon gained my affection; and, strange as it may seem, I loved him! To me he was ever kind in sickness, and always treated me with gentleness; in fact, he was an agreeable husband, and a comfortable companion.

1771

 The 3,000 Salinan Indians in California find their lives changing dramatically with the founding of Mission San Antonio de Padua. The northwestern group of Salinans are required to work at the mission; they become known as the Antoniaños. As the decades pass, they begin to lose their cultural identity and assimilate to first Spanish, then Mexican culture.

1773

 Iroquois Indians resent colonists disguising themselves as Indians before throwing British tea into Boston Harbor.

1774

 Shawnee warriors fight colonists when the governor of Virginia ignores the legal boundary between Indian and settlers' land and grants land to war veterans west of the Appalachians. Shawnees beg their traditional allies, the Iroquois, to fight with them, but the British convince the Iroquois to refuse. Cornstalk, a Shawnee chief, and his warriors fight the British alone, and are defeated.

By 1775

 Three decades ahead of the first white explorers, smallpox arrives in the Plateau. By the time the first non-Indians appear, half the population of the Plateau has died.

"We Are Unwilling"

 As the Revolutionary War began, Oneidas told the colonists, "We are unwilling to join on either side of such a contest. . . . Should the great King of England apply to us for our aid—we shall deny him—and should the Colonists apply—we shall refuse."

The Continental Congress issued an announcement to Indian tribes in general that described the revolution as "a family quarrel between us and Old England. You Indians are not concerned in it. We don't wish you to take up the hatchet against the king's troops. We desire you to remain at home, and not join on either side, but keep the hatchet buried deep."

Even so, Indians from many tribes found themselves pressured to join sides. In the end, no matter which side they chose, they lost. Those who sided with the British were punished by having their lands taken away. Those who sided with the colonists found that their aid had gained them few friends, as settlers in the postwar era pushed onto their lands.

1775

 At George Washington's request, warriors from the Passamaquoddy, St. John's, Stockbridge, and Penobscot Tribes agree to fight with the colonists. The British court their longtime allies, the Iroquois, to fight against the colonists, but Chief Cawconcaucawheteda (Flying Crow) tells them, "You say their Powder is rotten—We have found it good. You say they are all mad, foolish, wicked, and deceitful—I say you are so and they are wise for you want us to destroy ourselves in your War and they advise us to live in Peace. Their advice we intend to follow."

 Thayendanégea, Mohawk chief, travels to London with a British officer who is determined to convince the Iroquois to ally themselves with the British. Under the name Joseph Brant, Thayendanégea socializes with aristocrats and sits for famous portraitist George Romney. He returns to America and urges his tribespeople to fight on behalf of the King.

1776

The Tubatulabal Indians experience their first cultural disruptions by non-Indians when an exploring party led by Francisco Garcés arrives in the Kern River area of California.

 A delegation of Shawnees, Delawares, and Mo hawks arrives in Cherokee country and urges the Cherokees to fight against the colonists. Angry at colonists for settling on Indian lands, the Cherokees begin attacking white settlements along the frontier.

COMANCHE

The nomadic Comanches, about 25,000 strong, once roamed in small bands from the Rocky Mountains deep into Mexico. Cultural ties, family connections, and a common language linked the bands, but each band had its own leader.

In the 1700s, Comanches were famous among Indians and non-Indians of the Southwest and Great Plains as traders. They arrived at the annual trade fairs in Taos each year bringing guns, powder, tobacco, hatchets, tin cooking vessels, and other trade items.

In 1867, the Medicine Lodge Treaty required Comanches to move to a reservation in southwestern Oklahoma, but Quanah Parker and his band of Kwahadi Comanches didn't surrender until 1876. The General Allotment Act of 1887 resulted in the Comanches losing all their communally held lands.

During World War II, seventeen young Comanches worked as "code talkers" in Europe, sending messages in the ancient language of the Comanches.

Today the Comanche language survives, and ancient art forms, music, dances, and ceremonies are being preserved. Comanche artists are especially noted for their fine feather and bead work.

"We did not know there were other people besides the Indian until about one hundred winters ago, when some men with white faces came to our country. They brought many things with them to trade for furs and skins. They brought tobacco, which was new to us. They brought guns with flintstones on them, which frightened our women and children."
— Chief Joseph, recounting the history of the Nez Perce Indians, 1879

1777

The Six Iroquois Nations give up hope of remaining neutral and split into two factions. The Mohawks, Cayugas, Senecas, and Onondagas fight alongside the British. The Oneidas and Tuscaroras join the colonists.

Before 1778

The Piscataway Tribe of Maryland emerges as an amalgam of Indians and people of part Indian, part black, and part white ancestry.

1778

Cherokees, Creeks, Choctaws, and Chickasaws receive gifts valued at 75,000 pounds sterling from the British as a reward for remaining allied with England during the Revolutionary War.

> **"When your army entered the country of the Six Nations, we called you Town Destroyer; and to this day when that name is heard, our women look behind them and turn pale, and our children cling close to the necks of their mothers."**
> **—Cornplanter, Seneca chief, to George Washington, about 1790, regarding attacks of colonial soldiers on the Senecas in the late 1770s**

1779

Seneca Indians pay a high price for allying with the British against the rebelling colonists when George Washington sends an army up the Susquehanna to invade their territory. Unable to stop the invaders, the Senecas flee. Soldiers destroy their homes, crops, and food stores, causing the Senecas much suffering long after the invaders leave. Following this and related battles, the Iroquois Confederacy never recovers completely.

1780

An army of Creek warriors, 2,000 strong, aids the British in successfully defending Pensacola against Spanish allies of the American colonists.

Cherokees pay for their alliance with the British when an army of Virginians and North Carolinians sweeps into

Cherokee country, destroying Cherokee villages, including Chote, the central village.

1781

 Four hundred Choctaws and one hundred Creeks fight beside the British to save Pensacola, but it falls to the Spanish.

1783

 Indians who fought with Great Britain against the colonists find themselves betrayed by the Treaty of Paris when Great Britain makes no provisions for their protection against vengeful colonists. The English simply transfer their claims to Indian lands east of the Mississippi to the United States. Settlers attempt to seize land from Natives in western New York and along the Ohio River, but they resist. By 1789, settlers return to the colonial practice of buying Indian land.

1784

 The trading patterns of Alaska Natives change permanently when Russians establish their first trading post in Alaska on Kodiak Island. Alaskans trade furs to the outsiders in exchange for iron, copper kettles, knives, and other items.

1785

 The Wyandotte (Wendat) Indians of Michigan are forced to sign a treaty acknowledging themselves to be under the protection of the United States.

Greatest Land Grab in History

 Between 1784 and 1871, Indian tribes across the country were forced to sign away 2 billion acres of tribal land in 720 separate treaties and land cessions.

"THERE WERE THREE REASONS"

 "I wish now to acquaint you with what happened to one of my people about four years ago, four miles above Fort Pitt: A young man who was married to my wife's sister, when he was hunting, was murdered by a white man. There were three reasons for his being killed: In the first place he had a very fine riding horse; secondly, he was very richly dressed, and had about him a good deal of silver; and thirdly, he had with him a very fine rifle. The white man invited him to his house, to light from his horse, and as he was getting off his horse, his head being rather down, the white man struck him with a tomahawk on the head and killed him, and having plundered him dragged him into the river."

—Ki-on-twog-ky (Cornplanter), Seneca chief, orator, and peacemaker, addressing white leaders in Philadelphia, October 29, 1790

 Twenty Tanaina Indians living along Cook Inlet are seized by Russians and held hostage.

1788

 The Onondaga Indians lose much of their ancestral land but receive a hundred-square-mile tract by provision of the Treaty of Fort Schuyler.

1789

 Comanches face starvation following the famine of 1788. Chief Ecueracapa rides to Santa Fe to ask for Spanish assistance. The governor and citizens donate 360 bushels of food.

1790

 Miami leader Little Turtle heads a force of Miamis, Shawnees, Potawatomis, and Chippewas against an American army sent into Indian lands in Ohio. Little Turtle and his army pretend to flee into the forest, then turn and rout their pursuers. Hoping to avoid further battles, Little Turtle allows the invaders to retreat.

Late 1700s

 Population pressures from other Yuman tribes force the Pee-Posh (Maricopa) Indians to leave the Colorado River area and migrate upstream along the Gila River.

1791

Once again, Little Turtle and his confederacy of Potawatomis, Chippewas, Miamis, Shawnees, and others face an American army sent to gain control of Indian lands in the Northwest Territory (Ohio, Indiana, Illinois, Michigan, and Wisconsin). Again, Little Turtle and his army rout the Americans.

1792

The Twana (Skokomish) people in western Washington meet their first non-Indians, but the strangers' diseases have preceded them. Already smallpox has shrunk the tribe.

1794

Russian Orthodox priests arrive in Alaska and begin introducing Christianity to Alaska Natives. Those who adopt the new religion add it to their ancestral shamanism, rather than replacing the old beliefs. In some villages, shamans become devout Christians while continuing their shamanistic rituals.

Little Turtle watches as the Americans amass a third army, this one highly disciplined and well trained, to invade the lands of the allied tribes. Little Turtle advises his allies to seek peace instead of fighting. But the other chiefs replace him with Turkey Foot, and the Indians are defeated at Fallen Timbers, near present-day Toledo, Ohio.

LITTLE TURTLE

Little Turtle, great warrior of the Miami Indians of Ohio, Indiana, and Illinois, was born to a Miami chief and a Mahican woman about 1747. When whites began invading the ancestral lands of the Miamis, Shawnees, Potawatomis, and others, it was Little Turtle who rallied the tribes to form a confederacy and fight the invaders. Again and again, he and his warriors and allies defeated the army. But in the end, neither Little Turtle nor any other leader could stop the advance of the settlers.

After the 1795 Treaty of Greenville, in which the confederated tribes lost much of their ancestral land, Little Turtle continued to give speeches in support of the Indians' right to their land. His own ancestors, he said, had kindled their fires on the site of Detroit.

A writer of Little Turtle's era called the chief "the bravest among the brave, and wisest among the wise . . . leading an army of braves to sure victory one hour—cutting and slashing, as with the ferocity of a tiger, at one moment—and as passive and gentle as a child the next."

"OUR PATIENCE IS WORN OUT"

"Brother: We are of the same opinion with the people of the United States; you consider yourselves as independent people; we, as the original inhabitants of this country, and sovereigns of the soil, look upon ourselves as equally independent, and free as any other nation or nations. This country was given to us by the Great Spirit above; we wish to enjoy it, and have our passage along the lake, within the line we have pointed out.

"Brother: The great exertions we have made, for this number of years, to accomplish a peace, and have not been able to obtain it; our patience, as we have already observed, is exhausted, and we are discouraged from persevering any longer. We, therefore, throw ourselves under the protection of the Great Spirit above, who, we hope, will order all things for the best. We have told you our patience is worn out; but not so far, but that we wish for peace, and whenever we hear that pleasing sound, we shall pay attention to it."
—Thayendanégea (Joseph Brant), Mohawk leader, at a council with whites, April 21, 1794

"You have told us to speak our minds freely, and we now do it. This line takes in the greater and best part of your brothers' hunting ground."
—Little Turtle, Miami leader, objecting in vain to the boundary lines of the Treaty of Greenville, August 1795

1795

On August 7, the defeated leaders of the confederated tribes of the Northwest Territory are forced to sign the Treaty of Greenville. Signers include Little Turtle and representatives of the Shawnee, Wyandotte,

Miami, Potawatomi, Chippewa, Ottawa, Delaware, Kickapoo, Piankashaw, Kaskaskia, Wea, and Eel River Indians. The treaty gives the U.S. government Indian lands in southeastern Indiana, southern Ohio, and other parts of the Northwest Territory. A full-scale migration of non-Indians to the former tribal homelands begins.

1796

 The Otoe and Missouria peoples of Kansas and Nebraska unite against the Sac and Fox, who have been forced into Otoe and Missouria territory from farther east. This common bond forges a new tribe, the Otoe-Missouria.

 The Penobscot Indians are forced to sign over title to most of their land in Maine. They keep only the islands in the Penobscot River and about 100,000 acres of hunting lands.

1797

 The southern branch of Salinan Indians in California finds its traditional lifestyle disrupted with the establishment of Mission San Miguel Arcángel. They become known as the Migueleños and begin the painful process of adjusting to first Spanish, then Mexican rule.

By 1799

 Navajos begin weaving blankets specifically to sell to Spanish settlers.

1799

 Handsome Lake, a Seneca, sees visions that convince him that the Iroquois can regain their cul-

Friends and Enemies

 Warfare against some tribes and friendship with others was the norm in North America for thousands of years. At first, after the arrival of non-Indians, many tribes continued to war more intensely against each other than against the outsiders.

 In the Plains, the Sioux were known as fierce warriors. In the early 1800s, their enemies included Pawnees, Crows, Shoshones, and Kiowas. Among their friends: Assiniboines, Northern Arapahos, Northern Cheyennes, and Blackfeet.

tural and political power. He forbids drinking alcohol and teaches traditional rituals and values. He urges the Iroquois to learn from the white man, but to maintain their tribal and cultural integrity. His teachings become known as the Handsome Lake or Longhouse religion and continue to attract followers for the next two centuries.

1800

Eighty percent of land in what will become the lower forty-eight states of the United States still belongs to Indians and is largely undisturbed by whites.

The Pueblo Indians have suffered another decline in population, dropping from 14,000 to 10,000 since 1700.

1802

The U.S. government enters an agreement with Georgia to move the Cherokees out and turn their territory over to the state.

1803

Removal, the government policy of forcibly removing entire tribes from ancestral lands, gathers momentum with the Louisiana Purchase, when President Thomas Jefferson suggests moving eastern Indians west of the Mississippi.

The Kaskaskia (Illinois) people sign a treaty agreeing to obtain the consent of the United States before making war, either on other tribes or on foreign nations.

BLACK HAWK'S WAR

Between 1804 and 1832, 150,000 white settlers moved into Illinois and settled on land claimed by the Sac and Fox. Each spring, when the Sac and Fox returned from their winter hunt, they found more villages destroyed, more settlers living on their land. Again and again, Black Hawk and other leaders protested, but settlers kept coming, and Sac and Fox found themselves forced to relocate farther west, among tribes who resented having to share their traditional land with these strangers.

Finally, in the spring of 1832, Black Hawk led 1,000 Sac and Fox men, women, and children back into Illinois, hoping to reclaim and resettle their former lands. But the government sent troops to attack the Indians. After an initial battle at Stillman's Run, in which 40 warriors easily defeated 250 half-drunk soldiers, Black Hawk and his people turned on the settlers and rampaged across the countryside, trying to drive the invaders out of their homeland.

After that, Illinois militia and U.S. troops hunted down Sac and Fox mercilessly, and newspapers called for a "war of extermination." On August 3, Black Hawk tried to surrender, but troops clubbed, stabbed, and shot the Sac and Fox until the Mississippi ran red with their blood.

Two hundred escaped by swimming the river, but Sioux attacked them on the other side. Black Hawk escaped to the Winnebago Indians of Wisconsin, but they handed him over to government authorities. After a year in jail, the government sent the prisoner on a tour of eastern cities.

Following the war, the government seized all remaining Sac and Fox lands in Illinois and eastern Iowa and Winnebago land in southern Wisconsin. Unnerved by the war and the brutality of the peace, other tribes fled westward.

1804

At a conference in St. Louis, Sac and Fox leaders sign a document that they believe permits whites to enter their lands only to hunt, but that in fact turns over

50 million acres of land to white settlers. Black Hawk and other leaders who have signed repudiate the treaty. Other bands who have not participated in the conference likewise repudiate it. The government insists that the treaty is final and that the leaders who signed spoke for all Sac and Fox Indians. The Sac and Fox are forcibly removed to Iowa.

1805

   Sacajawea, the Shoshone wife of a French-Canadian fur trader, assists the Lewis and Clark expedition as an interpreter and peacemaker during the explorers' trek from North Dakota to the Pacific Ocean.

> **"I have heard many great orators, but I never saw one with the vocal powers of Tecumseh."**
> **—Captain Sam Dale of Mississippi, who fought against Indians in the early 1800s**

1807

The Cayugas of New York are forced to turn over their last surviving traditional territory in the Finger Lakes area to the state of New York, making them homeless. Eventually some Cayugas move to Canada, others to Oklahoma. Others settle among the Senecas.

> **"Forget not, O Choctaws and Chickasaws, that we are bound in peace to the Great White Father at Washington by a sacred treaty, and the Great Spirit will punish those who break their word."**
> **—Pushmataha, Choctaw leader, urging his people not to join Tecumseh's rebellion, 1811**

1808

 Shawnee leader Tecumseh and his brother, the prophet Tenskwatawa, establish a multitribal community of Ojibwas, Kickapoos, Ottawas, Delawares, and Wyandottes (Wendats), near the confluence of the Wabash and Tippecanoe Rivers in present-day Indiana. Non-Indians call the village Prophetstown.

1809

 Territorial governor William Henry Harrison orders Native American leaders to Fort Wayne, Indiana, where he gets them drunk and tricks them into signing over 3 million acres of Indian lands. Tecumseh, Shawnee leader, gathers 1,000 warriors in Prophetstown to protest the governor's treachery and prevent Harrison from taking possession of the land.

1810

 Tecumseh brings four hundred warriors to parley with Harrison at Vincennes, Indiana. Harrison invites Tecumseh to sit in a chair beside territorial officials, saying the "Great Father, the President of the United States," wants it so. Tecumseh refuses and sprawls on the ground saying, "My Father? The Sun is my father, the Earth is my mother—and on her bosom I will recline." The parley ends in a stalemate.

1811

 In Illinois, Potawatomis kill settlers. Governor Harrison decides the murderers are followers of

"THEY HAVE VANISHED"

  "Where today are the Pequot? Where the Narragansetts, the Mohawks, Pocanokets, and many other once powerful tribes of our people? They have vanished before the avarice and oppression of the white man, as snow before a summer sun. . . .

"Sleep not longer, O Choctaws and Chickasaws, in false security and delusive hopes. Our broad domains are fast escaping from our grasp. Every year our white intruders become more greedy, exacting, oppressive, and overbearing. . . .

"Are we not being stripped day by day of the little that remains of our ancient liberty? Do they not even kick and strike us as they do their black-faces? How long will it be before they will tie us to a post and whip us, and make us work for them in their corn fields as they do them? Shall we wait for that moment, or shall we die fighting before submitting to such ignominy?"
—Tecumseh, Shawnee leader, appealing to the Choctaws and Chickasaws for support in fighting Americans, spring 1811

Tenskwatawa, Tecumseh's brother, and he orders the Prophetstown Shawnees to turn the murderers over.

Tecumseh sets out on a six-month journey across the Carolinas, Mississippi, Georgia, Alabama, and Florida, asking Natives of many different tribes to put aside their differences and fight. Before he leaves, he asks Tenskwatawa not to fight while he is gone.

While Tecumseh is gone, Harrison marches on Prophetstown. Tenskwatawa and his warriors attack Harrison in the night, but Harrison's men withstand the attack and destroy Prophetstown in fighting that comes to be known as the Battle of Tippecanoe.

"Farewell, Tecumseh. You will see Pushmataha no more until we meet on the fateful warpath."
—Pushmataha, Choctaw leader, as he parts with Tecumseh, 1811

1812

Little Turtle, famed Miami leader, warrior, and peacemaker, dies at about age sixty-five at his lodge near the junction of the St. Mary and St. Joseph Rivers.

"Our lives are in the hands of the Great Spirit. We are determined to defend our lands, and if it be his will, we wish to leave our bones upon them."
—Tecumseh, Shawnee leader, September 1813, a month before his reported death

1812–13

Tecumseh returns from the South, enraged at Ten-skwatawa for fighting in his absence, and sends his brother into exile. In the ashes of Prophetstown, he swears eternal hatred of the Americans. Then he and his allies—Wyandottes, Chippewas, Sioux, Shawnees, and others—join the British in fighting Americans in the War of 1812.

A great military strategist, Tecumseh parades the same army of six hundred warriors across a clearing in front of Fort Detroit three times, so that the Americans will think his army three times stronger than it is. The ruse works, and the commander of Detroit capitulates without a fight.

Tecumseh's victories continue, but control of British forces falls to an anti-Indian officer, who, in spite of Tecumseh's victories, withdraws.

On October 5, 1813, Harrison's troops attack a combined force of British soldiers and Tecumseh's warriors. The British fall, but Tecumseh and his warriors continue fighting. The great leader of the Shawnees is last seen with blood covering his face as he yells enthusiastic shouts of support to his men.

1813

Red Eagle, a follower of Tecumseh, rallies Creek Indians of Alabama and Georgia to fight against the Americans. Red Eagle and his warriors capture Fort Mims, near Mobile, Alabama.

TECUMSEH

 One of the warriors fighting in vain at Fallen Timbers in August 1794 was a six-foot-tall Shawnee named Tecumseh, twenty-six years old. Helplessly he watched as a brother died, and his people and their allies, under Little Turtle, faced defeat.

Over the next few years, Tecumseh, whose name means "Cougar Crouching for his Prey," studied the white man's ways and history. He learned all he could about Alexander the Great, Caesar, and other military heroes. He dreamed of forming a great union of tribes that would drive the whites out, and he maintained that no tribe should sell land to whites without permission from all Indian tribes. Along with his brother, a prophet named Tenskwatawa, who preached a return to traditional Indian ways, Tecumseh founded a religious community, which non-Indians called Prophetstown. Then he traveled across the Northwest Territory—the present states of Ohio, Indiana, Illinois, Michigan, and Wisconsin—and among the Indians of the Southeast, urging Indians everywhere to unite.

When William Henry Harrison, a longtime fighter against Indians who would eventually become President of the United States, tricked some old chiefs into turning over millions of acres of Indian land while they were drunk, Tecumseh gathered a thousand warriors to prevent Harrison from claiming the land. As war broke out between the British and the Americans in 1812, Tecumseh rallied Wyandottes, Chippewas, Sioux, and others to fight on behalf of the British. That summer the great Indian leader and an army of 15,000 warriors roamed the lands around the Great Lakes, seizing American outposts.

In the end, though, Tecumseh could not overcome the obtuseness of his British allies, or offset the cultural and political forces separating tribes, or drive the whites out.

Harrison's troops believed they killed Tecumseh in battle in October 1813. But among Indians, the legend grew that Tecumseh still lived.

Tecumseh's teachings, his courage, and his belief in the right of the Indians to reclaim their ancestral lands inspired a struggle by Indians of many tribes east of the Mississippi that lasted for decades after he was gone.

Even Harrison, Tecumseh's great enemy, called him "one of those uncommon geniuses which spring up occasionally to produce revolutions and overturn the established order of things. If it were not for the vicinity of the United States, he would perhaps be the founder of an Empire that would rival in glory Mexico or Peru."

The Tennessee legislature authorizes 3,500 militia and $350,000 to fight the Creeks. Andrew Jackson leads the Americans. Creeks lose many men but continue fighting.

"I have done the white people all the harm I could. I have fought them, and fought them bravely. If I had an army, I would yet fight, and contend to the last. But I have none. My people are all gone. I can now do no more than weep over the misfortunes of my nation."
—Red Eagle, Creek leader, surrendering to Andrew Jackson, 1814

1814

At Horseshoe Bend along the Tallapoosa River in Alabama, surviving Creeks under Red Eagle meet Andrew Jackson's troops in the final battle of the Creek War. More than five hundred warriors die.

Jackson gives Red Eagle his freedom but forces the starving Creeks to sign over 23 million acres of Creek land in Georgia and Alabama to the United States. Many of the dispossessed Creeks drift into Florida and join the Seminoles.

CHOCTAW

  After centuries of living in their Mississippi homeland, the Choctaw Indians were forced to sign over their tribal lands in 1830 and agree to move to Indian Territory (Oklahoma). Of the 19,500 Choctaws alive at that time, 12,500 moved. Another 5,000 escaped relocation and remained on their ancestral lands. Because of the stress of the cultural upheavals and the traumas of forced removal, 2,500 Choctaws—more than one Choctaw in eight—died during the relocation.

As one of the Five Civilized Tribes, which also include the Cherokees, Chickasaws, Creeks, and Seminoles, the Choctaws lost most of their collective lands following the General Allotment Act of 1887 and the subsequent work of the Dawes Commission.

Today the Choctaws exist in many separate groups in Oklahoma, Louisiana, Alabama, and Mississippi. The Mississippi Band of Choctaws is descended from those who avoided relocation, and the Choctaw Tribe of Oklahoma is descended from those who submitted to relocation. Only these two groups have received federal recognition as tribes.

1815

 Sac and Fox in Illinois watch helplessly as settlers pour into their territory following the War of 1812.

1817

 The United States declares war on the Indians of Florida, which is still Spanish territory. General Andrew Jackson and his troops burn every Seminole village they encounter. They destroy food and capture runaway slaves who have been given sanctuary by Seminoles.

The campaign becomes known as the First Seminole War and leads Spain to hand Florida over to the United States.

1819

 After being forced onto a reservation in central Florida, hundreds of Seminoles die of starvation. Survivors raid white settlers, who begin lobbying for forced removal of the Seminoles to lands west of the Mississippi.

Cherokees are forced to cede much of their remaining territory to whites.

 Congress establishes a "civilization fund" to subsidize religious schools that enroll Indian children. This funding remains in effect until 1873.

1820

 Penobscots lose control of their lands when Maine becomes a state and becomes guardian of tribal holdings.

1821

 Petalesharo, Pawnee leader, travels from Nebraska to Washington, D.C., as a guest of President James Monroe.

 After twelve years of work, Sequoyah finishes developing the Cherokee language. The Cherokee Nation adopts the new alphabet, and tribe members learn to read and write.

SEQUOYAH

 Sequoyah, a Cherokee from eastern Tennessee, spent the years 1809 to 1821 developing an alphabet of the Cherokee language. The eighty-six-character alphabet made it possible to publish books and newspapers in Cherokee and for Cherokees across the United States to write letters to one another.

Born sometime between 1760 and 1776, Sequoyah spoke only Cherokee. He could not speak, read, or write English. But he was a talented painter and silversmith, and he understood the value of "talking leaves," as Cherokees called the printed word. At first he tried to transcribe Cherokee into pictographs. But that made an inefficient, cumbersome system, so he started again, adapting letters from the English, Greek, and Hebrew alphabets to form the Cherokee alphabet.

Once he completed the alphabet, Sequoyah became a leader among the Western Cherokees and traveled widely on behalf of his people. Although he reportedly kept a diary, it has never been found.

After his death, Sequoyah's name, respelled Sequoia, was given to the giant redwoods of California and to Sequoia National Park.

"The Great Spirit made us all—he made my skin red, and yours white; he placed us on this earth, and intended that we should live differently from each other. He made the whites to cultivate the earth, and feed on domestic animals; but he made us, red skins, to rove through the uncultivated woods and plains; to feed on wild animals; and to dress with their skins. He also intended that we should go to war—to take scalps—steal horses from and triumph over our enemies—cultivate peace at home, and promote the happiness of each other."
—Petalesharo, Pawnee leader, speaking to President James Monroe, February 4, 1822

1822

 Georgia urges Congress to cancel Cherokee land titles and turn the Indian's territory over to the state. Rather than fight a shooting war, the Cherokees spend the next ten years fighting for their rights through the courts.

1823

 The acting governor of Arkansas Territory demands that Quapaw Indians give up their land in Arkansas so that white farmers can plant more cotton crops.

 In a ruling that sets the pattern for the next century and a half, the U.S. Supreme Court decrees in *Johnson v. M'Intosh* that Indians have fewer rights to their own lands than do the "discoverers" of the Americas, white Europeans. The court determines that only the United States government has the right to decide the disposition of Indian lands. The case, in effect, makes the federal government the landlord and Indians the tenants.

1824

 The Bureau of Indian Affairs, soon renamed the Indian Office, is established as a branch of the War Department. Transferred twenty-five years later to the Department of the Interior, it comes to affect every aspect of Native American life by 1900.

The Indian Office continues the practice of bringing Indian leaders to Washington at government expense and hires artist Charles Bird King to paint portraits of the visitors. Over the next twenty years, King immortalizes more than 140 Indian leaders on canvas.

Pushmataha, aging Choctaw leader, arrives in Washington, D.C., with eight other Choctaws from Mississippi to negotiate a settlement regarding Choctaw lands. After three months of futile negotiating, Pushmataha falls ill and dies in his room at the Indian Queen Hotel on Christmas Eve.

1827

Armed with the written language invented by Sequoyah, the Cherokee Nation holds a constitutional convention and drafts a constitution. At this time, Cherokee holdings include 22,000 cattle, 7,600 horses, 46,000 pigs, 2,500 sheep, 762 looms, 2,488 spinning wheels, ten sawmills, thirty-one gristmills, sixty-two blacksmith shops, and eighteen schools.

Creeks living in Georgia are forced to relocate to Alabama.

> **"I had no father. I had no mother. The lightning rent the living oak, and Pushmataha sprang forth."**
> —Pushmataha, Choctaw leader born about 1764

1828

 Native Americans find themselves in trouble when Andrew Jackson, renowned for fighting Indians, is elected to the White House.

The first Native American newspaper, the *Cherokee Phoenix*, appears in Georgia. Thanks to the written alphabet devised by Sequoyah, it includes articles in Cherokee as well as English.

GALAGI'NA

*When the first native newspaper, the Chero-*kee Phoenix, *was published in 1828, the editor was a Cherokee named Galagi'na (Elias Boudinot). In 1833, during a period of great upheaval for his people, while he was still editing the newspaper, Galagi'na wrote a book in Chero-kee called* Poor Sarah; or the In-dian Woman.

As someone who had been ed-ucated among non-Indians and understood their ways, Galagi'na believed it was futile to resist the changes whites were determined to force on the Cherokee people. When the order came to move to Indian Territory, he urged people not to fight it. This made Gala-gi'na so unpopular that on June 22, 1839, another Cherokee mur-dered him.

Many Plains tribes wore feather-filled warbonnets as part of their war uniform. Following the customs of his people, Iron Tail, a Sioux leader of the mid-1800s, wore a warbonnet in which each feather stood for a courageous act during battle.

 Trading patterns and lifestyles among the Assiniboines, Crows, Crees, Blackfeet, and other tribes of the northern Plains change as Fort Union is erected at the confluence of the Misssouri and Yellowstone Rivers. The fort becomes a center in the fur trade. It also brings two great destroyers—smallpox and alcohol.

1829

 A century and a half after the murder of Wampanoag leader Metacomet, his life is dramatized in a popular New York stage play.

More and more white settlers invade Sac and Fox territory in Illinois. Black Hawk, Sac and Fox leader, returns from his winter hunt to find white squatters living in his lodge. Black Hawk protests, but the General Land Office ignores him and puts his village and other usurped land up for sale to whites. Black Hawk and other Sac and Fox are forced to move westward.

 When gold is discovered on Cherokee land in Georgia, whites increase pressure on Cherokees to give up their land and move west.

> **"The Great Spirit made the white man and the Indian. He did not make them alike."**
> —Daykauray, Winnebago, 1829

1830

 President Jackson warns Chickasaws either to emigrate from Mississippi or to give up tribal customs and acquiesce to Mississippi's claim that it has the legal right to control the Indians.

"WHEN WE ARE GONE"

"Here, my Great Father, is a pipe which I present you, as I am accustomed to present pipes to all the red skins in peace with us. It is filled with such tobacco as we were accustomed to smoke before we knew the white people. It is pleasant, and the spontaneous growth of the most remote parts of our country. I know that the robes, leggings, moccasins, bear claws, etc., are of little value to you, but we wish you to have them deposited and preserved in some conspicuous part of your lodge, so that when we are gone and the sod turned over our bones, if our children should visit this place, as we do now, they may see and recognize with pleasure the deposits of their fathers; and reflect on the times that are past."

—Petalesharo, Pawnee leader, giving President James Monroe a peace pipe and other traditional Pawnee gifts, Washington, D.C., February 1822

The Indian Removal Act authorizes President Jackson, a former Indian fighter, to relocate Indian tribes living in the Southeast.

The Treaty of Dancing Rabbit Creek forces Choctaws to agree to forfeit tribal lands in Mississippi and other areas east of the Mississippi River and move to Indian Territory (Oklahoma).

An epidemic of intermittent fever, probably malaria, decimates the Shoalwater band of the Lower Chehalis, the Willapa Chinook, the Lower Chinookans, and the Athabaskan-speaking Kwalhioqua in western Washington. Survivors merge and form a new tribe, the Shoalwater people.

"When returning from an ill-fated day's hunt, wearied and hungry, with my feet stumbling with the weight of sixty-four winters, I was basely charged by two palefaces of killing their hogs, which I indignantly denied because the charges were false, but they told me I lied, and then they took my gun, powderhorn, and bullet-pouch from me by violence, and beat me with a hickory stick until blood ran down my back like drops of falling rain, and my body was so lame and sore for a moon that I could not hunt or fish."

—Black Hawk, Sac leader, describing an 1831 encounter with white settlers

1831

 Black Hawk, sixty-four-year-old Sac leader, is accosted by white settlers, falsely accused of theft, and beaten severely.

Members of the Brothertown tribe of upstate New York emigrate to Wisconsin and establish the community of Manchester, later known as Brothertown.

 The Supreme Court refuses to hear the case *Cherokee Nation v. Georgia*, and states that the Cherokee Nation is, in effect, a ward of the U.S. government. "They occupy a territory to which we assert a title independent of their will," the court's ruling reads.

 Five hundred Odawa (Ottawa) Indians are forced to agree to leave Michigan and move to Kansas.

1832

 In *Worcester v. Georgia*, the U.S. Supreme Court acknowledges limited sovereignty of the Cherokee Nation, stating that the laws of Georgia have no force in Cherokee territory and that Georgia citizens may not enter without Cherokee permission. President Andrew Jackson says, "[Chief Justice] John Marshall has made his decision. Now let him enforce it." Congress and the state of Georgia proceed to seize Cherokee land.

 Black Hawk, Sac chief, leads 1,000 Sacs (Sauks) back to Illinois with the intention of reclaiming Sac land from white settlers. White soldiers attack and kill more than 850 men, women, and children. Survivors scatter. Black Hawk is taken prisoner and transported to Washington, D.C.

In a treaty with the Winnebago Indians, the federal government agrees to provide health services in exchange for land ceded. This sets the precedent for government health care of Native Americans.

"Sir, you are a man; so am I. But fortune has placed us in different circumstances. Your people are stronger than mine. You can dictate your terms. I am your prisoner, and must submit, but I am still a man, the same as you."
—Black Hawk, Sac leader and prisoner of the U.S. government, speaking to President Andrew Jackson following the Sac and Fox surrender in 1832

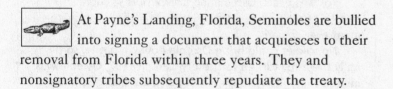 Creeks from Georgia who have been relocated in Alabama are forced to move again, this time to Indian Territory (Oklahoma). Many die. The Yuchi people of Georgia are required to move westward with the Creeks.

 At Payne's Landing, Florida, Seminoles are bullied into signing a document that acquiesces to their removal from Florida within three years. They and nonsignatory tribes subsequently repudiate the treaty.

 The Kickapoo in Illinois are forced to accept the Treaty of Castor Hill, which requires them to move to northeast Kansas.

OSCEOLA

 When General Wiley Thompson called a council of Seminole leaders in the spring of 1835 and intimidated them into signing a removal agreement, one young leader stepped forward and stabbed the treaty with his knife. "That's your heart," he said, "and my work."

The young man, Osceola, was a transplanted Creek who had suffered in encounters with whites during the Creek War, the First Seminole War, and afterward. In Florida, white slavers had stolen his wife, Chechoter, a Seminole of mixed Indian and black ancestry, and sold her as a slave in Georgia. According to the white man's law, the slavers' act was legal, but it added to Osceola's hatred of whites.

After he plunged his knife into the treaty paper, Osceola continued, "The white man says I shall go, and he will send people to make me go; but I have a rifle, and I have some powder and some lead. I say, we must not leave our homes and lands. If any of our people want to go west we won't let them; and I tell them they are our enemies, and we will treat them so, for the Great Spirit will protect us."

General Thompson jailed Osceola until he signed the document. "The agent has had his day. I will have mine," Osceola said. He disappeared into the swamps and reemerged fighting. He and his warriors killed Thompson and decimated soldiers sent against them. Seminoles who didn't want to fight turned to the U.S. government for protection.

For two years, Osceola led his warriors so successfully that this became the costliest Indian war the U.S. government ever waged.

No soldier could bring Osceola down in battle, so finally the army turned to trickery. Late in 1837, Osceola was invited to negotiate under a flag of truce that guaranteed his freedom. But once at the parley, he was captured and imprisoned. Many Americans protested this treachery, but the army refused to release Osceola. His warriors continued fighting under the Seminole leader Bowlegs.

While in prison at Fort Moultrie in South Carolina, Osceola grew weak with malaria and grief. On January 30, 1838, he dressed himself in his war clothing, put on his war belt, and painted himself with red war paint. Then he lay down on his prison bed, closed his eyes, and died.

In a final macabre brutality that violated ancient Native beliefs, an attending officer cut off the dead warrior's head and saved it as a souvenir.

 "Some time back beyond our old homes I heard a man preach from a book that he called a Bible, and although that book was read by a white man, I believe there is something better in it than the way the white man acts."
—Kanchi, a Choctaw, as the Choctaws prepare for forcible removal from Mississippi, spring 1834

1833

The Penobscot Indians lose 100,000 more acres of land when the state of Maine decides unilaterally to sell it. Penobscots are left with fewer than 5,000 acres.

Keokuk replaces Black Hawk as leader of the Sac Indians.

1834

Mission Indians of California who have finally adjusted to mission life find their lives disrupted again when the Mexican government secularizes the missions. Many Salinan and other Mission Indians drift away from their former mission communities and become further assimilated into mainstream Hispanic culture.

The Potawatomis of Wisconsin are ordered to move west of the Mississippi. Some comply. Some stay and go into hiding. Others flee to Canada or migrate to the Cedar River area of northern Michigan.

1835

Seminole chiefs are told that if they do not sign a document agreeing to their eviction from Florida, they will be removed as leaders of their people. One by one they sign, until Osceola, a Creek who has joined the

Seminoles following the Creek War, stabs his hunting knife into the document and issues his famous call to war. Osceola becomes head war chief of the Seminole warriors, who number under five hundred. On December 28, Seminoles under Micanopy, a fellow war chief, decimate two companies of white soldiers. On New Year's Eve, Osceola's warriors defeat a force of eight hundred more soldiers.

Five hundred Cherokees are forced to sign a treaty agreeing to sell all remaining Cherokee land east of the Mississippi and move to Indian Territory (Oklahoma). They are promised the freedom to establish their own country and their own laws, as long as those laws harmonize with the U.S. Constitution. More than 15,000 Cherokees protest the treaty, but President Jackson orders them out and sets a deadline of May 23, 1838.

The Kadohadachos (Caddos) are forced to give up their land in Louisiana and move to Texas.

Coharie and other Indians in North Carolina lose many rights when the state constitution is changed to define them as "people of color."

1836

Cayuse people along the upper Walla Walla River find their traditions and customs challenged as Presbyterian missionaries arrive and settle among them.

Ki-on-twog-ky, longtime leader of the Senecas, dies at about age one hundred.

Smallpox breaks out in Alaska. It passes from family to family, village to village, and cultural group to cultural group. The outbreak lasts for four years and kills more than 4,000 people.

1837

 Osceola is invited to a peace parley, then seized and imprisoned. Seminole warriors fight on, under Bowlegs and other leaders.

 Smallpox hits the Mandans of the upper Missouri region again, annihilating the remaining 1,600 tribespeople. Fewer than 200 survive. Other tribes in the northern Plains lose an additional 13,000 members to the deadly pustules.

Social and geographical disruptions caused by the epidemic allow the Sioux to push the Kiowas from the Black Hills and force the Crows out of the Powder River area.

"We, the People"

  "Therefore we, the people composing the Eastern and Western Cherokee Nation, in National Convention assembled, by virtue of our original and inalienable rights, do hereby solemnly and mutually agree to form ourselves into one body politic, under the style and title of the Cherokee Nation.

"In view of the union now formed, and for the purpose of making satisfactory adjustment of all unsettled business which may have arisen before the consummation of this union, we agree that such business shall be settled according to the provisions of the respective laws under which it originated, and the courts of the Cherokee Nation shall be governed in their decisions accordingly."

—Eastern and Western Cherokees agreeing to join and create the Cherokee Nation, July 12, 1839

1838

 Black Hawk, vanquished Sac and Fox leader, dies.

The treaty of Buffalo Creek forces the six Iroquois tribes, along with Brothertowners and others, to agree to abandon their land and move to Kansas.

  Osceola dies in prison. The Seminoles fight on. Zachary Taylor, future U.S. President, becomes commander of field operations. He rounds up Seminoles and ships prisoners west. He uses bloodhounds to track remaining resisters through the swamps. Newspapers in the North protest this ploy, to no effect. Seminoles continue fighting.

By the May 23 deadline, only 2,000 Cherokees have moved from Georgia to Oklahoma; 15,000 remain in Georgia and refuse to leave. Soldiers under Winfield Scott ride into Cherokee territory and force the Cherokees out of their homes at gunpoint. Captured Cherokees spend the summer in a concentration camp, then are loaded into 645 covered wagons and forced to ride and walk westward toward Oklahoma. Four thousand die along the way. The brutal removal of the Cherokees and other tribes becomes known as the Trail of Tears.

 The people of Pecos Pueblo find their life and customs disrupted by smallpox epidemics, passing wagon trains, and Comanche raids. Once the largest Pueblo village in the Southwest, Pecos dwindles to fewer than two dozen residents, and the sacred fire, which has burned uninterrupted for centuries, dies. Survivors abandon their ancestral home and move west to the Pueblo community of Jemez, the only other village that speaks Towa.

 "If I could . . . I would remove every Indian tomorrow beyond the reach of the white men, who, like vultures, are watching, ready to pounce on their prey and strip them of everything they have. . . ."
—General John Ellis Wool, on being ordered to force the Cherokees to leave their Georgia homeland, 1838

1839

  The Eastern and Western Cherokees assemble at a National Convention of Cherokees at Illinois Campground and declare themselves one nation, acting in unison. Sequoyah signs as president of the Western Cherokees; George Lowrey signs as president of the Eastern Cherokees.

 The army tries to force Potawatomis of Michigan to move west of the Mississippi. Those who escape the roundup flee back to Michigan.

The Brothertowners win a battle in Congress, which allows them to remain on their lands in Wisconsin and grants them citizenship. It is later argued that this legislation deprives the Brothertowners of tribal status.

  After two centuries of cultural upheavals and migrations, a band of Texas Kickapoo, originally from the Great Lakes region, flees into Mexico and settles in Coahuila.

Apache Arrows

 Apaches made their bows and arrows with such craftsmanship and used them with such skill that the ancient weapon flew accurately for more than one hundred yards. A well-trained archer could shoot so fast that he would be drawing the bow for his ninth arrow before the first hit its mark.

RAPE OF THE SACRED LAND

 Throughout the West, the biggest danger Native peoples faced in preserving their right to live on the sacred lands of their ancestors was the discovery of minerals on that land. Again and again, land that treaties had already confirmed as belonging to Indians was seized by force or treachery, usually with the loss of hundreds of lives and the further deterioration of ancient customs and cultures.

In the Great Plains, the Sioux lost the sacred Black Hills following the discovery of gold there in 1874. In the battles and upheavals that followed, many Sioux died or found their lives destroyed, and many ancient lifeways were lost forever. In the Plateau region, Nez Perce lost much of their land to money-hungry miners; the tragic flight of the Nez Perce under Chief Joseph and others followed. In the Great Basin, Utes found their sacred land stolen. And in the Southwest and California, the discovery of gold in Arizona brought in floods of miners that changed the Natives' lives forever.

About 1840

 Kitzn-jin-jn, a headman of the Coos Indians, marries Gishgewe, daughter of an Upper Co-quille chief, uniting the two tribes. Their daughter Susan Adulseh Wasson becomes a noted oral historian, court translator, and storyteller.

1840

Comanche chiefs bolt from a peace parley when Texas Rangers try to seize them. Rangers shoot them. In revenge, five hundred Comanche warriors attack and destroy the towns of Linnville and Victoria, killing twenty-four whites.

1841

 The Second Seminole War ends officially, but skirmishes continue for another seventeen years. Four thousand Seminoles have been shipped west. A few bands manage to escape army detection by slipping deep into the swamps.

1842

Three and a half centuries after the arrival of Europeans in the Americas, another mass invasion is set to begin: of white settlers pushing west of the Mississippi into lands already occupied by Indians. In the trans-Mississippi West, the Native American population is estimated at 360,000. The Plains peoples, who live scattered from Montana to Minnesota, and from the Canadian border to Texas, number only about 75,000. By contrast, the government has moved 84,000 Indians from the Five Civilized Tribes—Cherokee, Creek, Choctaw, Chickasaw, and Seminole—from the Southeast into Oklahoma. In the Southwest, about 12,000 Navajos live in the Colorado Plateau. Their linguistic and cultural cousins, the Apaches, number an estimated 8,000.

Sequoyah, Cherokee leader, now an old man, travels to Mexico to try to persuade Cherokee refugees there to return to the United States.

Bostons

In the 1840s and later, Indians living along the Oregon Trail in the Plateau and Great Basin called the white people flooding into their territory Bostons, no matter where the outsiders came from.

"THE BUFFALO COULD BE SEEN"

 In 1846, at a time when millions of buffalo still pounded across the flat plains, Old Smoke and Whirlwind, two Oglala Sioux leaders, allowed historian Francis Parkman to participate in a buffalo hunt. Wrote Parkman:

Amid the trampling and the yells I could see their dark figures running hither and thither through clouds of dust, and the horsemen darting in pursuit. . . . The uproar and confusion lasted but a moment. The dust cleared away, and the buffalo could be seen scattering as from a common centre, flying over the plain singly, or in long files and small compact bodies, while behind them followed the Indians riding at furious speed, and yelling as they launched arrow after arrow into their sides. The carcasses were strewn thickly over the ground. Here and there stood wounded buffalo, their bleeding sides feathered with arrows; and as I rode by them their eyes would glare, they would bristle like gigantic cats, and feebly attempt to rush up and gore my horse.

1843

 While in Mexico visiting Cherokee refugees, Sequoyah dies and is buried there.

  After being pushed from their St. Lawrence River homes to Ohio and Michigan by the Iroquois, the Wyandottes (Hurons) find themselves forced to move again, this time by the U.S. Army, which resettles them in Kansas. Only fourteen years later, in the upheavals that precede the Civil War, they relocate again, to Indian Territory (Oklahoma).

1845

 Moguago and Pamptopee, leaders of the Potawatomi refugees in southern Michigan, purchase eighty acres of land for their people to live on. The state of Michigan donates another forty acres.

  The Sac and Fox Tribes are forcibly resettled on a reservation in Kansas.

1846

  The Miami Tribe, which is scattered across Ohio, Indiana, and Illinois, is forcibly divided into two groups. About six hundred are shipped by canal boat to a reservation in Kansas, and eventually on to Oklahoma. The other group is allowed to remain in north-central Indiana.

MISSIONARIES

 From the beginning of Native contacts with Europeans, missionaries disrupted Native cultures and lives.

 The Plateau region provides a good example, even though missionaries bringing the white man's religion arrived relatively late, in the 1800s. Used to the laissez-faire attitude of white trappers, the Indians couldn't at first comprehend the missionaries' rejection of Native values, beliefs, and customs. For instance, Tilokaikt, leader of the Cayuse, was stunned when Narcissa Whitman refused a gift he brought for her newborn: a pair of coyote paws.

In the Plateau as in other parts of the country, the presence of missionaries led to the development of two factions in tribe after tribe: Christians and non-Christians. In this way, the missionaries disrupted the political structures of the Native peoples as well as their cultures and traditions.

In the 1860s, about two-thirds of the 4,000 Nez Perce Indians belonged to the Christian faction. Their leader was Hallalhotsoot, called Lawyer by whites, who admired his skills as a debater. The remaining Nez Perce, labeled heathens by the missionaries, followed Old Joseph, Eagle from the Light, White Bird, Old Looking Glass, Young Looking Glass, and other leaders in continuing their ancient beliefs and customs.

When the U.S. Army seizes New Mexico from Mexico, Navajos provide the first resistance the army encounters when they steal cattle from the beef herd of General Stephen Watts Kearny. They also steal thousands of cattle, sheep, and horses from Hispanic settlers under his protection.

1847

In Oregon, the Cayuse people, already suspicious of the missionaries and settlers who are flooding their traditional territory, contract measles from an infected traveler in a passing wagon train. Approximately half the Cayuse near Waiilatpu die in the epidemic. Survivors suspect Marcus and Narcissa Whitman, Presbyterian missionaries, of poisoning them and vow revenge. To avenge the deaths of so many Cayuse by measles, Tilokaikt and Tomahas lead a party of Cayuse on an attack at the Whitmans' mission at Waiilatpu in November. They kill the Whitmans and nearly a dozen others and take thirty-nine hostages, most of them children.

1848

  Keokuk, Sac leader, dies in Franklin County, Kansas, without being allowed to return to his native land.

Indians living in central Oregon face unexpected upheavals when Colonel Cornelius Gilliam, a proponent of extermination of all Indians, leads 550 citizen soldiers on a government-sanctioned rampage to avenge the Whitmans' deaths. He attacks peaceful Indians who had nothing to do with the massacre, and soon the Cayuse, Nez Perce, Palouse, and other tribes of the Columbia Basin are on the verge of uniting for war. But Gilliam dies in an accident, and in June the soldiers withdraw. Peace returns.

"His chest and arms were naked; the buffalo robe, worn over them when at rest, had fallen about his waist, and was confined there by a belt. This, with the gay moccasins on his feet, completed his attire. For arms he carried a quiver of dog-skin at his back, and a rude but powerful bow in his hand."
—Francis Parkman, on his encounter with an Oglala Sioux Indian at Fort Laramie in 1846

Pueblo Indians, who have full citizenship under Mexican rule, are promised continued full citizenship when Mexico turns over New Mexico to the United States in the Treaty of Guadalupe Hidalgo. Their ancient landholdings are also protected by treaty. Neither provision of the treaty is subsequently honored.

Cocopah Indians of southern Arizona and northern Mexico find themselves separated from relatives and tribal members by the new international border.

 In New York State, the Seneca Nation votes to establish its own republic and adopt a constitution. The Senecas eliminate the system of traditional chiefs. That act is considered to constitute their withdrawal from the ancient Iroquois Confederacy. Other bands of Senecas, including the Tonawanda, continue their membership in the confederacy and the tradition of the council of chiefs.

1849

At the moment before gold is discovered in California, the Native American population there stands at 300,000. As thousands of gold seekers and settlers arrive, they disrupt Indian lifestyles, seize their land, destroy their food supplies, transmit diseases to them, and wage an open war of extermination against them. By 1860, only 30,000 Indians survive.

  Treaties with the Navajos and Utes give the U.S. government the right to pass laws governing Indian activities and lands.

 Navajos living in Canyon de Chelly find their territory invaded by three hundred soldiers seeking stolen stock. Navajos blame the Apaches, and the soldiers leave, but not before Narbona, a prominent Navajo leader, dies in a skirmish.

About 1850

 Navajo artisans adopt silversmithing from Hispanic silversmiths.

1850

 Witthae, daughter of a chief of the Iowas, marries Rudolph Friedrich Kurz, a Swiss-born artist. Within a week, she decides she has made a mistake and returns to her tribe. Kurz goes on to draw hundreds of illustrations depicting Plains Indians and their customs and lives.

 Tilokaikt, Tomahas, and three other Cayuse Indians turn themselves in to white authorities for killing the Whitmans in 1847. Tried and convicted of murder, they are sentenced to hang. On June 3, they accept last rites from a Catholic priest and die.

   Congress enacts the Land Donation Act, which opens all land in Oregon and Washington, including Indian lands, to homesteading by white settlers.

1850–63

 Under the Act for the Government and Protection of Indians, an estimated 10,000 California Indians, many of them children, are kidnapped and sold as de facto slaves or forced to work as indentured servants.

THE TREATY OF FORT LARAMIE

In 1851, the U.S. government invited 10,000 Plains Indians to a treaty council near Fort Laramie. Bands of Sioux, Arapahos, Cheyennes, Gros Ventres, Crows, Shoshones, Assiniboines, and Arikaras attended the September meeting, but Pawnees, Comanches, and Kiowas stayed away, saying they did not trust the Sioux and Crow.

Tribes attending the council were required to elect one person to serve as head chief. These newly elected head chiefs signed the Treaty of Fort Laramie. The government expected their signatures to bind all Sioux, all Shoshones, all Arapahos, and so on to honor the terms of the treaties, but the notion of a single leader for an entire Indian nation contradicted centuries of social and political customs. Bands not represented at the council, and bands other than those to which the new head chiefs belonged, did not consider themselves to be partners to the agreement.

The Treaty of Fort Laramie called for Indians and whites to live in peace forever. It allowed whites to build roads and forts on Indian land, and it delineated boundaries of white and Indian territories. The treaty later became known as the first in a series of treaties that alternated with uprisings, leading to the Battle of Little Bighorn in 1876 and culminating in the destruction of the Plains Indians' way of life.

The Treaty of Fort Laramie reflected new realities. No longer could Indians hope that by moving west of the Mississippi they would be free from white invasions into their lands, their cultures, and their lives.

Tribes protest but are helpless. In desperation, parents among the Wailaki people begin tattooing their children, so that if the children are stolen and grow up among strangers, they will always know who their people were. Only after the passage of federal legislation freeing slaves during the Civil War is the act repealed.

Hoping to reduce intertribal warfare and make the Oregon Trail and the Santa Fe Trail safe for white travelers, government officials call a treaty council at Fort Laramie, Wyoming. Misunderstandings that arise out of the subsequent treaty set the stage for later bloodshed and cultural disruptions.

The Santee Sioux of Minnesota, under Little Crow and other leaders, succumb to the pressure of white settlement and agree to sell their hunting grounds for $3 million, broken into fifty annual installments.

The Cheyenne are formally split into Northern Cheyennes and Southern Cheyennes.

 In California, thirteen chiefs of the Shasta peoples meet with government representatives and agree to live on a reservation to be set aside for them. When the signing is completed, the hosts prepare a feast of barbecued meat for the chiefs and their followers—and lace the food with strychnine. Thousands of Shasta die. To complete the genocidal brutality, white vigilantes attack and torch Shasta villages, raping and killing the inhabitants.

 "That the war of extermination will continue to be waged until the Indian race becomes extinct, must be expected."
—Governor Peter H. Burnett of California, 1851

1852

 In Maine, the Passamaquoddy split into two factions, progressives and traditionalists. The traditionalists, who favor as little contact with whites as possible, found the village of Motahkokmikuk. Progressives, who favor assimilation, remain at Sipayik.

> "Revenge by young men is considered gain, even at the cost of their own lives, but old men who stay at home in times of war, and mothers who have sons to lose, know better."
> —Attributed to Seattle, chief of the Suquamish and Duwamish, 1853 or 1854

1853

  Since 1846, nearly half of all remaining Plateau Indians have died in a series of smallpox epidemics. Epidemics also ravage tribes along the Northwest Coast. Among the Stillaguamish of western Washington, approximately 85 percent perish.

 The San Sebastian Indian Reserve is established for the Kitanemuk and other Indians at Rancho El Tejón in California. The reserve is voided when it is determined that this is part of an older land grant, but the Kitanemuk continue to reside at Rancho El Tejón. Gradually they become known as Tejón Indians.

In northern California, 450 Tolowas are slaughtered by white settlers, who also destroy the Tolowas' ancestral spiritual center, Yontockett. This genocidal attack occurs during performance of the sacred Naydosh, a ceremony that renews and honors Mother Earth.

 Tribes who refused to attend the Fort Laramie treaty council in 1851 convene at Fort Atkinson on the Arkansas River and are forced to agree to similar terms.

 ## "THE WHITE MAN WILL NEVER BE ALONE"

"When the last Red Man shall have perished, and the memory of my tribe shall have become a myth among the White Men, these shores will swarm with the invisible dead of my tribe, and when your children's children think themselves alone in the field, the store, the shop, upon the highway, or in the silence of the pathless woods, they will not be alone. In all the earth there is no place dedicated to solitude. At night when the streets of your cities and villages are silent and you think them deserted, they will throng with the returning hosts that once filled them and still love this beautiful land. The White Man will never be alone.

"Let him be just and deal kindly with my people, for the dead are not powerless. Dead, did I say? There is no death, only a change of worlds."
—Attributed to Seattle, chief of the Suquamish and Duwamish, 1853 or 1854

THE SPEECH OF CHIEF SEATTLE

 In 1853 white settlers in western Washington State named a small community on Puget Sound for Chief Seattle, noted leader of the Suquamish and Duwamish Tribes. At a ceremony in his honor, Chief Seattle addressed the settlers in the Duwamish language. Dr. Henry Smith, who spoke both Duwamish and English, attended the ceremony and translated the speech into English.

Nearly a century and a half later, the speech has become a major source of argument among non-Indians. Some say that Dr. Smith wrote the speech down immediately, in as accurate a rendition of the great chief's words as was possible, given the differences in cultures and worldviews. Others believe that Dr. Smith waited more than three decades before recording the speech, from memory, and that he altered Seattle's meaning to reflect his own views.

Complicating the issue, in 1972 a non-Indian writer rewrote Seattle's speech to match ideas prevalent among non-Indians in the 1970s. That fictitious oration has circulated widely.

The quotations presented in this book are from Dr. Smith's rendition of the speech. Even if they contain embellishments added by Smith, they have had a major effect on Indians and non-Indians for more than a century.

 The Makah Indians are allowed to preserve a portion of their ancestral lands on the Pacific coast of Washington when the Treaty of Neah Bay is signed. Subsequent treaties bring other traditional Makah villages into the reservation.

The town of Seattle is laid out and named after the chief of the Suquamish and Duwamish Tribes.

1854

 The Oto and Missouri Treaty authorizes the U.S. president to circumvent tribal policies and allot ownership of tribal lands to individual Indians. The treaty becomes the forerunner of the disastrously destructive General Allotment Act of 1887.

The Dakota Sioux are forced to sign over rights to 21 million acres of ancestral lands.

As wagon trains pass through Sioux territory in the North Platte Valley, High Forehead, a Sioux warrior, kills a traveler's ox. Soldiers respond by killing Brave Bear, the designated head chief of the Brule Sioux. Brave Bear's warriors and other Sioux attack and kill all but one of the soldiers in revenge. General William S. Harney, known to Indians as the Butcher, marches up the Oregon Trail to take revenge. Little Thunder succeeds Brave Bear.

 "By God, I'm for battle—no peace."
—General George William S. Harney,
called by Sioux the Butcher, as he
marches out of Fort Kearny, Nebraska, to
slaughter Sioux, August 24, 1855

 Even though the Steilacoom Indians of western Washington agree to the Medicine Creek Treaty, they are left landless because of white plans to settle on traditional Steilacoom land. Some Steilacooms leave and join nearby tribes; others remain in the land of their ancestors, hoping that a better day will come.

> "My people, what have you done? While I was gone, you have sold my country. Go home to your lodges. I will talk to you."
> —Looking Glass, Nez Perce leader, begging his people to reconsider their choice to acquiesce to Governor Isaac Stevens's demand that they give up their ancestral lands in Washington Territory and move to reservations, May 1855

1855

Isaac Stevens, governor of Washington Territory, invites 5,000 Indians to the Walla Walla Valley for a treaty council. The Wanapam refuse to participate. Chief Peo-peo-mox-mox of the Wallawallas arrives, but refuses to eat with the whites. A thousand Nez Perce warriors thunder into camp dressed in full war regalia. After Stevens tells the assembly they must agree to move to reservations, or be overrun by white settlers, Nez Perce chief Looking Glass begs his people not to sign. But other leaders agree to the enforced move. Stevens promises it will be two or three years before they have to move, but then opens their land for settlement two weeks later.

Following U.S. government policy of combining small tribes into large ones, fourteen distinct tribes and bands, including the Yakimas, are merged into one unit and placed on a reservation in Washington State. Henceforth, all are called Yakimas. All together, they have lost more than 29,000 square miles of land—an area larger than West Virginia—to non-Indians.

When gold is discovered on Yakima lands, Chief Kamiakin responds to invading white miners by creating an alliance of Plateau tribes to keep the whites west of the Cascade

Mountains. Kamiakin's nephew Qualchin participates in a massacre of whites, and Kamiakin warns that any "Bostons" (whites) who cross the Cascades will die. A party of five hundred warriors chases soldiers sent to test Kamiakin's ultimatum back to Fort Dalles, and the Yakima War begins.

> "Why should I mourn at the untimely fate of my people? Tribe follows tribe, and nation follows nation, like the waves of the sea. It is the order of nature, and regret is useless. Your time of decay may be distant, but it will surely come, for even the White Man whose God walked and talked with him as friend with friend, cannot be exempt from the common destiny. We may be brothers after all. We will see."
> —Attributed to Seattle, chief of the Suquamish and Duwamish, 1853

While attending a truce parley, Chief Peo-peo-mox-mox of the Wallawallas is seized and killed by the Oregon militia. The settler-soldiers scalp Peo-peo-mox-mox, cut off his ears, and send these grisly souvenirs home for display.

The Flathead Reservation is established in western Montana. Here Salish, Kootenai, Pend d'Oreille (Kalispel), Spokane, Flathead, and other Indian groups are merged into a single tribal unit by treaty.

The Cayuse, Umatilla, and Wallawalla Indians are forced to give 4 million acres of tribal lands to the United States and resettle on a 250,000-acre reservation in northeastern Oregon. A few Palouse and Nez Perce Indians join them. As white settlers move in, they take away more land, until only 95,000 acres remain. Eventually the combined tribes become known as the Confederated Tribes of the Umatilla Indian Reservation.

Des Chutes, Tenino, Dock-spus, Dalles, Kigaltwalla, Wasco, and Dog River peoples are forced to abandon their homelands and move to the Warm Springs Reservation in northern Oregon. They become known as the Confederated Tribes of the Warm Springs Reservation.

 Ojibway politician William W. Warren publishes the classic *History of the Ojibway People*. With George Copway's *Traditional History and Characteristic Sketches of the Ojibway Nation*, it stands among the first written works of Native American history produced by Native American historians.

> "Why do you ask us to leave the rivers, the sun, and the wind, and live in houses? Do not ask us to give up the buffalo for the sheep. The young men have heard talk of this, and it has made them sad and angry."
> —Comanche warrior protesting the government's insistence that his people live on a reservation, mid-1800s

In the Rogue River area of southern Oregon, settlers kill twenty-three old people and children. When a war party responds by killing twenty-seven settlers, settlers vow to exterminate the Indians. Two hundred and thirty members of the Cow Creek Band of Umpqua Indians flee into the mountains, where they remain in hiding for decades.

Many Samish Indians of the San Juan Islands refuse to move, as required by the Treaty of Point Elliott. Although they cannot know it, this decision will cost their descendants the right to governmentally recognized tribal status.

The Klallam Indians of western Washington are ordered to move to the Skokomish Reservation following the Treaty of Point No Point. They refuse to go, and for the next several decades successfully resist attempts to enforce their removal.

MEDICINE SONGS

 Traditionally there were two kinds of Native songs: songs consciously composed by people and songs that came to a person in visions or dreams.

 In revealing the words of his own medicine song, Goyahkla (Geronimo), famous Apache leader, said, "The song tells how, as I sing, I go through the air to a holy place where Yusun [the Creator] will give me power to do wonderful things. I am surrounded by little clouds, and as I go through the air I change, becoming spirit again."

O, ha le
O, ha le!
Through the air
I fly upon a cloud
Towards the sky, far, far, far,
O, ha le
O, ha le!
There to find the holy place,
Ah, now the change comes over me!
O, ha le
O, ha le!

 "The sun is our father."
—White Bird (Otank), Kiowa medicine man, speaking through Kiowa leader Lone Wolf, at a peace council with representatives of the U.S. government, 1866

The Quinault Indians lose most of their ancestral lands to the government, but are able to preserve the core of the most important ceremonial lands.

On September 3, a band of 250 Sioux men, women, and children are attacked in their village along Blue Water Creek by soldiers under General William S. Harney, known by Sioux as the Butcher. Eighty-five

CONFEDERATED TRIBES OF GRAND RONDE

In the mid-1800s, Indians from five Oregon groups were required to leave their traditional homelands and merge into one unit, the Confederated Tribes of Grand Ronde. They included Shasta, Kalapuya, Rogue River, Molalla, and Umpqua Indians, as well as a few Chinook, Clackamas, and others.

They settled together on a 59,000-acre reservation and worked to preserve ancient traditions while forming a new collective identity.

At the turn of the century, the confederated tribes lost most of their joint lands because of the U.S. government's cruel allotment policy. Finally, in the 1930s, following the Indian Reorganization Act, they received 537 acres for a reservation. A generation later, in 1954, when the government reversed its policy again, it confiscated the land and legislated the Grand Ronde tribes out of existence.

Not until 1983 were the Grand Rondes allowed to regroup as a tribal unit. They regained many former rights, except hunting, fishing, and trapping. In 1988, Congress transferred 9,800 acres of land within the original reservation from the Bureau of Land Management to the tribe.

Today the Grand Rondes operate a tribal council and tribal court system and work to restore a sense of cultural heritage. Three thousand people are enrolled as Grand Rondes.

Sioux die; 70 women and children are taken prisoner. The Butcher challenges other Sioux to fight. None do.

1856

Members of a dozen groups of Oregon Indians, most of them Athabaskans, are forcibly marched and moved by ship from their homelands to the newly established Siletz Reservation. The refugees include Galice Creek, Chetco, Mishikwutinetuhne, Kwatami, Tututni,

Kwaishtunnetunne, Shasta Costa, Mikonotunne, Chetleshin, Yukichetunne, and Chemetunne peoples. Many die. Survivors are resettled along the Siletz River near the Pacific Ocean and become known collectively as the Siletz Indians.

On May 27, Rogue River chiefs Old John, George, and Limpy attack soldiers in the Battle of Big Meadows but are beaten back when reinforcements arrive. They and their people surrender and are moved to a reservation along the Oregon coast.

The Bureau of Indian Affairs and the U.S. Army forcibly resettle Coos Indians of Oregon at the mouth of the Umpqua River among the Lower Umpqua Indians. Hundreds die in the brutal upheaval.

 In March, chiefs of the Teton Sioux attend a peace council called by the Butcher (General William S. Harney). Harney orders them to sign a peace treaty, and they do. With the Sioux defeated, Cheyennes move up from the south and harass wagon trains along the Platte Road in Nebraska.

 Embattled Yakima chief Kamiakin and other war leaders flee eastward. In July, settler-soldiers kill forty Wallawalla Indians and pronounce the Yakima War over. But as settlers and gold seekers flood Indian lands, Kamiakin and other leaders prepare for the next confrontation.

1857

In New York, the Tonawanda Band of Senecas signs a treaty that requires them to gain approval of the Secretary of the Interior for any attorneys they appoint. This treaty becomes a forerunner of government policies toward tribes across the United States.

On the Solomon River in western Kansas, three hundred Cheyenne warriors face soldiers under Colonel Edwin V. Sumner. Medicine men have prepared warriors for battle by having them wash their hands in sacred water to gain protection from bullets, and they face soldiers without fear. But Sumner learns of the rite and orders soldiers to attack with sabers. Cheyennes flee.

"Now the woods is full of indian sine [signs of Indians] in one mile of my house I dare not to leave my house to go one mile on aney business for fear my familey is murde[red] before I can get back I pay my taxes as any other citisons for protection and has failed to get it."
—Settler in a letter to the governor of Texas, begging for protection from Comanches, 1858

1858

In early May, Comanches living along the Canadian River near Oklahoma's Antelope Hills look up to see a hundred Texas Rangers swooping down on them. For seven hours, the Comanches fight their attackers, but seventy-six villagers die, and Comanches finally flee. Rangers burn the village and return to Texas.

In mid-May, warriors of the Palouse, Spokane, and Coeur d'Alene Tribes attack and nearly annihilate three companies of dragoons and a detachment of infantry under Lieutenant Colonel Edward J. Steptoe. Yakima chief Kamiakin, his nephew Qualchin, and his brother-in-law Owhi are singled out as villains. In early September, in the Battle of Spokane Plain and the Battle

IÑUPIAQ

For centuries, the Iñupiat (singular: Iñupiaq), known to outsiders as Eskimos or Inuit, have lived scattered across Alaska, northern Canada, Greenland, and the far eastern tip of Russia. In Alaska, their picturesque lifestyle—including snow block houses called igloos, animal skin boats called kayaks, and heavy fur clothing—have fascinated outsiders for many decades. The most recent newcomers to the Americas before Europeans, the Iñupiat are called Alaska Natives, but in a nuance of the anthropology of non-Native people, they are not considered to be Indians.

Earlier in this century, the federal government worked systematically to wipe out both the Iñupiaq language and the culture. Schoolchildren caught speaking their own language had their mouths washed out with soap and their hands slapped and were required to write, over and over, in English, "I will not speak Eskimo."

During the 1960s, without the knowledge or permission of the Iñupiat, the Atomic Energy Commission dumped unsealed, unprotected nuclear waste on Iñupiaq land. The waste exposed both animals and humans to dangerous levels of radiation.

Traditions that remain strong among Alaska Iñupiat include the winter Messenger Feast and the summer trade fair. Held in January in Barrow, the Messenger Feast includes social and sacred rituals that have survived from pre-European days. In 1991, Iñupiat from Russia came from Chukotka to celebrate the summer trade fair with Alaska Inupiat for the first time in a century.

The Iñupiat today also observe ancient rituals related to whaling. The People believe that whales will not give themselves to hunters who do not have a properly prepared home. So when the spring sun appears after the long winter night, householders clean their ice cellars and line them with fresh snow to prepare a place for the whale.

Following the whale hunt comes the Blanket Toss. Whale meat is divided among villagers, and a blanket made from whale skin is used to toss people into the air, one at a time.

of Four Lakes, soldiers with new long-range infantry rifles easily defeat an alliance of six hundred Indian warriors fighting with short muskets and bows and arrows. A badly wounded Kamiakin flees to Canada. At a peace conference, soldiers seize Owhi, force him to send for his son Qualchin, then murder both leaders.

In September, Buffalo Hump, Comanche chief, pledges peace and friendship with soldiers at Fort Arbuckle, but on October 1, troops under Major Earl Van Dorn attack Buffalo Hump's village on Rush Creek, killing fifty-eight. Comanches flee and vow revenge.

"Your friend is your enemy."
—Saying among the San Juan Paiutes,
as a reminder that the only people you
can really count on are family

Congress authorizes the Commissioner of Indian Affairs to forcibly remove individuals, both Indians and non-Indians, from reservation land if the commissioner considered that person "detrimental to the peace and welfare of the Indians."

Bowlegs, Seminole chief, gives in to years of pressure from the U.S. government. He agrees that the Seminoles will leave Florida and resettle in Oklahoma.

1859

At Crooked Creek, ninety-one Comanche men, women, and children trapped in a ravine fight another desperate battle against troops led by Major Earl

Van Dorn. The fighting ends only when all ninety-one have been killed or captured.

The Tonkawa people of Texas find that decades of aiding whites against the Comanches have earned them no advantage. They are forced to leave their ancestral homeland and move to Indian Territory (Oklahoma).

 Three years after their last forced relocation, Coos Indians are marched northward and resettled on the Siletz Reservation. Once again, many perish.

 Congress ratifies treaties negotiated with Yakimas, Wallawallas, and other Plateau tribes four years earlier by Governor Stevens. Their spirit broken by the Yakima War of 1855–56 and the conflicts of 1858, people retreat to the reservations assigned to them.

 Delaware (Lenape) Indians living with the Caddo in western Oklahoma are forced to move again, this time to Anadarko.

 "The Indians are children."
—Horace Greeley, noted white editor and politician, 1859

 The Shinnecock Indians of Long Island find their ancestral holdings further reduced, to under 1,000 acres.

1860

While religious leaders of the Wiyot of California are performing ancient ceremonies on Indian Island in California's Humboldt Bay, whites from Eureka at-

Big Mouth

 From the beginning, Native peoples often couldn't agree among themselves about how to deal with the non-Indians invading their continent. Some counseled adapting to Europeans and their strange ways. Others begged their people to turn their backs on these outsiders and preserve their traditions. Often the division resulted in bloody fights or murders.

 In the 1860s, Big Mouth, leader of the Brule Sioux, urged his people to honor the old ways and to refuse to give in to the demands of the whites. Spotted Tail, another leader, agreed with Big Mouth. But then Spotted Tail was invited to Washington and other cities in the East, and when he returned, he had switched to the side of those who advocated accommodation and adaptation. When Big Mouth publicly made fun of Spotted Tail's new views, Spotted Tail shot and killed Big Mouth.

In this way, Big Mouth became a martyr to the cause of cultural preservation and a symbol of the overwhelming challenges faced by those who wanted to maintain traditional ways.

tack them without provocation, and 250 Wiyot are slaughtered. The *New York Century* writes, "In the Atlantic and Western States, the Indians have suffered wrongs and cruelties at the hands of the stronger race. But history has no parallel to the recent atrocities perpetrated in California."

 On the Yakima Reservation in Washington State, the first federal boarding school for Indians opens. Over the next decades, similar schools are established across the country, both on and off the reservation. In an attempt to speed up assimilation with non-Indian culture, Indian children are forcibly removed from their homes and placed in the schools, where they are required to speak English and forbidden to practice traditional rituals.

THE SANTEES REBEL

In 1851, the Santee Sioux of Minnesota agreed to turn their traditional hunting grounds over to the government. That opened the land for settlement. For ten years, Little Crow and other Santee leaders convinced their people to live at peace with the German and Scandinavian settlers, with the missionaries who tried to convince them to abandon their traditional beliefs, and with the traders who sold them shoddy goods for outrageous prices. But it created a miserable existence that disrupted tribal traditions and life. Sometimes the Santees went hungry, as game that had once been plentiful fled the advancing farms.

Finally, in August 1862, four hungry young Santee hunters, returning discouraged and empty-handed from a hunt, killed five settlers. In the intense council fire meeting that followed, militant Santees demanded that the peace-loving Little Crow lead his people into war. Seeing his people determined to fight, Little Crow agreed.

The next day, Santees killed four hundred whites. By the end of the week, Santees under Little Crow, Big Eagle, and other leaders had killed four hundred more. Thirty thousand settlers abandoned their homes and fled.

In the end, though, Santees were too few and poorly armed and the whites too numerous and well armed. Little Bear and other leaders escaped and fled west to Dakota Territory, but 2,000 Sioux surrendered. Of these, 303 were sentenced to hang for their part in the uprising, but President Abraham Lincoln protested that most had been convicted hastily and on inadequate evidence. He spared all but 38. On December 26, 1862, the condemned men swung dead at a specially constructed public scaffold at Mankato. It was the largest mass execution in U.S. history.

The Santees were beaten, but their rebellion turned out to be merely the first phase of a war that lasted eight years and cost the lives of hundreds of Native Americans.

Two Northern Paiute girls disappear. Their parents believe them drowned, but the girls are found being held prisoner for sexual purposes by two white brothers in a whiskey shop along the Carson River. Warriors burn the shop and kill the brothers. Whites attempt to take revenge for the death of the brothers, and the Pyramid Lake War begins. Although the Paiutes have no tradition of warfare, they outfox four companies of regular troops and five hundred volunteer soldiers, then accept offers of peace. Increasingly the Northern Paiute people suffer hunger, assaults, and further disruptions of their way of life.

 In April, about 2,000 Navajo warriors attack Fort Defiance but are repelled. By August, fifteen companies of soldiers fan out across Navajo country.

1861

 Bowlegs, Seminole leader, sides with the Union in the Civil War. He and other chiefs lead 2,000 warriors in holding off a Confederate attack.

The Cherokee Nation, in exile in Oklahoma, recognizes its long ties to the South. John Ross and other Cherokee leaders urge Cherokees to ratify a treaty with the Confederacy that will allow the Cherokees to send a delegate to the Confederate Congress. A regiment of Cherokee soldiers joins the Confederate army.

 Six decades after enduring forced removal to Iowa from the Great Lakes region, the Sac and Fox are required by the government to relocate again, this time to Kansas.

 When Apaches steal livestock and kidnap a child, Chiricahua leader Cochise is wrongly accused of the crimes. An army officer threatens to take Cochise

 "The Cherokee people stand upon new ground. Let us hope that the clouds which overspread the land will be dispersed, and that we shall prosper as we have never before done. New avenues to usefulness and distinction will be opened to the ingenuous youth of the Country. Our rights of self government will be more fully recognized, and our citizens be no longer dragged off upon flimsy pretexts to be imprisoned and tried before distant tribunals."
—John Ross, Cherokee leader, describing the benefits of a Cherokee alliance with the Confederacy, October 9, 1861

hostage, but the Apache leader slashes the wall of the officer's tent and escapes. Both sides take hostages, and when negotiations fail, Cochise and his followers begin ambushing stagecoaches of the Butterfield Overland Mail lines, which until then have passed peacefully for three years through Chiricahua Apache territory.

1862

 Tired of brutal, unjust treatment and treaty violations by their white neighbors, the Santee Sioux rebel. They kill more than eight hundred men, women, and children before the army stops them. As punishment, they are forcibly resettled in the territories of Dakota and Nebraska.

After being attacked by other Indians, the relocated Tonkawa Indians flee Indian Territory (Oklahoma) and return to Texas.

Survivors of the decimated Mandans move in with the Hidatsa and Arikara peoples in the village of Like-a-Fish-hook.

 In July, Mangas Coloradas, Apache leader, is hit in the chest by a bullet from a carbine. His warriors take him to Mexico, where a physician extracts the bullet. The leader recovers and returns to battle miners and troops. In September, he agrees to a peace parley, but treacherous soldiers capture and shoot him.

 Bear Hunter, a Shoshone leader, and his people watch helplessly as Mormon settlers and gold hunters invade their territory in southern Idaho.

1863

Four hundred Mescalero Apache men, women, and children of southern New Mexico are forced to leave their homes and move to a concentration camp on the Pecos River at a place called Bosque Redondo. Their persecutors: General James Carleton, whom later historians know as "the military dictator of New Mexico," and the former friend of Indians, Kit Carson.

In June, the Navajo Nation, 12,000 strong, receives an ultimatum from General Carleton to give up their homeland and join the Mescalero Apaches incarcerated at Bosque Redondo. They have twenty days to surrender peacefully, says Carleton. Any Navajo who doesn't will be considered to be at war with the United States, and will be shot.

When Navajos refuse to leave their homeland willingly, Kit Carson and a regiment of 1,000 soldiers begin shooting Navajos on sight. They burn Navajo crops, destroy Navajo hogans, and seize Navajo goats and sheep. As the months pass, the hungry, homeless, terrorized survivors turn themselves in to Fort Wingate and Fort Canby and wait.

The Pee-Posh (Maricopa) Indians of Arizona, friendly to the army and passing travelers, receive guarantees of protection from white settlers, through formation of the Gila River Indian Reservation.

Only nine years after acquiescing to reservation life, the Nomlaki people of California find their reservation lands snatched by white settlers. Surviving Nomlaki are forcibly moved away.

When Bear Hunter, Shoshone leader, learns that soldiers are marching toward his winter encampment through heavy winter snows, he and his warriors

"I LIVED HAPPILY"

"I was born upon the prairie, where the wind blew free, and there was nothing to break the light of the sun. I was born where there were no enclosures, and where everything drew a free breath. I want to die there, and not within walls. I know every stream and every wood between the Rio Grande and the Arkansas. I have hunted and lived over that country. I lived like my fathers before me, and like them, I lived happily."
—Ten Bears, Yamperethka Comanche leader, at Medicine Lodge Creek council, October 1867

Fight Indians or Rot in Prison Camps

 During the Civil War, captured Confederate soldiers were sometimes given the choice of remaining in prison camps or going west to fight Indians. Those who chose to fight formed six regiments and were known as Galvanized Yankees. When the Civil War ended in 1865, the reluctant fighters were released from service and allowed to return home. The loss of these troops contributed to the government's willingness to make peace with the tribes of the northern and southern Great Plains— Cheyennes, Arapahos, Sioux, and others—following the war.

build rock and earthen fortifications around the village, which lies in a steep ravine on the Bear River 140 miles north of the Great Salt Lake. When the enemy attacks, the Shoshones fight fiercely, but the soldiers are better armed. Within hours, 224 Shoshones die, including Bear Hunter. Another 164 are taken prisoner.

Nez Perce Indians disagree about whether to allow the U.S. government to change its treaty with them and take away land where gold has been discovered. The Christian faction, led by Hallalhotsoot, whose land is safe, signs the treaty. Other leaders, including Old Joseph, whose bands will lose their traditional lands, refuse to sign.

> "The white people have looked for me long. I am here! What do they want? They have looked for me long; why am I worth so much? If I am worth so much why not mark when I set my foot and look when I spit?"
> —Cochise, Chiricahua Apache leader, about 1866

  Leaders of the Modocs, Klamaths, Northern Paiutes, Pit River, Shasta, and the Yahooskin Band of Snake People find themselves forced to sign over their traditional tribal lands to the U.S. government and live on the Klamath Reservation in southern Oregon. Tribes are ordered to move at once, even before Congress ratifies the treaty. Eventually these different cultural groups merge and form a new cultural identity as the Maklaks, or Klamath Tribe.

"There Was No Suspicion Among Us"

 "We have warred against the white man, but never because it gave us pleasure. Before the day of oppression came, no white man came to our villages and went away hungry. It gave us more joy to share with him than it gave him to partake of our hospitality. In the far-distant past there was no suspicion among us. The world seemed large enough for both the red man and the white man. Its broad plains seem now to contract, and the white man grows jealous of his red brother. He once came to trade; he comes now to fight. He once came as a citizen; he now comes as a soldier. He once put his trust in our friendship, and wanted no shield but our fidelity, but now he builds forts and plants big guns on their walls. He once gave us arms and powder, and bade us hunt the game. We then loved him for his confidence. He now suspects the faith we pledged, and drives us to be his enemies. He now covers his face with a cloud of jealousy and anger, and tells us to be gone, as the offended master speaks to his dog."

—Satank, Kiowa leader, at Medicine Lodge Creek council, October 1867

"I Will Not Lie to You"

 "Speak, Americans and Mexicans, I do not wish to hide anything from you nor have you hide anything from me; I will not lie to you; do not lie to me. I want to live on these mountains; I do not want to go to Tularosa. That is a long ways off. The flies on those mountains eat out the eyes of horses. The bad spirits live there. I have drunk of these waters and they have cooled me; I do not want to leave here."

—Cochise, Apache leader, at a peace council, September 1866

1864

Arapahos and Cheyennes refuse to agree to demands by Colorado governor John Evans and territorial military leader John M. Chivington to sign away their hunting grounds and move to reservations. Evans and Chivington declare the Cheyennes to be at war and order soldiers to "burn villages and kill Cheyennes wherever and whenever found."

Black Kettle, a chief of the Tsitsistas, the Cheyennes, camps along Sand Creek in southeastern Colorado with his people and some Southern Arapahos. Black Kettle believes he and the army are at peace, but at dawn on No-

"When I was young, I walked all over this country, east and west, and saw no other people than the Apaches. After many summers I walked again and found another race of people had come to take it. How is it? Why is it that the Apaches wait to die—that they carry their lives on their finger nails? They roam over the hills and plains and want the heavens to fall on them. The Apaches were once a great nation; they are now but few, and because of this they want to die and so carry their lives on the finger nails."
—Cochise, Apache leader, at a peace council, September 1866

vember 29, an army of citizen soldiers under Colonel Chivington attacks, killing two hundred people, two-thirds of them women and children. Refugees flee to the Yellowstone, Powder, and Tongue Rivers and recount the story of the massacre to Teton Sioux and Northern Cheyennes.

Little Crow, leader of the Santee Sioux rebellion, is murdered in exile while picking berries in the Dakotas, shot down by a white settler.

 After losing more than 830,000 acres of land to white settlers, the Chehalis people of western Washington receive a 4,215-acre reservation. Twenty-two years later, President Grover Cleveland confiscates this land, too, and offers it to homesteaders.

 Kintpuash, Modoc leader known to whites as Captain Jack, leads Modocs as they escape from the hated Klamath Reservation. They return to their homeland, a region of grassy plateaus on the California-Oregon border. The refugees settle along the Lost River north of Tule Lake.

 Six thousand Navajos surrender to soldiers at Fort Wingate and Fort Canby and begin the long walk to Bosque Redondo, hundreds of miles to the east. Soldiers shoot stragglers, including pregnant women. At Bosque Redondo, prisoners build 1,276 hogans.

 "As there has been a great deal said about my killing women and children, I will state to you that we killed in this Scout 22 Bucks 5 women & 3 children. We would have killed more women [if they had been present]. For my part I am frank to say that I fight on the broad platform of *extermination*."
—King S. Woolsey, Arizona rancher and volunteer soldier, March 29, 1864

The Hupa people receive permission to live on a portion of their ancestral land in northwestern California along the lower Trinity River. Their 89,000-acre reservation becomes the largest in California.

1865

 Enraged by the massacre at Sand Creek, Arapahos, Cheyennes, and Sioux meet in a council on the upper Republican River and smoke a pipe of war. During January and February, they burn ranches, attack stagecoaches, cut telegraph lines, and kill fifty whites in the South Platte Valley. In July, they strike a military station on the Upper Platte Bridge. Then, considering the score settled and the war over, they ride off to hunt buffalo. Short of soldiers following the end of the Civil War, the army agrees to peace.

Kicking Bird, Kiowa leader, decides that resistance to whites will fail. He becomes the first Kiowa leader to agree to accept reservation status and persuades his people that the transition to reservation life is inevitable. Kiowas from other bands oppose him.

 Twenty-four years after being forcibly removed from their Wisconsin homeland to Iowa, the Winnebagos are required to move again, this time to Nebraska. As time passes, some are able to escape and return to Wisconsin, resulting in the formation of two separate Winnebago tribes, the Hochungra of Nebraska and the Wonkshieks of Wisconsin.

THE WHITE MAN'S PEACE:
MASSACRE AT SAND CREEK

 In September 1864, Black Kettle, a peace-loving leader of the Southern Cheyennes, attended a peace meeting in Colorado with Governor John Evans and territorial military commander Colonel John M. Chivington, a former Methodist preacher who believed that even Native American babies should be killed because "Nits make lice."

Black Kettle left the meeting reassured that if he and his people camped near a fort and submitted to the authority of the soldiers there, they would be able to live in peace. In November, he brought six hundred men, women, and children to Sand Creek, in southeastern Colorado, and he traveled to Fort Lyon, forty miles away, to remind the soldiers there that he and his people wanted peace.

Colonel Chivington didn't care. Late in November, he arrived at Fort Lyon and announced that he planned to attack Black Kettle. When soldiers there protested that Black Kettle and his people were at peace, and under the protection of the fort, Chivington replied, "Damn any man that is in sympathy with Indians."

On November 29, Chivington deployed seven hundred volunteer soldiers and four howitzers around Black Kettle's village. Black Kettle assured the terrified Cheyennes that it was just a misunderstanding, and he raised the American flag and a white flag above his tepee.

Chivington ignored the flags. With orders not to spare any lives, his soldiers opened fire and charged into the village. About two-thirds of the Cheyennes were able to escape. The rest, including nine chiefs, died at the hands of Chivington and his soldiers.

John Smith, an army interpreter, later gave this account of the deaths of Black Kettle's people at Sand Creek: "They were scalped, their brains knocked out; the men used their knives, ripped open women, clubbed little children, knocked them in the head with their guns, beat their brains out, mutilated their bodies in every sense of the word."

After the massacre, one hundred Cheyenne scalps were displayed at a theater in Denver, and soldiers who had participated in the massacre at Sand Creek paraded proudly through the streets.

Black Kettle escaped and fled with eighty families to a hideout south of the Arkansas River, where he continued to long for peace.

Although both the U.S. Congress and the War Department investigated the Sand Creek Massacre, neither ever took any action against Chivington or his soldiers.

"I once thought that I was the only man that persevered to be the friend of the white man, but since they have come and cleaned out our lodges, horses, and everything else, it is hard for me to believe white men anymore."
—Black Kettle, Cheyenne leader, addressing U.S. government officials at a peace council on the Little Arkansas River, October 12, 1865

Whites accuse Northern Paiutes of cattle rustling. While hunters are gone, soldiers enter the Pyramid Lake Reservation of the Northern Paiutes and attack thirty men, women, and children. Only one person, sister of Paiute spokesperson Sarah Winnemucca, escapes murder, as she flees pursuing soldiers. In a subsequent attack, another twenty-three die. Then thirty-five more. Then 115. The starving, broken survivors face extinction.

After enduring two years of hunger, disease, and humiliation at the concentration camp on the Bosque Redondo, surviving Mescalero Apaches escape and flee back to their mountain homeland.

Land on both sides of the Colorado River in Arizona and California is set aside for a reservation for Mojave and Chemehuevi Indians. Mojave leader Arateba agrees to move south, but most Mojaves side with Chief Homose Kohote and refuse to leave their traditional homeland.

"YOUR YOUNG MEN MUST NOT SHOOT US"

"You sent for us; we came here. We have made the treaty with our agent, Colonel Wynkoop. We never did the white man any harm; we don't intend to. Our agent told us to meet you here. Whenever you want to go on the Smoky Hill you can go; you can go on any road. When we come on the road, your young men must not shoot us. We are willing to be friends with the white man. . . . Your young men must not fire at us; whenever they see us they fire, and we fire on them."

—Tall Bull, leader of the Dog Soldiers of the Cheyennes, speaking to General Winfield Hancock, March 1867

 "There, at Sand Creek, is one chief, Left Hand; White Antelope and many other chiefs lie there; our women and children lie there. Our lodges were destroyed there, and our horses were taken from us there, and I do not feel disposed to go right off in a new country and leave them. What I have to say, I am glad to see you writing down to take to the Big Chief in Washington."
—Little Raven, Arapaho leader, reminding U.S. officials at a peace council on the Little Arkansas River in October 1865 of the tragic 1864 massacre at Sand Creek

1866

 Cherokees in exile in Oklahoma are forced to give the U.S. President power to veto Cherokee Nation laws and control the actions of the tribal council. In exchange, they secure some protection and recognition for Eastern Cherokees.

 Chief Seattle, longtime leader of the Suquamish and Duwamish Tribes, dies at age eighty.

 "When my time comes to die, I intend to die and not wait to be killed by the white men."
—Otank (White-Bird), Kiowa medicine man, at a peace council with representatives of the U.S. government, 1866

Red Cloud, Oglala Sioux, and other Sioux leaders ride into Fort Laramie to ask the government not to allow wagon trains filled with miners and settlers to cross through Teton Sioux territory on the newly opened

Bozeman Trail. A few chiefs sign an agreement not to bother travelers, but Red Cloud and others refuse and ride away in frustration.

Oglala Sioux war leader Crazy Horse and other warriors watch Fort Phil Kearny in hopes of teaching whites a lesson so that they will abandon the Bozeman Trail. On December 21, Crazy Horse attacks a wood train and sends a decoy party to lure soldiers into battle. Led by Captain William J. Fetterman, who has boasted that he could safely cross the entire Sioux territory with only eighty men, the soldiers ride into a trap. Fifteen hundred warriors swarm toward them from all sides; Fetterman and all eighty soldiers die.

> "The Great Father sends us presents and wants us to sell him the road, but White Chief goes with soldiers to steal the road before Indians say Yes or No."
> —Red Cloud, Oglala Sioux, protesting the government's decision to open the Bozeman Trail across Teton Sioux territory with or without the Indians' permission, June 1866

After two years of living on the run and in hiding, 4,000 Navajos under Barboncito and Manuelito turn themselves in and prepare to join other Navajos at the concentration camp at Bosque Redondo. Only a few Navajos remain in Navajo land, where they live hidden deep in the canyons.

Transplanted Seminoles from Florida living in Indian Territory (Oklahoma) move to the area that eventually becomes known as Seminole County, Oklahoma. There they struggle to preserve the Muskogee language and their traditional beliefs and practices, including Apuskita, the Green Corn ceremony.

> "I am the man who makes it rain. . . .
> If I have any difficulty with anyone
> and wish them to perish with thirst, I
> stop the rain, and if I wish them well, I
> cause it to rain so that the corn can grow."
> —Otank (White Bird), Kiowa medicine man,
> speaking through Kiowa leader Lone Wolf, at a
> peace council with representatives of the U.S.
> government, 1866

1867

On August 1 and 2, Sioux and Cheyenne warriors attack small parties of soldiers outside Fort C. F. Smith and Fort Phil Kearny. Warriors discover too late that soldiers have new weapons: breech-loading rifles instead of the cumbersome muzzle-loaders. Despite defeat, Red Cloud and other leaders vow to continue fighting the opening of the Bozeman Trail.

> "The white man has the country
> which we loved and we only wish to
> wander on the prairie until we die."
> —Ten Bears, leader of the Yamperethka
> Comanches, at Medicine Lodge Creek council,
> October 1867

Sioux and Cheyenne inhabitants of an intertribal village outside Fort Larned, Kansas, panic when soldiers who have promised peace march toward them. Remembering the Sand Creek Massacre, they flee northward. Soldiers destroy the villages. In the following months, Cheyennes and Sioux terrorize white settlers across Kansas in retaliation.

At Medicine Lodge Creek, Kansas, the largest number of warriors and chiefs ever assembled gather for a peace conference with government officials. Cheyennes, Arapahos, Kiowas, and Comanches sign a treaty that gives Kansas to whites. In exchange, the Indians receive two large tracts of land in Indian Territory (Oklahoma). The Cheyennes and Arapahos agree to live on one; the Kiowas, Comanches, and Kiowa-Apaches on the other. Few signing the treaty realize they are agreeing to major cultural upheavals, the inevitable result of being forced to switch from the nomadic life of hunters to the settled life of farmers.

> **"We do not break treaties. We make but few contracts, and them we remember well. The whites make so many they are liable to forget them."**
> —**Satank, Kiowa leader, at Medicine Lodge Creek council, October 1867**

Athabaskans of the Alaska Plateau, accustomed to more than a century of interaction with Russian traders and explorers, watch Russians leave and Americans arrive when the United States purchases Alaska from Russia. Only the Russian Orthodox Church remains. American traders bring an abundance of formerly scarce firearms. The guns change centuries-old hunting customs and eliminate caribou, the traditional food staple, from coastal areas and lower rivers. Under the terms of the sale, Alaskan Natives lose their right to hold the status of citizens.

> **"My band is not going to live on the reservation. Tell the white chiefs that Kwahadies are warriors."**
> —**Quanah Parker, leader of the Kwahadi Comanches, refusing to sign the peace treaty at Medicine Lodge Creek, 1867**

DOG SOLDIERS

 Among the Cheyennes who signed the Medicine Lodge Treaty in 1867, three war chiefs—Bull Bear, White Horse, and Tall Bull—refused to agree to give up their nomadic lives as hunters and settle in as farmers. Together they led a special band of Cheyenne warriors known as the Dog Soldiers. During the summer and fall of 1868, the Dog Soldiers raided white settlements in western Kansas and eastern Colorado. As other Cheyennes surrendered, the Dog Soldiers continued to insist on their right to live and hunt in Kansas. Only after Tall Bull's death in 1869 did the Dog Soldiers give up and agree to move to the reservation assigned to Cheyennes in Indian Territory (Oklahoma).

 Odawa (Ottawa) Indians are forced to relocate to Oklahoma three decades after being relocated to Kansas from Michigan.

The Peoria Indians, who a few decades earlier endured forced removal from Illinois to Kansas, now find themselves required to move again, this time to Indian Territory (Oklahoma). They resettle among the Miami, Wea, and Piankashaw Tribes. Collectively these groups become known as the United Peoria and Miami Tribe.

Lenape (Delaware) Indians buy the right to live among the Cherokees in Oklahoma.

1868

 Oglala Sioux leader Red Cloud is invited to a peace council at Fort Laramie, but he refuses to talk peace until the army abandons all its posts in the Powder River country. In a rare instance in the history of Indian dealings with whites, the Red Cloud War ends on

Red Cloud's terms. The army abandons its Bozeman Trail forts. The Powder River country is acknowledged to belong to Indians, not whites, and the Sioux receive all of South Dakota west of the Missouri River as the Great Sioux Reservation.

Cheyenne leader Black Kettle and his people are camped on the Washita River of Oklahoma. Once again, Black Kettle believes there is peace between his people and whites. Once again, at dawn, the cavalry attacks, this time led by a white man whom the Tsitsistas know as Long Hair, George Armstrong Custer. Stunned by the new brutality, Black Kettle stands numbly in front of his lodge. He dies in the attack, a victim not just of a bullet wound, but of his own good faith and of the white man's lies. The attack takes place on November 27, almost exactly four years after the Sand Creek Massacre.

> "You fought me, and I had to fight back: I am a soldier. The annuities you speak of we don't want. Our intention is to take no present."
> —Gall, Hunkpapa Sioux leader, speaking to army generals at a peace conference, 1868

In September, a band of Cheyennes called Dog Soldiers, under the leadership of Tall Bull, joins its southern Oglala Sioux allies to battle soldiers in western Kansas. The fight turns into an eight-day siege. Just as the Indians are about to win, army reinforcements arrive from Fort Wallace and drive the warriors away. Whites commemorate the incident as the Battle of Beecher's Island, but Cheyennes name it the Fight Where Roman Nose Was Killed, in honor of fallen war chief Roman Nose.

Navajo leaders Manuelito, Barboncito, and others travel to Washington, D.C., to plead for release of their people from the concentration camp at Bosque

The Price of Breaking Taboos

 In a battle in eastern Colorado in September 1868, Cheyenne leader Roman Nose realized he couldn't fight because he had accidentally eaten bread that had touched a metal fork. White Contrary, another Cheyenne, taunted Roman Nose for not fighting, but Tall Bull begged Roman Nose to stay out of the battle until he could undergo a purification ceremony. Although Roman Nose believed that he would die if he fought, he chose to join the next charge of his comrades against the soldiers. Within minutes, a bullet tore into Roman Nose's chest and killed him.

"I was in hopes that you would continue the war, and then, though I were to kill only one of your warriors while you killed a hundred of my men, you would have to wait for those little people [children] to grow up to fill the place of your braves, while I can get any number of soldiers the next day to fill the place of my hundred men. In this way it would not be very long before we would have you all killed off, and then the government would have no more trouble with you."

—General George Crook, addressing eight hundred Paiutes led by Weawea when they surrender to him at Camp Harney, Oregon, July 1, 1868

GALL

On a winter night at 2 A.M., probably sometime in the late 1860s, one hundred soldiers rode into a Sioux village searching for a young Hunkpapa leader named Gall, born about 1840. He was accused of having stolen some ponies.

Gall was sleeping in his tepee. When he stuck his head out to see what was going on, a soldier shot at him. Gall slashed a hole in the back of the tepee and tried to escape, but soldiers with rifles and bayonets surrounded him. They stomped him, stabbed him, and beat him with clubs until they were convinced he was dead. One soldier thrust his bayonet so deeply into Gall that he had to stand on the body to tug it out.

The soldiers left Gall's body lying in the snow and rode away. The other villagers, thinking their leader dead, packed up their tepees and moved away in case the soldiers came back.

But Gall wasn't dead. When he finally regained consciousness, he walked and crawled twenty miles through the cold and snow until he reached the lodge of a friend.

From then on, Gall hated and mistrusted all whites.

Redondo. When peace commissioners visit Bosque Redondo and see the squalor in which the prisoners are forced to live, Navajos are finally freed and allowed to return to their home. A treaty grants them 3.5 million acres, only a fraction of their traditional lands. The horrifying years at Bosque Redondo remain in tribal memory as Nahondzod, the Fearing Time.

 After several years of skirmishing and running from soldiers, Northern Paiutes decide to stop fighting. They have fought forty battles, in which 329 Paiutes have died and another 225 have been captured.

Led by Weawea, 800 Paiutes surrender at Camp Harney, Oregon, on July 1.

1869

 Only eight years after their last forced removal, the Sac and Fox are required to move once again, this time from Kansas to Indian Territory (Oklahoma). In spite of the deep cultural disruptions, they continue to preserve their heritage, including the Sac and Mesquakie (Fox) languages and traditional dances.

 President-elect Ulysses S. Grant announces a new policy regarding Native Americans. It includes peace toward Indians willing to live on reservations, where they are expected to farm, become Christians, and imitate white ways. For all others, he orders "a sharp and severe war policy." To implement the brutal, culturally destructive policy, he establishes an all-white Board of Indian Commissioners to monitor the handling of Indian affairs by the Department of the Interior.

In March, Cheyennes living at the villages of Medicine Arrows and Little Robe on Sweetwater Creek send chiefs out to talk peace with soldiers who have tracked them down. The soldiers' leader, George Custer, seizes three chiefs and threatens to hang them. The Cheyennes surrender and agree to honor the Medicine Lodge Treaty and move onto their designated reservation in Indian Territory (Oklahoma). Only the militant Dog Soldiers under Tall Bull refuse to submit; instead, they rampage along the Kansas-Colorado border.

"THE GREAT SPIRIT MADE US BOTH"

 "The Great Spirit made us both. He gave us land, and he gave you land. You came here and we received you as brothers. When the Almighty made you, He made you all white and clothed you. When He made us, He made us with red skins and poor. When you first came, we were very many and you were few. You do not know who appears before you to speak. He is a representative of the original American race, the first people on this continent. We are good, and not bad. The reports which you get about us are all on one side. You hear of us only as murderers and thieves. We are not so. If we had more lands to give you, we would give them, but we have no more. We are driven into a very little island, and we want you, our dear friends, to help us with the Government of the United States."

—Red Cloud, Sioux leader, speaking to a white audience at Cooper Institute in New York, June 16, 1870

"NOT AN UNREASONABLE REQUEST"

 "No one who listened to Red Cloud's remarkable speech yesterday can doubt that he is a man of very great talents. . . . He has spent his life fighting the battles of his people, and one day he is transplanted to Cooper Institute, and asked to put on a clean shirt, a new waistcoat, a high crowned hat, and then make a speech. . . . His earnest manner, his impassioned gestures, the eloquence of his hands, and the magnetism which he evidently exercises over his audience, produced a vast effect on the dense throng which listened to him yesterday. 'You have children, and so have we. We want to rear our children well, and ask you to help us in doing so.' It seems to us that this is not an unreasonable request even though it does come from a 'savage.'"
—*New York Times,* June 17, 1870, in a front-page story on a speech by Sioux leader Red Cloud to a white audience in New York

 In July, in a surprise attack on the Dog Soldiers by the cavalry, Tall Bull finds himself trapped in a ravine at Summit Springs, Colorado. Tall Bull shoots his horse in the mouth, a sign that he knows death is near, then dies fighting. The Dog Soldiers leave western Kansas forever.

Southern Arapahos are forced to sign away their traditional lands in eastern Colorado and western Kansas and agree to join the Cheyennes on a reservation in western Oklahoma.

 The Nipmuc Indians, landless since 1800, formally become citizens of Massachusetts but remain landless and unrecognized by the federal government.

1870s

 Among the Potawatomis of Michigan and neighboring tribes, the Drum Cult blossoms. In addition to metaphysical prophecies, it promises that lost lands will be regained. Flourishing into the 1880s and after, it provides a renewed sense of cultural identity that outlives the cult.

1870

 Red Cloud, Sioux leader and warrior, travels to Washington, D.C., where he talks with President Grant and speaks to white audiences about the plight of the Sioux. Other Indian leaders travel with him, but the trip becomes known as Red Cloud's Peace Crusade.

Spotted Tail, nephew of Crazy Horse and leader of the Lower Brule Sioux, finds himself accused by Red Cloud of selling Sioux land and pocketing the money.

 Modoc Indian refugees from the Klamath Reservation find their white neighbors in the Tule Lake area of northeastern California increasingly determined to force them to leave their homeland once more and return to the Klamath Reservation.

 Five years after Mojave chief Homose Kohote refuses to lead his people south to live on the Colorado River Indian Reservation, the Fort Mojave Reservation is established along the Colorado River at the junction of California, Nevada, and Arizona. It allows the Mojave Indians to continue living on a small portion of their ancestral lands.

1871

Eskiminzin, Apache leader, and his people, five hundred strong, live at Camp Grant at peace with

"THE WHITE MEN FOUND GOLD"

"After a while the white men found gold in our country. They took the gold and pushed the Indian from his home. I thought Washington would make it all right. I am an old man now. I have been waiting many years for Washington to give us our rights. The Government sent agents and soldiers out there to us, and both have driven us from our lands. We do not want to fight. The white man has taken away everything."
—Little Raven, Arapaho leader, addressing a white audience in New York, 1871

the soldiers. But at daybreak on April 30, a group of citizens from Tucson, aided by traditional enemies of the Apaches, the Tohono O'odham (Papago) Indians, storm the camp. They kill an estimated 150 men, women, and children. They mutilate the bodies of the dead, rape surviving Apache women, and kidnap twenty-nine Apache children as slaves.

"One infant of some ten months was shot twice and one leg nearly hacked off."
—Lieutenant Royal E. Whitman, describing the brutal massacre of peaceful Apaches at Camp Grant on April 30, 1871

The era of treaty making ends officially with the Indian Appropriations Act, when Congress decides that Indians shall no longer be construed as independent nations or sovereign powers with the right to enter into treaties. Congress may now dictate to Indians without their approval. In theory, the act upholds the validity of previously ratified treaties. In practice, the treaties offer little protection.

Kiowas led by Satanta head south from their reservation in Fort Sill and ambush a caravan of ten wagons in Texas. The ambush becomes known as the Salt Creek Massacre. Satanta and two other Kiowa leaders, Satank and Big Tree, are arrested for murder. While riding shackled in a wagon on his way to prison, Satank sings his death song. Then he pulls out a hidden knife and stabs a guard. Another guard shoots him.

"You are fools to make yourselves slaves to a piece of fat bacon, some hard-tack, and a little sugar and coffee."
—Sitting Bull, Hunkpapa Sioux leader, scolding other Sioux for agreeing to give up their traditional lifestyle and live on a reservation, about 1870

SATANTA: "ORATOR OF THE PLAINS"

Among the Kiowas in the 1860s, no leader could speak more eloquently than Satanta, a man with a large chest and strong voice whom whites called the Orator of the Plains. Satanta lived in a red tepee and delighted in attention. Although he agreed to move to the Kiowa-Comanche Reservation in Indian Territory, he believed in the Kiowas' right to continue to wander the Great Plains. At the signing of the Medicine Lodge Treaty in 1867, Satanta explained his position this way: "I love to roam the wide prairie, and when I do it, I feel happy, but when we settle down, we grow pale and die."

A fighter at heart, Satanta couldn't bear to give up the practice of his forefathers: raiding against those who intruded into Indian lands. While planning a raid on wagon trains at Salt Creek Prairie in Texas, in May 1871, Satanta received advice from a medicine man to let the first group of travelers pass and attack the second. Satanta did, and in this way inadvertently spared the life of General William Tecumseh Sherman, who went on to enforce the destruction of the Kiowas' traditional lifeways.

When questioned about the Salt Creek Massacre, Satanta replied, "If any other Indian claims the honor of leading the party, he will be lying to you. I led it myself."

Arrested for murder, Satanta was tried and sentenced to death. Under pressure from Quakers and others, the governor of Texas commuted his sentence, and in 1873, Satanta was freed and allowed to return to his people. In 1874, fearing further harsh treatment at the hands of whites and longing for a return to the old lifestyle, he bolted from the reservation with other refugees.

In 1875, when General Sherman forced Kiowas and others to identify their best fighters, Satanta was arrested again. Instead of being sent with his friends to prison in Florida, he was returned to the Texas penitentiary. In 1878, in despair at the death of the way of life he so loved, Satanta killed himself by jumping from a window at the penitentiary.

LOZEN

 Among the Apaches, women sometimes became warriors. The most famous was Lozen, sister of noted Apache leader Victorio. Born about 1840 to the Warm Springs Band, she lived in times so troubled that children grew up thinking bullet wounds were the only reason people died. Sometimes alone, sometimes with her people, she traveled thousands of miles on foot and horseback in Texas, New Mexico, Arizona, and Mexico.

Once when her people were fleeing soldiers, the Rio Grande stopped them. The muddy water was running hard and rising fast, and their horses refused to cross. Finally Lozen rode up on a magnificent black stallion. Holding her rifle high, she kicked the horse's right shoulder hard. He plunged in and swam across, and the other horses followed.

Another time, soldiers ambushed Lozen and other warriors. The men scattered, leaving their ammunition pouch and five hundred cartridges. Lozen crawled back through cross fire and rescued the cartridges, saving her companions.

One time when soldiers were chasing them, a woman went into labor. Lozen sent her own horse and the woman's horse on with the others, so the soldiers wouldn't realize anyone had broken off from the group. She hid the woman, helped with the birth, then walked many miles until she could steal more horses and a rifle.

Because Lozen stopped to aid this woman, she escaped the Battle of Tres Castillos, in which her brother died. Afterward, survivors who believed in the power of her medicine said that if Lozen had been there, she would have sensed the approach of the soldiers. The Apaches would have been able to flee, and Victorio would have survived.

Nana, an aging Apache leader, once said, "There is no warrior more worthy than Lozen."

But even the most worthy warrior couldn't slow the arrival of white settlers and soldiers or save her people from their fate. When Geronimo surrendered in 1886, Lozen surrendered with him. She died of tuberculosis in a prison camp in Alabama and was buried in an unmarked grave.

On the Staked Plains of Texas, Quanah Parker, leader of the Kwahadi Band of Comanches, successfully evades troops under R. S. Mackenzie, a soldier described by Ulysses S. Grant as "the most promising young officer in the Army."

Buffalo robes become fashionable in the East. Plains Indians watch in horror and frustration as white hunters begin slaughtering more than 1 million buffalo a year, solely for their hides. The white hunters are not merely driving the buffalo toward extinction but also depriving Native peoples of what has been a major food source for 10,000 years.

Little Raven, Arapaho leader, travels to Washington, D.C., with a delegation of Cheyenne, Arapaho, and Wichita leaders. Little Raven speaks to white audiences about the injustices done to his people.

 Old Joseph, Nez Perce leader, dies without fulfilling his dream to regain the high, grassy lands of his ancestors in eastern Oregon for his people. Young Joseph, only thirty-one, takes over leadership of the band. With Young Looking Glass, whose father has also died, Chief Joseph becomes a leader of the nontreaty, non-Christian faction of the divided Nez Perce.

1872

 The Colville Reservation of northeastern Washington is formed by executive order from President Ulysses S. Grant.

> "Why not give me Apache Pass? Give me that, and I will protect all the roads. I will see that nobody's property is taken by Indians."
> —Cochise, Chiricahua Apache leader, negotiating with General Oliver Howard for a place to live in peace, autumn 1872

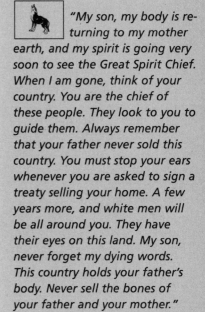

In November, Lieutenant Colonel George Crook strikes out against Apaches living in the Tonto Basin below the Mogollon Rim in Arizona. Over the next months, commando units sweep across the basin nine times, hunting down men, women, and children. Twenty times they attack, killing two hundred Apaches.

Cochise, leader of the Chiricahua Apaches, has successfully eluded soldiers ever since they attempted to imprison him at a peace conference eleven years earlier. Now he agrees to meet General Oliver Howard alone in a secret hideout in the Chiricahua Mountains. For two weeks the two leaders negotiate. Howard wants the Chiricahuas to move to a reservation in New Mexico. Cochise refuses to ask his people to leave their native Arizona. Finally Cochise offers to settle at Apache Pass and protect wagon trains. Howard accepts. Cochise keeps his word, but other whites refuse to honor Howard's agreement with Cochise.

 In late November, Modoc refugees from the Klamath Reservation living along the Lost River, north of Tule Lake, wake up to find soldiers from Fort Klamath attacking. Instead of returning to the reservation as the government requires, the 175 Modocs, of whom more than a hundred are women and children, flee south to the Land of Burnt-Out Fires, the lava beds on the south shore of Tule Lake. There they live in hiding among the twisted black boulders, hoping to outwit and outwait the whites until they can return to their beloved Lost River homeland.

 Pocatello, Shoshone leader, is forced to move his band to the Fort Hall Reservation in Idaho. A decade later, Pocatello, Idaho, is named in his honor.

Ten Bears, eighty-year-old chief of the Yampe-rethka Comanches, travels to Washington to discuss peace agreements between the U.S. government and the Comanches. The trip exhausts him, and he dies on October 23.

The Santee Sioux embrace the new Drum Cult, also known as the Dream Dance. Tallfeather Woman, a Sioux (Dakota) woman, is credited with being one originator of the new religion.

 After being forcibly resettled several times, the Kadohadacho (Caddos) lose more land under an agreement that lumps them with Wichitas, Hasinai, Nachi-toches, Anadarkos, and Ionies. The new treaty provides a much diminished reservation for the Wichitas and Affiliated Bands in Indian Territory (Oklahoma).

1873

 The U.S. Supreme Court rules in *United States v. Cook* that tribes must have permission of the U.S. government before they can cut timber on tribal land, except to clear land for farming.

 The U.S. Cavalry rides into Mexico and kidnaps forty Kickapoo women and children from the refugee band that settled in Texas thirty-four years earlier. The hostages are imprisoned at Fort Gibson, Oklahoma. The move is calculated to force the Kickapoo to return to the United States. Some do, but many remain in Mexico, or return there in following decades.

> "They are a sorry, pitiful-looking set to have given so much trouble."
> —Army officer describing a group of 155 Modoc men, women, and children who held off the army for more than four months in early 1873 before being captured and exiled

On January 16, a force of fewer than seventy-five Modoc warriors defeats four hundred attacking soldiers sent to return them to the Klamath Reservation. The warriors are such skilled fighters and know the art of hiding in the lava land of the Land of Burnt-Out Fires so well that the wounded soldiers retreat without ever having seen a Modoc face.

Two years after the death of Old Joseph, Nez Perce leader, President Ulysses S. Grant belatedly confirms the chief's assessment that the grassy Wallowa Valley in northeastern Oregon should belong to the Nez Perce. Grant sets aside land in the Wallowa for the band, now led by Young Joseph.

> "I can see how I could give up my horse to be hanged; but I can't see how I could give up my men to be hanged. I could give up my horse to be hanged, and wouldn't cry about it; but if I gave up my men I would have to cry about it."
> —Captain Jack (Kintpuash), Modoc leader, March 6, 1873, seven months before he and three other Modoc leaders were hanged

Modoc Indians hiding in the Land of Burnt-Out Fires in northeastern California divide into factions as peace commissioners led by General Edward Canby ask them to surrender unconditionally. Kintpuash (Captain Jack) advises persistence and patience in trying to gain a reservation on

Between Two Worlds: Toby Riddle, Modoc Woman

In April 1873, as Modoc refugees hiding in the lava beds south of Tule Lake argued among themselves about whether to surrender, Toby Riddle, a Modoc woman married to a white man, listened and worried. As the niece of Modoc leader Kintpuash (Captain Jack), she understood the Modocs' longing to return to their homeland near the Oregon-California border. But as the wife of the interpreter for peace commissioner General Edward Canby, she was an outsider among her own people, a Modoc who traveled with the enemy. She longed to see peace between the whites of her husband's world and the Modocs of her family's world.

When Toby learned that militant Modocs had persuaded her peace-loving Uncle Kintpuash to join them, she warned General Canby to expect treachery. But the white man ignored her, and on the morning of Good Friday, April 11, 1873, General Canby died at her Uncle Kintpuash's hand.

Canby's refusal to pay attention to the Modoc woman's warning led not only to his death but to the execution of her uncle and the exile of her people.

A photograph of Toby Riddle, taken shortly before the general's murder, shows a beautiful young woman with her dark hair pulled back and her face tense and solemn.

their ancestral homeland along the Lost River. Others advise murdering the commissioners as a message to Washington. On April 11, Kintpuash gives in. He shoots Canby in the face, stabs him to death, and removes the officer's dress uniform. Modocs flee deeper into the lava land south of Tule Lake.

With only twenty-two warriors, Modoc military leader Scarfaced Charley ambushes sixty-six soldiers, including five officers, and twelve Indian scouts sent to find the Modocs hiding in the Land of Burnt-Out Fires in April.

All five officers die, along with twenty men. Scarfaced Charley permits survivors to retreat. Disagreements about what to do next grow among the Modocs. They scatter.

Exhausted Modoc refugees find themselves seized by soldiers, a few at a time. On June 1, Kintpuash (Captain Jack) and his family are captured. On October 3, four Modoc leaders swing dead by their necks at Fort Klamath: Kintpuash, Boston Charley, Schonchin John, and Black Jim. In actions that violate ancient Modoc taboos, the dead men's heads are severed from their bodies and sent to the Army Medical Museum in Washington, D.C. The 155 surviving Modocs, who wanted only to be allowed to stay in their native land, are shipped east to the Quapaw Reservation in Indian Territory (Oklahoma).

The Coeur d'Alene Indians, who once roamed 3 million acres in the Plateau region, find their holdings reduced to a 600,000-acre reservation in northern Idaho. Over the next century, they lose nearly 90 percent of even this reduced amount of land.

 "All you fellows that ain't dead had better go home. We don't want to kill you all in one day."
—Scarfaced Charley, Modoc leader, permitting defeated soldiers, who had been sent to destroy the Modocs, to retreat in safety, April 26, 1873

 Apaches in the Tonto Basin have endured six months of being terrorized by Lieutenant Colonel Crook's soldiers. Starving and demoralized, they begin surrendering in April. By autumn, 6,000 Apaches have moved onto reservations, and Crook has been rewarded for his part in destroying the Apaches by being promoted to brigadier general.

INDIAN AGENCIES

In the 1800s, the U.S. government forced Native peoples across the country to give up their ancestral homelands, live on reservations, and submit to the control of non-Indian outsiders. In order to govern the reservations, the Indian Office (the predecessor of the Bureau of Indian Affairs) created Indian agencies on the reservations. Non-Indians known as Indian agents ran the agencies. Often agents had life-and-death control over the Native peoples. Brutalities and abuses abounded, and Indian agents were directly or indirectly responsible for many deaths.

Kiowa leaders Big Tree and Satanta are released from prison and return to their people at the Kiowa-Comanche Reservation in Indian Territory (Oklahoma).

> "A long time ago this land belonged to our fathers; but when I go up to the river I see camps of soldiers on its banks. These soldiers cut down my timber; they kill my buffalo; and when I see that, my heart feels like bursting; I feel sorry. I have spoken."
> —Satanta, Kiowa leader known as the Orator of the Plains, at Fort Larned, Kansas, May 1867

Kiowa leader Kicking Bird lobbies for the establishment of the first school on the Kiowa-Comanche Reservation in Oklahoma.

Enraged that white hunters are exterminating buffalo while they themselves are denied the right to leave the reservation to hunt buffalo, Kiowas and Comanches continue their raids on white settlements.

"THE SUN AND MOON LOOK AT US"

 "We always give the Great Spirit something. I think that is good. We see the sun, we give him something; and the moon and the earth, we give them something. We beg them to take pity on us. The sun and moon look at us, and the ground gives us food. You come and see us, and that is why we give you something. We are men like each other; our religion is different from yours."
—Blackfoot, Mountain Crow leader, at a peace council in Montana, August 1873

 "We have often wished for the Sioux and Northern Cheyennes not to come down here. They steal our horses when they come here, and we do not want them to come."
—Kicking Bird, Crow leader, at a peace conference, April 1867

Oglala Sioux leader Red Cloud and Brule Sioux leader Spotted Tail agree to report to Indian agencies on the upper White River, far from military supervision. Hunting bands of Sioux, Northern Cheyennes, and other groups continue to follow buffalo through the area recognized by treaty as unceded Indian territory.

Surviving Kaw (Kansa) Indians of Kansas are forced to move to a small reservation in Oklahoma. Since 1700, cultural upheavals and disease have reduced their population from about 5,000 to under 700.

Congress repeals the "civilization fund" of 1819, by which it subsidizes religious schools that enroll Native American children. It continues to contract with the schools on an individual basis, paying $167 per student annually.

 "This tobacco comes from the whites; we mix it with bark from the Indian trees and burn it together before Thee, O Great Spirit! So may our hearts and the hearts of the white men go out together to Thee and be made good and right."
—Blackfoot, Mountain Crow leader, offering a prayer to the Great Spirit before passing a peace pipe at a peace council in Montana, August 1873

Sarah Winnemucca, Toc-me-to-ne

Toc-me-to-ne was born in Nevada about 1844, to Chief Winnemucca, a shaman of the Northern Paiute People, or Numa. At that time, the Numa, who numbered about 6,000, still lived in small bands that drifted across northern Nevada and central Oregon. Nearly every day they traveled many miles looking for food and spent long hours gathering wild roots and hunting antelope and other game.

But non-Indian settlers, fishermen, and miners began to overrun Numa lands. As a young teenager, Toc-me-to-ne, renamed Sarah, worked as a servant for white families and learned to speak, read, and write English. After her mother and sister died of starvation and two brothers died in unprovoked attacks by whites, she vowed to devote her life to helping her people and to bringing peace between Indians and whites. While working intermittently as a translator and army scout, she wrote pleas on behalf of the Numa which were published in newspapers in the East. She visited generals and senators and barraged them with letters.

But still her people's circumstances were desperate. Many had lost their lands or their lives to whites, and hundreds had died of typhus, tuberculosis, and smallpox. Forced to live on reservations, and prohibited from foraging in their traditional hunting grounds, many had been reduced to a choice between starvation and stealing cattle. She wrote, "We would all much rather be slain and put out of our misery than to be lingering here—each day bringing new sorrows—and finally die of hunger and starvation."

In 1878, during the Bannock War, she rode 223 miles in two days in order to save her father and other Numa.

In 1880, she traveled to Washington, D.C., to convince the Secretary of the Interior to help the Numa. But she failed, and her people were forced to move 300 miles to another reservation through waist-deep snow.

Traveling east again in 1883, she lectured in Boston, New York, Philadelphia, and other cities, urging that Indians be granted citizenship rights. She testified to the Senate Subcommittee on Indian Affairs and wrote a short memoir, *Life Among the Piutes: Their Wrongs and Claims*.

When she died, in 1891, her detractors said she was too much like whites. But her admirers credited her with helping to save her people from extinction.

1874

For two decades, the Jamestown Band of Klallam Indians has successfully resisted government attempts to force them to leave their homeland on the Olympic Peninsula of western Washington and move to the Skokomish Reservation. Now the Jamestown Band is able to raise enough money to buy 210 acres of land east of Port Angeles.

The army forcibly moves the Hualapai Indians two hundred miles south from their homeland on the western edge of the Colorado Plateau to live with tribes along the Colorado River. For two years, the Hualapai live unhappily among these strangers before being allowed to return to their homeland.

Cochise, leader of the Chiricahua Apaches, dies. The people accept neither of his sons, Taza and Nachez, as leaders, and begin to quarrel among themselves.

The San Carlos Reservation is established in Arizona. It serves as a prison camp for Yavapai, Mojaves, and Apaches from many different bands.

Paiute leader Natchez, brother of Pauite spokeswoman Sarah Winnemucca, is charged with inciting his people against the Indian agent and is sent to Fort Alcatraz in San Francisco Bay. Both Paiutes and whites protest his arrest. Released soon after, he comes home to Nevada a hero, and, like his sister and father, continues to dedicate himself to improving life for his people.

QUANAH PARKER

During the 1830s, Comanches in Texas captured Cynthia Ann Parker, aged nine. As the years passed, she learned Comanche ways, forgot English, and married a Comanche chief. In 1845, their son was born. Whites later came to know him as Quanah Parker.

In an era when whites were encroaching on traditional Comanche territory, and tribes from one area were being pushed onto other tribes' lands, Quanah grew up fast. By age twenty-two, he had become a spokesman for his people, the Kwahadi Comanches. In 1867, he refused to attend the council at Medicine Lodge Creek or agree to live on a reservation.

For the next eight years, Quanah led raids across the Texas and Kansas countryside. Again and again, he and his warriors outsmarted soldiers who pursued them.

Finally, exhausted and worn down from living for so many years on the run, Quanah led the Kwahadies to Fort Sill, Oklahoma, in 1876 and surrendered.

Once he had accepted the hopelessness of fighting against reservation life, Quanah focused on succeeding at the white man's own game. Although he never learned to speak more than badly broken English, he transformed himself from warrior to businessman and politician. He lobbied for Indian rights, bought and traded railroad shares, leased lands to cattlemen, and served as chief judge for the reservation Court of Indian Offenses. He built himself the Star House, an elegant home with twelve rooms, and, in Comanche tradition, supported five wives.

A devotee of peyote, Quanah carried peyote buttons in a medicine bag on his chest to protect him in battle. While under the influence of peyote, he composed lively songs that one witness described as "beautiful just like race horses—go fast."

About a year before Quanah died, at age sixty-six, he had his mother's body exhumed in Texas and reburied in Oklahoma.

In Texas, the city of Quanah, near the Oklahoma border, carries his name.

Kicking Bird, Kiowa leader, is designated head chief of the Kiowas. Traditionalists distrust and oppose him.

In the Black Hills, sacred home of Sioux deities and long-time hunting ground for the Sioux, white explorers under George Custer discover gold. Even though the Black Hills are already off limits to whites by treaty, miners rush in. The U.S. government tries to buy the Black Hills from the Sioux, but the chiefs refuse to sell.

> **"What I say is law for the Comanches, but it takes half a dozen to speak for the Kiowa."**
> —Ten Bears, leader of the Yamperethka Comanches, October 1867

In June, Quanah Parker, leader of the Kwahadi Comanches, and an intertribal band of warriors attack a small group of white buffalo hunters at Adobe Walls in the Texas Panhandle. The Comanches and Kiowas are many—seven hundred—and the buffalo hunters few. But the Indians fight with lances, bows, arrows, and ancient guns, while the buffalo hunters fight with the newest white man's weapon: high-powered Sharps rifles outfitted with telescopes. When the warriors fail to defeat the hunters, they take revenge by slaughtering travelers and settlers in Kansas and Texas.

Following attacks by Quanah Parker and the Kwahadi Comanches on white intruders into land that has traditionally belonged to Indians, General Philip Sheridan receives orders to make war on all Indians perceived to be hostile, wherever they might be. Worried about what may happen next, about 4,000 Kiowa, Comanche, and Cheyenne men, women, and children flee their Indian Territory reservation. The refugees break up into small bands and scatter across the Texas Panhandle. Comanche leaders include Black Beard, Mow-way, Wild Horse, and Tabananaka. Cheyenne leaders include Gray Beard, Bull Bear, Stone Calf, Medicine Arrows, and Medicine Water. Kiowa leaders are Satanta, Lone Wolf, Woman's Heart, Big Tree, and Mamanti.

Pursued by five columns of soldiers under General Sheridan and others, Kiowa, Comanche, and Cheyenne refugees from Indian Territory find that the elements, too, are turning against them: dried water holes, plagues of locusts, and fiery temperatures in summer; snow, winds, ice, and subzero temperatures in winter. They begin surrendering in small groups.

In late September, soldiers attack a village of Kiowa, Comanche, and Cheyenne refugees in Palo Duro Canyon in Texas. Soldiers capture 1,500 horses, destroy the village, and leave survivors hungry and horseless.

1875

When white settlers in central Arizona complain that their lives would be easier without the presence of the longtime inhabitants of the region, the Yavapai, the Indians are forcibly removed to the San Carlos Apache Reservation. There they are required to live in exile from their homeland for more than two decades.

For the third time in twenty years, the Coos people find themselves deprived of homes and forced to move when Congress gives white settlers land previously granted to Coos, Lower Umpqua, and Siuslaw Indians.

By April, Kiowa, Comanche, and Cherokee refugees who fled reservation life the year before have surrendered. On May 5, Kicking Bird, Kiowa leader, dies suddenly at about age forty-five. Many suspect

CHIEF JOSEPH, IN-MUT-TOO-YAH-LAT-LAT

To Americans, the courageous leader of the Nez Perce was known as Young Joseph or Chief Joseph. But he called himself In-mut-too-yah-lat-lat (Thunder Traveling over the Mountains). His father, Old Joseph, received his American name from a missionary, and the name passed on to In-mut-too-yah-lat-lat.

Like all traditional Nez Perce leaders, Chief Joseph sought consensus from other leaders rather than trying to become the dominant chief of all the Nez Perce. From their fathers, Young Joseph and other leaders had inherited the most pressing social, political, and cultural crisis their people had ever known. Whites had seized their traditional territories and refused to allow the Indians to live there any longer.

All his adult life, Chief Joseph wanted little more than to return with his people to the grassy Wallowa Valley of his ancestors in eastern Oregon. Instead, in 1877, he and other leaders—Young Looking Glass, Toohulhulzote, White Bird, and others—found themselves and their people hunted down by heavily armed soldiers, who were eager to shoot them and drag survivors off to a reservation that did not include their sacred homeland.

From June 17 until October 5, Chief Joseph and the other leaders alternately led their people and fought with soldiers as they fled across Idaho and into Montana. Even after he surrendered, on October 5, a few miles south of the Canadian border, Chief Joseph continued to press for his goal of leading his people back to the Wallowa Valley. Instead, they were exiled to Kansas and Indian Territory (Oklahoma). Many died. Others, including Chief Joseph, were sent to live on the Colville Reservation in Washington State.

Still longing to touch the ground where his ancestors walked, Chief Joseph died heartbroken on the Colville Reservation in 1904.

Today Chief Joseph's memory survives in the words of his surrender speech, among the most eloquent ever recorded. His memory also survives in the stories and hearts of his people. And it survives in the name of a dam on the Columbia River, near Bridgeport, Washington: Chief Joseph Dam.

that his enemies within his own tribe have poisoned him. The defeated bands are ordered to identify their best fighters. Those so identified—seventy-two in all—are shackled, chained to wagons, and sent on a twenty-four-day journey to a centuries-old prison in St. Augustine, Florida, El Castillo de San Marcos. Near Florida, Grey Beard, a Cheyenne leader grieving at the thousands of miles separating him from his family and homeland, tries to escape and is killed by guards.

Bands of Sioux and Cheyennes are hunting in the un-ceded Indian territory according to guidelines set by treaty. But in December, they are ordered by the U.S. government to turn themselves in to reservation officials by January 31, 1876, or be attacked by the military.

Nez Perce under Young Joseph are reminded of how provisional the white man's promises are when President Grant takes back the Wallowa Valley of their ancestors and turns it over to white settlers.

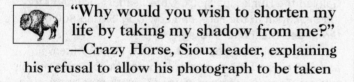

"Why would you wish to shorten my life by taking my shadow from me?"
—Crazy Horse, Sioux leader, explaining his refusal to allow his photograph to be taken

In the fifteen years since 1860, epidemics have de-creased the Tanaina population in southern Alaska from about 5,000 to about 1,500.

1876

Kwahadi Comanches of the Staked Plains in west Texas, who have avoided treaties and reserva-tions until now, find themselves victims of the army's cam-paigns against Kiowa, Comanche, and Cheyenne refugees

THE BATTLE OF GREASY GRASS
(LITTLE BIGHORN)

 In late June 1876, Sioux and Cheyenne families, with 1,800 warriors among them, were camped in eastern Montana along a stream called Greasy Grass, which whites called the Little Bighorn. Although treaties had given the Indians the right to hunt and camp in the unceded Indian area, as it was called, the U.S. government had decided to cancel that right unilaterally and had sent soldiers out to hunt down and attack the Indian families.

The Indians watched, waited, performed ceremonies, and talked about the powerful vision seen by Sitting Bull, leader of the Hunkpapa Sioux, in which dead soldiers fell into the Indians' camp.

On June 24, the soldiers arrived within a few miles of the village, led by a man the Indians called Long Hair, General George Armstrong Custer. The next day, Custer divided his troops among himself and two officers, Major Marcus Reno and Captain Frederick Benteen, for an attack planned in a pincer move.

Two Moon and Lame White Man led the Cheyennes. Crazy Horse and other chiefs led the Oglala Sioux warriors. Gall led the Hunkpapa Sioux. Other leaders included Kicking Bear, Rain in the Face, and Low Dog. Sitting Bull masterminded the Indian strategy.

As the soldiers prepared to attack, Lame White Man and Gall crossed the stream and routed Major Reno and his soldiers. Then they turned toward Custer's men and forced them onto a long high ridge. Crazy Horse and Two Moon and their warriors joined them, to create their own pincer effect. Indians attacked Custer's men from all directions. Within an hour, Long Hair and all his soldiers lay dead.

Meanwhile, the battered troops under Reno and Benteen, not knowing of Custer's fate, joined forces. Using mule packs, ammunition boxes, and shallow trenches for cover, they withstood the continuing siege of the warriors, but only with heavy losses.

Then Sitting Bull received the news that more soldiers were on their way. On June 26, the warriors set the prairie grass on fire and joined a long caravan of Sioux and Cheyenne families moving toward the high country. The

Battle of Greasy Grass, known to whites as the Battle of Little Bighorn, was over. Reno and Benteen and their few surviving soldiers waited numbly for reinforcements.

The Indians had been fighting in self-defense. General Custer had come to attack them in their homes. The Battle of Little Bighorn was one of the greatest triumphs during centuries of Indians battling whites for the right to lead their own lives in their own lands. But the American public didn't see it that way. Stories told and retold about the Indians' great victory caused many white Americans to demonize Indians and to cry even louder for their extermination. In the end, the Battle of Greasy Grass, a battle the Indians didn't want and didn't ask for, speeded up the Sioux's and the Northern Cheyennes' loss of their right to roam free, to hunt in their traditional hunting grounds, to live their lives as their ancestors had lived.

The Battle Where the Sister Saved Her Brother

 In a battle at Rosebud Creek, Montana, on June 17, 1876, Cheyenne Chief Comes in Sight charged soldiers under General George Crook repeatedly. Finally a bullet downed his horse. Crow allies of the army headed for Comes in Sight, to kill him. But Comes in Sight's sister, Buffalo Calf Road, charged up on horseback and rescued her fallen brother. Following the battle, Cheyennes christened it the Battle Where the Sister Saved Her Brother; whites called it the Battle of Rosebud Creek.

from Indian Territory (Oklahoma). Facing no other choice but annihilation, they surrender and agree to give up their centuries-old lifestyle and live on a reservation.

At dawn on March 17, Oglala Sioux and Cheyenne Indians living in 105 lodges on the Powder River wake up to the sounds of guns as the army attacks them. Although unprepared for the assault, the villagers counterattack and force the soldiers to retreat. The Battle of Powder River teaches them that they will have to fight for their right to remain off reservation in the unceded Indian territory. Thousands of Sioux and Cheyennes leave the reservation and join Sitting Bull and Crazy Horse in camps in the unceded territory.

On June 17 at Rosebud Creek, Sioux and Cheyenne warriors preempt the army and attack soldiers sent out to attack them. Only the fighting prowess of Crow and Shoshone auxiliaries, traditional enemies of the Sioux, keep Crazy Horse and his followers from annihilating the bluecoats. The battle ends in a draw.

KICKING BEAR

 One of the warriors who charged the soldiers of the 7th Cavalry in the Battle of Little Bighorn in June 1876 was an artist named Kicking Bear. Years later, Kicking Bear painted the battle. In a turbulent scene, Sitting Bull, Rain in the Face, and Crazy Horse give orders to the warriors. Soldiers fall beneath Indian horses or lie with throats slit or heads severed. General George Custer lies dead in his buckskins, and the spirits of those who have died, both Indians and whites, rise in ghostly outline toward the heavens.

In late June, 7,000 Sioux and Cheyennes, many of them refugees from the reservation, converge in the valley of Greasy Grass Stream, where they feast, dance, and celebrate their determination to preserve their lifeways and keep the whites out of the sacred Black Hills. On the maps of the white soldiers pursuing them, Greasy Grass Stream is labeled "Little Bighorn."

On June 25, 1,800 Sioux and Cheyenne warriors, camped with their families on Greasy Grass Stream, defeat the 7th Cavalry under General George Armstrong Custer in a battle that whites come to know as the Battle of Little Bighorn. As fighting with Custer's officers continues, the chiefs learn that more soldiers are approaching. After defeating the soldiers, the Indians set fire to the prairie, pack up their camp, and begin walking deeper into the wilderness, hoping to find safety.

> "Indians covered the flat. They began to drive the soldiers all mixed up— Sioux, then soldiers, then more Sioux, and all shooting. The air was full of smoke and dust. I saw the soldiers fall back and drop into the river-bed like buffalo fleeing. They had no time to look for a crossing. The Sioux chased them up the hill."
> —Two Moon, Cheyenne chief, recalling the early part of the 1876 Battle of Greasy Grass, the Battle of Little Bighorn

Brule Sioux chief American Horse and about two hundred men, women, and children, camped at Slim Buttes, South Dakota, wake up before dawn on September 9 to the sound of gunshots, as a party of soldiers rampages through the camp. In the ensuing battles, American Horse is wounded. He surrenders and dies. The ambush leads to the Black Hills Agreement of September 26, 1876, which robs the Sioux of one-third of their land.

"This is a good day to die. Follow me."
—Low Dog, Sioux leader, calling his men
to follow him into battle at Greasy Grass
(the Little Bighorn), June 25, 1876

On November 25, Dull Knife and 1,000 Cheyenne men, women, and children living in a canyon of the Bighorn Mountains are attacked by soldiers. Their village and food supplies destroyed, survivors flee deeper into the snowy wilderness.

The Ponca Indians of Nebraska are forced to leave their homes and relocate to Oklahoma when the government gives their reservation to the Sioux.

"They say we massacred him
[Custer], but he would have done the
same thing to us had we not defended
ourselves and fought to the last. Our first
impulse was to escape with our squaws and
papooses, but we were so hemmed in that we
had to fight."
—Crazy Horse, Sioux leader, describing the
1876 Battle of Greasy Grass, the Battle of Little
Bighorn

Chiricahua Apaches receive orders to move to the San Carlos Apache Reservation. About half move unhappily to San Carlos. The other half flee to Mexico to join Juh, leader of the Nednhi Band of Chiricahuas. Goyahkla (Geronimo) is among them.

The U.S. Supreme Court decides that Pueblo Indians are different from other Indians and may sell their land to non-Indians if they wish.

"I am here by the will of the Great
Spirit, and by his will I am a chief."
—Sitting Bull, Hunkpapa Sioux leader, 1883

"WE MASSED OUR MEN"

"We massed our men, and that no man should fall back, every man whipped another man's horse and we rushed right upon them. . . . the white warriors dismounted to fire, but they did very poor shooting. They held their horses' reins on one arm while they were shooting, but their horses were so frightened that they pulled the men all around, and a great many of their shots went up in the air and did us no harm. The white warriors stood their ground bravely, and none of them made any attempt to get away."
—Low Dog, Sioux leader, recalling the 1876 Battle of Greasy Grass, the Battle of Little Bighorn

"We were happy when he [the white man] first came. We first thought he came from the light; but he comes like the dusk of the evening now, not like the dawn of the morning. He comes like a day that has passed, and night enters our future with him. . . . 'To take' and 'to lie' should be burned on his forehead, as he burns the sides of my stolen horses with his own name. . . . No, no; his course is destruction; he spoils what the spirit who gave us this country made beautiful and clean."
—Charlot, Flathead chief, 1876

The Ute Indians, who belong to seven different bands and live in western Colorado and eastern Utah, worry as Colorado miners pressure the government to confiscate 4 million acres of Ute land and exile the Utes to Indian Territory (Oklahoma). Miners and settlers hope to invade the country of arches, canyons, mountains, and plains, all sacred to the Utes.

Nez Perce under Young Joseph (Chief Joseph) and others win the government's admission that it has stolen their ancestral lands. In November, General Oliver O. Howard tries to force them to sell the land in a conference at Lapwai, Idaho. Young Joseph and other leaders argue that the people and their land are inseparable and that the land where their ancestors lived, loved, and died must be returned to them.

"Here's your gun. Fight!"
—Wife of Nez Perce leader Chief Joseph, after he dashed unarmed through soldiers to reach his lodge, where she and their children were trapped, 1877

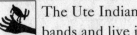

1877

On January 8, Crazy Horse and five hundred Sioux and Cheyenne warriors flee artillery shells and charging infantrymen at the Battle of Wolf Mountain. Sitting Bull leads about 2,000 Sioux north to freedom in Canada. Remaining off-reservation Sioux begin surrendering, a few at a time, at the Red Cloud Agency. On May 6, 1,000 Sioux men, women, and children under Crazy Horse arrive at nearby Camp Robinson and surrender themselves and 2,500 ponies to General Crook. Three hundred warriors among them sing their war songs one final time. Crazy Horse throws his rifle on the ground. Four months later, Crazy Horse is seized by soldiers sent to imprison him as a threat to the peace. He resists arrest and is bayoneted by a guard. He dies that night, and his parents bury him in a secret spot in the hills. No one is ever arrested or tried for the death of the great Sioux leader.

In the spring, Northern Cheyennes surrender on the Yellowstone River. A few weeks later, about 1,000 Cheyenne men, women, and children are forced to leave their northern homeland and walk from northern Nebraska to central Oklahoma. The journey takes seventy days. In crowded conditions in Oklahoma, the people suffer from summer's heat, winter's cold, hunger, and sickness. Many die.

>
> **"When the Crows meet a friend, they always give him something."**
> —Blackfoot, Mountain Crow leader, 1873

Blackfoot, leader of the Mountain Crows, dies of pneumonia in Wyoming in the autumn, at about age eighty-two, and is buried in a cave.

In Canada, Sitting Bull receives a visit from General Alfred Terry in October. Since Crazy Horse's death, the number of Sioux refugees with Sitting Bull has grown to 4,000. They live at peace with the Canadian government, but fight Canadian tribes for the right to hunt and eat scarce game. Terry tries to talk Sitting Bull into returning to the United States and living on a reservation. Sitting Bull refuses. Terry leaves, and U.S. soldiers patrolling the Canadian border receive orders to shoot any Sioux who tries to cross into the U.S.

>
> **"They tried to confine me. I tried to escape, and a soldier ran his bayonet into me."**
> —Crazy Horse, Sioux leader, on his deathbed, September 5, 1877

"WE PREFERRED OUR OWN WAY"

"We had buffalo for food, and their hides for clothing and for our tepees. We preferred hunting to a life of idleness on the reservation, where we were driven against our will. At times we did not get enough to eat, and we were not allowed to leave the reservation to hunt.

"We preferred our own way of living. We were no expense to the government. All we wanted was peace and to be left alone. Soldiers were sent out in the winter, who destroyed our villages."
—Crazy Horse, Sioux leader, on his deathbed, September 5, 1877

OLLOKOT: HE WHO LED THE YOUNG MEN

 Like other Nez Perce chiefs, Joseph led his people by consensus, and by mutual agreement with other chiefs. When young men among the nonreservation Nez Perce defied the older chiefs and started a rampage in June 1877, Joseph and the other chiefs stood behind them. Together young and old fled. As the Nez Perce struggled across Idaho, Montana, and a corner of Wyoming, the young man who became a spokesman for the other young men was Ollokot, Chief Joseph's younger brother. Above all others, it was Ollokot who masterminded the Nez Perce flight. And when Chief Joseph said in his surrender speech, "He who led the young men is dead," he was referring to Ollokot, who died fighting soldiers.

A photograph of Ollokot on file at the Montana Historical Society shows a smooth-faced young man with long black hair hanging down below his shoulders and piled high on his head. Ollokot looks at the camera with sad, earnest eyes.

In Oklahoma, the relocated Poncas from Nebraska celebrate the harvest. The event becomes an annual festival known as the Ponca Powwow and continues uninterruptedly for the next 120 years.

 "It is good. He has looked for death, and it has come."
—A fellow Sioux on Crazy Horse's death, September 5, 1877

 In the spring, Goyahkla (Geronimo) appears at the Warm Springs Apache Reservation just as the 450 Apaches there are being forced to move to San Carlos. He is arrested, put in irons, and imprisoned in San Carlos.

On September 2, Warm Springs Apache leader Victorio and three hundred Warm Springs and Chiricahua Apaches break out of the San Carlos Reservation and flee northward. A few weeks later, they give themselves up at Fort Wingate, New Mexico, and are allowed to return to their homeland at Ojo Caliente, New Mexico.

 "Crazy Horse always led his men himself when they went into battle, and he kept well in front of them. He headed many charges."
—He Dog, Oglala war leader, describing Crazy Horse, noted for his skill in guerrilla warfare, his modesty, and his courage

In May, Nez Perce leaders meet General Howard again; again he tries to bully them into selling their ancestral land. Again Young Joseph and other leaders refuse. Old Toohulhulzote argues so eloquently that General Howard throws him in the guardhouse. Then he gives the Nez Perce thirty days to renounce their claims and move onto a reservation that doesn't include their homeland. After that, he warns, soldiers will hunt them and kill

"CHIEF JOSEPH SURRENDERS"

"I am tired of fighting. Our chiefs are killed. Looking Glass is dead. Toohulhulzote is dead. The old men are all dead. It is the young men who say no and yes. He who led the young men is dead. It is cold and we have no blankets. The little children are freezing to death. My people, some of them, have run away to the hills and have no blankets, no food. No one knows where they are—perhaps they are freezing to death. I want to have time to look for my children and see how many of them I can find. Maybe I shall find them among the dead. Hear me, my chiefs, I am tired. My heart is sick and sad. From where the sun now stands, I will fight no more forever."

—Chief Joseph, Nez Perce leader, aged thirty-six, at his surrender, October 5, 1877

them. To save the lives of their families, Nez Perce leaders decide to submit to General Howard's demands. But en route to the reservation in June, young warriors begin rampaging. When one hundred soldiers arrive, warriors drive them back, killing a third of the troops. Knowing that more soldiers will come after them now, the Nez Perce, numbering three hundred warriors and five hundred women and children, abandon their plan to go back to the reservation. Now they flee. Leading them are Toohulhulzote, Young Looking Glass, Young Joseph, and others.

"You come here to tell us lies. Go home where you came from."

—Sitting Bull, Hunkpapa Sioux leader, refusing General Alfred H. Terry's request that he return to the United States from Canada and move to a reservation, October 1877

THE BANNOCK WAR

  Throughout the 1870s, Northern Paiutes and Bannocks often found themselves on the verge of starving. At their reservations on the Malheur and Snake Rivers, they didn't receive enough rations to survive, so they continued foraging as their ancestors had. But game was becoming scarcer as white settlements increased. The settlers' hogs destroyed a staple, the camas root, even though the right to collect the root was guaranteed by treaty.

Among the Northern Paiutes, Oytes, a shaman, urged revolt. Among the Bannocks, it was young Chief Buffalo Horn, who saw too late that he should not have worked as a scout for the U.S. Army against Nez Perce and Sioux.

On May 30, 1878, two hundred hungry young Bannock warriors under Buffalo Horn began raiding across southern Idaho. On June 8, soldiers shot Buffalo Horn, but his warriors continued on into Oregon. There Northern Paiutes under Oytes joined them, to create a force of 700 rebels, 450 of them warriors. At the group's insistence, a peace-loving Paiute chief named Egan took Buffalo Horn's place.

With soldiers behind them, the combined Bannock-Paiute force alternately fled, raided, and survived surprise attacks by soldiers. In July, they outwitted the soldiers by starting toward Nez Perce country, then doubling back toward the Umatilla Reservation near Pendleton. They hoped to gain allies, or at least find refuge among the Umatillas. Instead, on July 12, warriors battled soldiers as Umatillas watched. When the Umatillas entered the bloody battle, six hours later, they sided with the soldiers, to whom they presented Egan's scalp. In violation of ancient Native taboos, an army surgeon cut off Egan's head to send to the Army Medical Museum.

Oytes and surviving Northern Paiutes scattered. The Bannocks fled and raided eastward across Idaho.

On August 12, Oytes surrendered. The army rounded up six hundred Northern Paiute prisoners, many from peaceful bands uninvolved in the war. Forced to leave their reservation on the Malheur, they were sent to the Yakima Reservation in Washington State.

Meanwhile, the Bannocks were hunted down, killed, or captured. A few, trying to flee to Canada, made it as far as six-year-old Yellowstone National Park before being caught. The 131 surviving Bannocks were imprisoned throughout the winter, then sent back to the Bannock Reservation on the upper Snake River in the summer of 1879.

A war that could have been averted if people had had enough food to eat left the lives of hundreds of Northern Paiute and Bannock families more disrupted than ever.

On July 11, fleeing Nez Perce are attacked by General Howard and four hundred soldiers. After fighting furiously for two days to allow women and children time to escape, the warriors retreat. The chiefs meet in council and decide to flee eastward toward Montana. Again and again, troops attack them. Again and again, the Indians fight, and flee, fight and flee. At first they hope to settle among the Crows in Montana, but when they arrive, the Crows fight against the Nez Perce, side by side with the soldiers. The desperate refugees turn northward, hoping to join Sitting Bull and other Sioux who have escaped into Canada. In late September, the exhausted Nez Perce refugees camp on the northern edge of the Bear Paw Mountain. On September 30, only a week after surviving the soldiers' last attack, they are hit by a different force of nearly four hundred soldiers. The warriors fight bravely, but the battle becomes a siege. During the six-day siege, White Bird and three hundred men, women, and children are able to flee north and make it into Canada. But on October 5, with most of the other leaders dead and his people starving, Chief Joseph surrenders with 86 men, 184 women, and 147 children. They have walked and ridden horses across 1,700 miles of mountains and plains. Only thirty more miles separate them from Canada and freedom.

1878

  Facing starvation because of disruptions to their lifestyle created by the presence of white settlers, the Bannocks begin raiding across southern Idaho in June. Joined by Umatilla and Northern Paiute warriors, they fight settlers and soldiers intermittently for months.

 "Our treatment of the Indian is an outrage."
—General George Crook, known for his numerous campaigns against Indians in the trans-Mississippi West, June 18, 1878

 Warms Springs Apaches of New Mexico receive orders to return to the hated San Carlos Reservation in Arizona. Apache leader Victorio and eighty followers flee into the mountains.

In early September, three hundred Northern Cheyennes follow Little Wolf and Dull Knife, two Northern Cheyenne chiefs, and flee northward from Indian Territory (Oklahoma). Those with Little Wolf make it 1,500 miles north to the Tongue River and sanctuary. Little Knife surrenders and hopes for the best.

After three years in prison in St. Augustine, Florida, Plains Indian captives are released. Most return home to their families and tribes. Meanwhile on October 11, Satanta, incarcerated Kiowa leader, jumps to his death from a window in the state prison in Huntsville, Texas.

 In honor of Washakie, Shoshone leader, a fort in the Wind River Valley is named Fort Washakie.

FLIGHT OF THE NORTHERN CHEYENNES

In the spring of 1877, 972 Cheyennes were forced to travel south to a reservation in Indian Territory (Oklahoma). The journey took seventy days.

On the reservation, they endured malaria and other illnesses, starvation, and homesickness. Finally in September 1878, Little Wolf and Dull Knife, two Northern Cheyenne chiefs, escaped with three hundred Cheyennes and fled northward.

Over the next six weeks, the Cheyennes eluded 10,000 soldiers sent to bring them back. Then in southern Nebraska, the two leaders parted. After walking more than 1,500 miles, those with Little Wolf reached the Tongue River, where a friendly army officer agreed to let them stay. Six years later, the area became the nucleus of the Northern Cheyenne Reservation.

Dull Knife and those who remained with him disassembled their rifles and hid the pieces among their possessions. Then they turned themselves in to Fort Robinson in Nebraska. They expected to be allowed to join the Pine Ridge Sioux. But instead, General Phillip Sheridan ordered them sent back to Oklahoma as an example to all Indians everywhere.

Dull Knife and his people decided they would rather die than go back. On January 9, 1879, the Cheyennes reassembled their rifles and shot their way out of the fort.

Within hours, most escapees were killed or captured. Only Dull Knife and six others made it to Pine Ridge.

"Our fathers were steadily driven out, or killed, and we, their sons, but sorry remnants of tribes once mighty, are cornered in little spots of the earth all ours by right—cornered like guilty prisoners and watched by men with guns."
—Washakie, Shoshone chief, 1878

"We Buried Them in This Strange Land"

 "At Leavenworth we were placed on a low river bottom, with no water except river water to drink and cook with. We had always lived in a healthy country, where the mountains were high and the water was cold and clear. Many of my people sickened and died, and we buried them in this strange land. I can not tell you how much my heart suffered for my people while at Leavenworth. The Great Spirit Chief who rules above seemed to be looking some other way, and did not see what was being done to my people.

"During the hot days [July 1878], we received notice that we were to be moved farther away from our own country. We were not asked if we were willing to go. We were ordered to get into railroad cars. Three of my people died on the way to Baxter Springs [Kansas]. It was worse to die there than to die fighting in the mountains.

"We were moved from Baxter Springs to the Indian Territory, and set down without our lodges. We had but little medicine, and we were nearly all sick. Seventy of my people have died since we moved there."

—Chief Joseph, Nez Perce leader, recounting in 1879 the abuse done to his people following their surrender in 1877

 The Pomo people of California begin a century-long struggle to buy back lands lost to white settlers.

1879

 Chief Joseph of the Nez Perce travels to Washington, D.C., with his friend Yellow Bull and an interpreter. Chief Joseph pleads for better treatment for his people to audiences that include congressmen and cabinet members.

  In January, more than five hundred Northern Paiutes, many of whom are mistakenly believed to have fought with the Bannocks against the army, are forcibly moved to the Yakima Reservation, 350 miles to the north, during the middle of winter. Newborn babies, children, and old people die en route. Others, their spirits and hearts broken, die soon after they arrive.

 The Bureau of American Ethnology is created as a branch of the Smithsonian Institution. One of its missions is to collect information on Indian languages across the country.

 A small band of Ponca Indians, led by Chief Standing Bear, sneaks back home to Nebraska from Oklahoma. They are arrested and jailed. Standing Bear is tried and exonerated; the court decrees the Ponca have a right to remain in Nebraska. From this point on, the Ponca are split into two tribes, the Northern Ponca in Nebraska and Southern Ponca in Oklahoma.

THE UTES LOSE THEIR ANCESTRAL LAND

 Throughout the 1870s, following the discovery of silver in Colorado, white miners and politicians tried to find a way to evict the Utes from the 4 million acres in western Colorado and eastern Utah that belonged to the seven Ute bands. The fact that the land was already protected by treaty and had belonged to the free-roaming Utes and their ancestors for centuries, meant nothing to the greed-inspired non-Indians, who reasoned that 4,000 Indians couldn't possibly need so much land.

In 1879, when Indian agent Nathan Meeker tried to force the Utes to start farming, the Utes refused. The government sent 175 soldiers under Major Thomas T. Thornburgh. On September 29, 100 Ute warriors led by a man known to whites as Chief Jack blocked the soldiers' entry onto Ute land. In the fighting that followed, known as the Battle of Milk Creek, a Ute bullet killed Thornburgh.

For five days, the Utes laid siege to the surviving soldiers. Even after reinforcements arrived, the Utes continued to defend their native land. Only on October 5, as more soldiers appeared, did the Utes retreat. Before fleeing, they killed Meeker and took his wife and daughter prisoner.

Although Ouray, leader of the Uncompahgre Band of Utes, was able to negotiate peace and avoid further battles with the soldiers, neither he nor Chief Jack nor any other Ute could avoid what happened next.

In the summer of 1880, under threat of extermination or exile, Ouray and other Ute leaders met with government officials in Washington, D.C., and signed over Ute lands. The seven Ute bands avoided exile to Indian Territory (Oklahoma) but found themselves moved to small reservations in Utah and southwestern Colorado.

"OUR FATHERS GAVE US MANY LAWS"

 "Our fathers gave us many laws, which they learned from their fathers. These laws were good. They told us to treat all men as they treated us; that we should never be the first to break a bargain; that it was a disgrace to tell a lie; that we should speak only the truth; that it was a shame for one man to take from another his wife or his property without paying for it. We were taught to believe that the Great Spirit sees and hears everything, and that he never forgets; that hereafter he will give every man a spirit-home according to his desserts: if he has been a bad man, he will have a bad home. This I believe, and all my people believe the same."
—Chief Joseph, Nez Perce leader, at a gathering of congressmen, cabinet members, and diplomats in Washington, D.C., January 1879

Utes balk as government agents insist they give up the lifeways of their ancestors and become farmers. Trouble begins on September 10, when a government agent arrives at the home of Johnson, a medicine man, and orders him to kill his beloved horses and plow

THE VICTORIO WAR

 For four months in 1877, Victorio, leader of the Warm Springs Apaches who had been forcibly relocated at San Carlos, Arizona, watched helplessly as malaria struck his people at the detention camp. Insects covered babies' bodies with bites, and the traditional songs and remedies of the medicine people couldn't help. In September, he and his people escaped from San Carlos, and Victorio vowed never to return.

Back at his homeland at Ojo Caliente, New Mexico, the following year, Victorio responded to the order to return to San Carlos by fleeing. In January 1879, he begged the Indian agent at the Mescalero Reservation, farther east in New Mexico, for permission to settle there. The agent agreed to seek approval, but permission never came.

On September 4, Victorio and sixty warriors attacked a camp of cavalry horses near Ojo Caliente, killing eight soldiers and capturing the troop's entire herd of horses. Joined by Mescalero and other Apache warriors, Victorio and his men attacked travelers, soldiers, herders, and settlers in Texas, Arizona, New Mexico, and Chihuahua. American and Mexican soldiers hunted them on both sides of the border, but Victorio and the men, women, and children with him escaped each time.

Still, by October 1880, the refugees were hungry, exhausted, and nearly out of ammunition. On October 15, Mexican soldiers under Colonel Joaquín Terrazas surprised the weary Apaches. In two days of vicious fighting, the soldiers killed seventy-eight men, women, and children and took sixty-eight prisoners. Among the dead was Victorio. Afterward Apaches said that the great warrior had chosen to kill himself rather than be taken prisoner again.

the meadows they graze on. Johnson throws the agent out of his house. The government sends troops.

 A landmark federal boarding school for Indians is established in Carlisle, Pennsylvania. Emphasis is on vocational training for boys and homemaking skills for girls. The Carlisle school and the two dozen other off-reservation schools that open in the next two decades are designed to promote assimilation into white culture and destroy traditional tribal values. But as young people from many different tribes come together for the first time, a common Native American consciousness, distinct from mainstream culture, is born.

1880

Early in the year, Juh, leader of the Nednhi Band of Chiricahua Apaches, returns from Mexico with 105 people and turns himself in at the San Carlos Reservation. Goyahkla (Geronimo) is among them.

> "Lozen is my right hand. Strong as a man, braver than most, and cunning in strategy, Lozen is a shield to her people."
> —Victorio, Warm Springs Apache leader, praising his sister Lozen, a warrior who helped three hundred Apaches escape from San Carlos on September 2, 1877

Victorio, fierce leader of a band of Warm Springs Apache refugees fleeing reservation life, dies in the Battle of Tres Castillos in northern Mexico in October. Leadership of the refugee Apaches passes to Nana, an aging warrior.

"LEARN ALL YOU CAN"

 "In my early days I was eager to learn and to do things, and therefore I learned quickly, and that made it easier for my teachers. Now I often pick up papers and books which have all kinds of pictures and marks on them, but I cannot understand them as a white person does. They have a way of communicating by the use of written symbols and figures; but before they could do that, they had to have an understanding among themselves. You are learning that, and I was very much pleased to hear you reading.

"In future your business dealings with the whites are going to be very hard, and it behooves you to learn well what you are taught here. But that is not all. We older people need you. In our dealings with the white men, we are just the same as blind men, because we do not understand them. We need you to help us understand what the white men are up to. My Grandchildren, be good. Try and make a mark for yourselves. Learn all you can."

—Sitting Bull, Hunkpapa Sioux leader, addressing a group of Sioux schoolchildren, 1880s

"THERE HAVE BEEN MANY WORDS"

 "There have been many words. Wichitas have sent many words from their tongues; they have said little. Osages have talked like blackbirds in spring; nothing has come from their hearts. When Osages talk this way, Wichitas believe they are talkers like blackbirds. I have listened long time to this talk of blackbirds, and I said when my people talk like blackbirds, Wichitas think they are women. I want to say few words, then Wichitas can go to their lodges and mourn for their chief. I want Wichitas to know this thing. I want them to know that Osage are great warriors. Today they have talked like women, but they are warriors. They have those things which Wah'Kon-Tah [the Great Spirit] gave to men, so that he could tell them from women. They know how to die in battle. I want Wichitas to know this thing. We will give ponies to Wichitas for this chief, then they can go home to their lodges. I have spoken."

—Pa-i'm-no-pa-she, also known as Governor Joe, Osage leader, negotiating with Wichita Indians after two young Osage warriors killed a Wichita chief, about 1880

1881

 Since 1877, all but a few of the Sioux in Canada with Sitting Bull have given up and returned to the United States and accepted the hated life of the reservation. Now, after four years of hunger and deprivation, Sitting Bull and the two hundred Sioux who remain with him turn themselves in at Fort Buford, Dakota, on July 19. In a gesture of surrender, Sitting Bull hands his rifle to his eight-year-old son and tells the boy to pass it on to the post's commander.

Spotted Tail, Lower Brule Sioux leader, prepares for a trip to Washington, D.C., but before he leaves, Crow Dog, a subchief, murders him on August 5.

The Quileute Indians of Washington, worried about the reduced runs of chinook and coho salmon, refuse to sell salmon to non-Indians.

 The Apache leader Nana, old and ill, leads forty warriors on a thousand-mile rampage that kills forty whites and wounds many others. He wins eight battles with soldiers, seizes two hundred horses, and escapes into Mexico without losing a warrior.

> "I wish it to be remembered that I was the last man of my tribe to surrender my rifle."
> —Sitting Bull, Hunkpapa Sioux leader, surrendering, July 19, 1881

On August 30, White Mountain Apache medicine man and prophet Nakaidoklini is seized by soldiers. His followers surround the soldiers, whose Apache scouts mutiny. In the ensuing fight, soldiers kill Nakaidoklini. Warriors storm Fort Apache but are unable to take it.

On September 30, Juh, Geronimo, Chato, Nachez, and seventy-four other Apaches break out of San Carlos and bolt to Mexico, where they join Nana and the survivors of Victorio's band.

> "The soil you see is not ordinary soil—it is the dust of the blood, the flesh, and bones of our ancestors. . . . You will have to dig down through the surface before you can find nature's earth, as the upper portion is Crow."
> —Curly, Crow Indian who served with General George Custer, about 1880

"THEY KNOW WHAT LOVE MEANS"

"My people are ignorant of worldly knowledge, but they know what love means and what truth means. They have seen their dear ones perish around them because their white brothers have given them neither love nor truth. Are not love and truth better than learning? My people have no learning. They do not know anything about the history of the world, but they can see the Spirit-Father in everything. The beautiful world talks to them of their Spirit-Father. They are innocent and simple, but they are brave and will not be imposed upon. They are patient, but they know black is not white."
—Sarah Winnemucca, Northern Paiute, in her autobiography, *Life Among the Piutes,* 1883

1882

 In April, Juh, Geronimo, and other warriors slip back into Arizona from Mexico and attack San Carlos. Loco, leader of the Warm Springs Apaches, and several hundred other Apaches break out of San Carlos and return to Mexico with Juh and Geronimo.

In July, followers of the martyred White Mountain Apache medicine man Nakaidoklini storm San Carlos but are turned back.

Hopi Indians, ancient inhabitants of the mesas of northeast Arizona, receive the core of their ancestral territory as a reservation. It lies in the heart of the land of the Navajos, whom the Hopis see as latecomers and land-grabbers.

 "An Indian respects a brave man, but he despises a coward. He loves a straight tongue, but he hates a forked tongue."
—Chief Joseph, Nez Perce leader, January 1879

 Tonkawa Indians are once again forcibly removed from their Texas homeland and relocated in Indian Territory (Oklahoma). This occurs in spite of years of dedicated service to the U.S. Army as scouts in campaigns against Kiowas and Comanches.

 John Slocum, a Salish Indian of the Squaxin Island Tribe, has a vision during a near-death experience and founds the Indian Shaker Church.

1883

 In March, Chato and twenty-five Apache warriors raid across Arizona and New Mexico, then disappear into Mexico. In May, General Crook and 193 Apache scouts cross into Mexico and hunt for the Apache stronghold in the Sierra Madre. A scout nicknamed Peaches leads the soldiers to Chato's camp. After a fight, the two sides talk. Crook threatens to exterminate them all if they don't agree to return to San Carlos. At first, only Nana, Loco, and their followers return, but gradually others follow.

The Commissioner of Indian Affairs issues a list of "Indian offenses" that will henceforth be punished. These include such traditional Native American practices as ceremonial dances and feasts. Courts of Indian Offenses, composed of Indians appointed by white officials, are created to enforce the new regulations.

Chippewa religious leader Peter Marksman lends homeless Potawatomi refugees money to establish a permanent settlement in Michigan. In gratitude, they name the village Hannahville after their benefactor's wife.

1884

 Indians are formally excluded from U.S. citizenship in a U.S. Supreme Court ruling, *Elk v. Wilkins.*

The Indian Homestead Act allows individual Indians to file for homesteads. The act contributes to the breakdown of a sense of tribal identity.

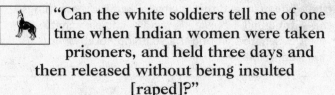
"Can the white soldiers tell me of one time when Indian women were taken prisoners, and held three days and then released without being insulted [raped]?"
—Chief Joseph, Nez Perce leader, in Washington, D.C., 1879

 White settlers seize Sauk-Suiattle (Sah-Ku-Mehu) land in Washington State and destroy the tribe's longhouses.

1885

 Apache leaders Geronimo, Nachez, Chihuahua, and Nana break out of San Carlos and flee back to Mexico. Forty-two warriors and ninety-two women and children bolt with them. Repeatedly they elude the hundreds of soldiers chasing them as they raid on both sides of the border.

 Near Lovelock, Nevada, Toc-me-to-ne (Sarah Winnemucca), a political activist of the Northern Paiutes, founds the bilingual Peabody Indian School, billed "the first school taught by an Indian." In a

GOYAHKLA (GERONIMO) SPEAKS

 During a peace conference on March 25, 1886, Apache leader Goyahkla, known to whites as Geronimo, speaks to General George Crook:

"While living I want to live well. I know I have to die sometime, but even if the heavens were to fall on me, I want to do what is right. I think I am a good man, but in the papers all over the world they say I am a bad man; but it is a bad thing to say so about me. I never do wrong without a cause. Every day I am thinking, how am I to talk to you to make you believe what I say; and, I think, too, that you are thinking of what you are to say to me. There is one God looking down on us all. We are all children of the one God. God is listening to me. The sun, the darkness, the winds, are all listening to what we now say.

"To prove to you that I am telling you the truth, remember I sent you word that I would come from a place far away to speak to you here, and you see us now. Some have come on horseback and some on foot. If I were thinking bad, or if I had done bad, I would never have come here. If it has been my fault, would I have come so far to talk to you?"

makeshift classroom in a brush arbor, twenty-six Paiute children learn to speak, read, and write English.

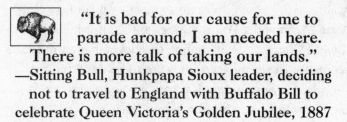

"It is bad for our cause for me to parade around. I am needed here. There is more talk of taking our lands." —Sitting Bull, Hunkpapa Sioux leader, deciding not to travel to England with Buffalo Bill to celebrate Queen Victoria's Golden Jubilee, 1887

 Alaska Natives find their lives disrupted after white prospectors discover gold, and the first waves of white miners flood into Native homelands.

Four years after his surrender, Sitting Bull accepts Buffalo Bill's offer to join the Wild West Show. Sitting Bull receives top wages for the era—fifty dollars a week.

Little Bear and two hundred Cree Indians flee Canada and move into Montana. Other Cree refugees of the Riel Rebellion join Chippewas under Little Shell. For the next three decades, the homeless, landless refugees wander Montana in search of food and a place to settle.

 The Lumbee Tribe of Cheraw Indians in North Carolina becomes one of the first Indian groups in the nation to operate its own school system, complete with a teacher-training college.

1886

 Geronimo, tired of living on the run, asks for peace talks. On March 25, Geronimo, Nachez, Chihuahua, and Nana meet with General Crook at Cañon de los Embudos. Crook threatens to continue hunting the Apaches down until they are all dead. Geronimo and the others agree to surrender, but then Geronimo changes his mind. Geronimo and Nachez flee back into the Sierra Madre with twenty men, thirteen women, and six children. Meanwhile, Warm Springs and Chiricahua Apaches living at San Carlos, including those who have worked as scouts for the army, learn they are to be deported to Florida. On September 4, Geronimo and thirty-six Apache men, women, and children surrender at Skeleton Canyon and are shipped to prison camps in Florida.

"I would like to know now who it was that gave the order to arrest me and hang me. I was living peaceably there with my family under the shade of the trees, doing just what General Crook had told me I must do and trying to follow his advice."
—Goyahkla (Geronimo), Apache leader, March 1886

With Geronimo captured, the futile battle of Native Americans across the West to live in their homelands in the style of their ancestors is almost over. Across the United States, there are now 187 reservations, home to 243,000 Native Americans. All together, the reservations cover 181,000 square miles of land.

The U.S. Supreme Court rules in *United States v. Kagama* that Congress has the power to control internal tribal affairs and to impose laws directly on tribes without seeking tribal approval.

With their ancestral land in Connecticut reduced from thousands of acres to a single quarter acre, the Paugusett union of five Algonquian-speaking tribes comes under the protection of the state of Connecticut.

"The Earth-Mother is listening to me, and I hope that all may be so arranged that from now on there shall be no trouble and that we shall always have peace."
—Goyahkla (Geronimo), Apache leader, speaking to General George Crook, March 1886

1887

Tsimshian Indians move from Metlakatla, Canada, to Alaska and establish the community of New Metlakatla.

"THE WASICHUS CAME"

"Once we were happy in our own country and we were seldom hungry, for then the two-leggeds and the four-leggeds lived together like relatives, and there was plenty for them and for us. But the Wasichus [white people] came, and they have made little islands for us and other little islands for the four-leggeds, and always these islands are becoming smaller, for around them surges the gnawing flood of the Wasichu; and it is dirty with lies and greed."

—Black Elk, Oglala Sioux, born in the Moon of the Popping Trees (December) on the Little Powder River in the Winter When the Four Crows Were Killed (1863)

GOYAHKLA (GERONIMO)

 The Chiricahua Apaches knew the short, intense man with a fierce scowl, probing eyes, and a bad temper as Goyahkla or Goyathlay. White Americans came to know him as Geronimo. After Mexican soldiers killed Goyahkla's children, wife, and mother in 1858, he became a master of guerrilla warfare, on both sides of the Mexican border, fighting and disappearing, fighting and disappearing.

Over the next twenty-eight years, he became known as the most elusive warrior of all times. Before his surrender in 1886, 5,000 troops chased him and his band of thirty-six men, women, and children without ever catching them. Perhaps he never would have been captured, but life on the run was no life at all, and he surrendered.

Geronimo's surrender symbolized the end of the long battle by western tribes for the right to live their traditional lifestyles in their traditional homelands instead of submitting to the indignities and cultural disruptions of life on the reservation. His surrender also marked the end of the Apaches' traditional way of life, which they had evolved during several hundred years of residence in the Southwest, and many hundreds of years in the north country before that.

After his surrender, Geronimo boarded the train at Fort Bowie, Arizona, a prisoner of war, destined never to see his homeland again. Incarcerated first in Florida, then in Alabama, he was eventually sent to live in Fort Sill, Oklahoma, and forced to become a farmer. A photograph from Fort Sill shows him standing in a pumpkin field, a hat in one hand and a pumpkin in the other. When he attended the inauguration of President Theodore Roosevelt in 1905, he received almost as much attention as the President.

Geronimo died of pneumonia at Fort Sill in 1909, still dreaming of returning to the land of his ancestors.

After Geronimo's death, his name became a synonym for fearlessness and bravery in battle. During World War II, hundreds of paratroopers leaped from airplanes shouting the name of the heroic Apache leader. Apaches today recall the reminiscences of their parents and grandparents, who remembered Geronimo as an intense man whom no one dared look in the eye.

Congress passes the General Allotment Act (Dawes Act). It requires reservation tribes to divide land among tribal members, in 160-acre parcels, and sell surplus lands to white settlers. In theory, the law allows tribal members to become private landowners and U.S. citizens. In practice, it undermines the tribe as a cultural, economic, political, and territorial unit; it causes poverty and further cultural upheaval and hastens the breakdown of traditional tribal values. Tribes are forced to submit to allotment even when they don't want to. The destructive legislation results in approximately 90 million acres—60 percent of remaining Indian land, including many sacred sites—being handed over to non-Indians.

The Indian Bureau passes a regulation requiring all Indian children to attend school.

> **"I know what the misfortune of the tribes is. Their misfortune is not . . . that they are a dwindling race; not that they are a weak race. Their misfortune is that they hold great bodies of rich lands."**
> **—Senator Eugene Casserly, 1871**

When the government offers to buy 10 million acres of Sioux lands at fifty cents an acre, Sitting Bull convinces the Sioux tribes not to sell.

Following years of unrest, guerrilla warfare, and harassment by the Mexican government, Yaqui Indian refugees begin fleeing north from Sonora and settle in southern Arizona near Phoenix and Tucson.

GHOST DANCE

 Beginning in the 1870s, a Paiute shaman named Wodziwob in Nevada predicted that Indian peoples across the country would experience great upheavals. Their deceased ancestors would return to guide them and turn the world into a paradise where no one would die, and there would be no distinction between races.

Meanwhile, Smohalla, of the Wanapum Tribe of the Plateau region, preached that if Native Americans returned to their original way of life, whites would vanish. Reminding his followers that the earth was their true mother, he urged them not to cut grass, because that shaved her hair, and not to plow the earth, because that broke through her skin. He taught sacred dances and urged people to maintain racial purity by protecting women from the sexual advances of white men.

Hundreds of miles to the south, Eschiti, or Isatai, a young Comanche shaman, announced in the 1870s that he could raise the dead, make people invincible against bullets, and deliver his people from white oppression.

The Apache medicine man Nakaidoklini made similar claims and announced that performing certain dances would force whites to depart.

From these and other teachings, the Ghost Dance tradition was born. In 1889, Wovoka, son of the Paiute shaman Wodziwob, became a leading prophet of the new faith. Like other shamans, he prescribed a healing dance.

As the movement spread, each tribe added its own interpretations and meanings. Although Wovoka preached peace, the Sioux predicted that a great whirlwind would annihilate whites, leaving Indians free to reclaim their ancient traditions and lands. Short Bull and Kicking Bear, two Sioux leaders, urged the Sioux to get the whirlwind going by donning a ghost shirt to protect them from bullets.

One belief, which remained consistent from tribe to tribe, was that the day would come when all Native Americans, not just those from one particular tribe, would live in their ancestral lands, free of whites and untroubled by misery, death, or disease. In this paradise, all the dead ancestors would return to life.

1888

Indian women married to white men are granted U.S. citizenship. Most other Indians are still considered noncitizens.

Felipe Roybal, nephew of the last *cacique* (religious leader) of the landless Tortugas Indians of southern New Mexico, leads his people in a campaign to regain a homeland and revive ancient traditions.

> **"When the English authorities were looking for me, I heard that the Great Father's people [white Americans] were looking for me, too. I was not lost. I knew where I was going all the time."**
> **—Sitting Bull, Sioux leader, reminiscing in 1883 about his flight to Canada and the years spent there**

1889

After a half century of uncertainty about their present and future, Cherokees living in North Carolina incorporate as the Eastern Band of Cherokee Indians.

Sitting Bull continues to urge the Sioux not to sign over any more land to the U.S. government, but when the government offers $1.25 an acre, the Sioux sign. The Great Sioux Reservation is divided into five parts. Teton Sioux are mixed with other groups and scattered among the new reservations.

> **"There are no Indians left now but me."**
> **—Sitting Bull, Sioux leader, berating the Sioux for having turned over 10 million acres of reservation land to the U.S. government, 1889**

Omaha Indian Susan La Flesche Picotte, the first Native American woman to earn an M.D. degree, begins practicing medicine on the Omaha Reservation in Nebraska.

Little Raven, leader of the progressive faction among the Arapahos, dies at about age seventy.

> "We could have escaped from Bear Paw Mountain if we had left our wounded, old women, and children behind. We were unwilling to do this. We had never heard of a wounded Indian recovering while in the hands of white men."
> —Chief Joseph, Nez Perce leader, recalling in 1879 his 1877 surrender

  Wovoka, Paiute shaman from the Walker River Reservation of Nevada, reports that during a solar eclipse he has traveled to the spirit world and found his people's dead living happily in a land of bountiful hunting. He teaches his people a dance to transform their lives. It becomes known as the Ghost Dance and spreads across the Great Basin, Great Plains, and beyond.

Thomas Morgan, Commissioner of Indian Affairs, organizes Indian schools into a three-tier system which requires students to attend boarding schools away from the influence of their parents and culture. The system is designed to instill the values of white people and destroy Indian culture and values.

> "The Indians must conform to 'the white man's ways,' peaceably if they will, forcibly if they must."
> —Thomas Morgan, Commissioner of Indian Affairs, 1889

THE BATTLE OF WOUNDED KNEE

 After Sitting Bull's murder on December 15, 1890, Red Cloud, a peacemaker at the Pine Ridge Reservation, sent a message to Big Foot, leader of the Miniconjou Sioux, asking for help. Red Cloud hoped that Big Foot, a former follower of the Ghost Dance religion who was known for his talents as a negotiator, could help calm whites' fears about the Ghost Dance religion and help negotiate the withdrawal of troops from Pine Ridge.

Big Foot was ill with pneumonia, but on December 23, he and 350 Miniconjou men, women, and children set out to join Red Cloud.

Assuming that Big Foot meant to cause trouble, General Nelson Miles panicked and sent out the 7th Cavalry to hunt for Big Foot and stop him. On December 28, the soldiers found him. The ill leader explained that he was on a mission of peace, and the two sides camped together along Wounded Knee Creek: 500 soldiers, 120 Sioux men, 230 Sioux women and children.

The next morning, the soldiers began taking away the Indians' guns. Yellow Bird, a medicine man, urged the warriors not to give up their arms. When a soldier seized a deaf warrior, the man's rifle went off. Moments later, a battle began. Soldiers and Indians shot, clubbed, and stabbed one another. Big Foot, almost too ill to stand up, rose from his bed to watch and was gunned down, with other Miniconjou leaders, including Yellow Bird.

Unprepared to fight, and lacking adequate weapons, the Sioux were slaughtered: 150 died outright, many of them women and children, and 50 were wounded.

Following the battle, 4,000 Sioux gathered in White Clay Valley north of Pine Ridge and talked of avenging the decimation of the Miniconjou Sioux. But the army was too powerful. On January 15, after only one token counterattack, the Sioux surrendered, and on January 21, General Miles paraded his soldiers past them, to remind them of his power.

The will of the Sioux was broken, but the memory of the brutality at Wounded Knee, the final battle in the Indian Wars of the nineteenth century, endured. In the years that followed this cruel butchery, Wounded Knee became a symbol for all the fatal and tragic encounters over the centuries between Indians and whites.

1890s

 Warfare, disease, and other disruptions have reduced the Kitikiti'sh (Wichita) people from about 4,000 to 153.

1890

 Kicking Bear and Short Bull, Sioux warriors, introduce the Ghost Dance religion to the Sioux at the Pine Ridge Reservation. They preach that the new religion will bring the buffalo back and make the white man disappear. On the Standing Rock Reservation, Sitting Bull promotes the new religion. On November 20, Sioux living on the Rosebud and Pine Ridge Reservations find a new burden added to reservation life. The cavalry and infantry arrive in response to white fears about the Ghost Dance religion. The Sioux split into two factions. About 3,000 followers of Short Bull, Kicking Bear, and the new religion flee to a far corner of the Pine Ridge Reservation known as the Stronghold. There they perform spiritual rituals and ceremonies designed to drive the whites away. The remainder, remembering the brutalities of the past, gather close to the Indian agencies and beg for peace.

> **"Come on now, let us protect our chief."**
> **—Catch the Bear, urging Sitting Bull's supporters to prevent his arrest, moments before Sioux policemen killed Sitting Bull, December 15, 1890**

In December, Short Bull and Kicking Bear invite Sitting Bull to join them in the Stronghold on the Pine Ridge Reservation, and he accepts. But on the morning of December 15, while Sitting Bull is still at his home on the Standing Rock Reservation, Indian Agent James McLaughlin sends two Sioux policemen, Bull Head and

PEYOTE

   By the early 1700s, the Indians of south Texas were using peyote cactus for ritual, spiritual, and medicinal purposes, but it was only in the late 1800s that its use became widespread across the Plains, Great Basin, and Southwest. Among the Wichitas and Winnebagos, peyote was used to cure blindness. Mescalero Apaches believed the fuzz from the peyote button could cure it. Kiowas used it as a cure-all: for toothaches, headaches, hemorrhages, tuberculosis, respiratory infections, fevers, hiccups, and more. Shawnees ate it for pneumonia and rheumatism. The Taos Indians used it to cure snake bites. The Otoe used it to treat mental illness, the Cheyennes to treat cancer.

Among the Mescalero Apaches, feuding shamans used peyote in trying to produce the most powerful songs. Shawnees carried peyote in their war bundles, and the spiritual powers of peyote included its ability to induce visions. Kiowas tell the story of Big Horse, a warrior in the mid-1800s, who could see events happening far away when he ate peyote. Jonathan Koshiway, Otoe peyote teacher, said, "The peyote spirit is like a little hummingbird. When you are quiet and nothing is disturbing it, it will come to a flower and get the sweet flavor. But if it is disturbed, it goes quick."

Contemporary tales about peyote include a story told by War Eagle, a Delaware, of an Indian soldier gassed in World War I who was cured by peyote after medical doctors said he was dying. Poncas talk about the time a man and his wife came home to find that a tornado had destroyed their home, leaving only a Bible and peyote paraphernalia untouched.

The use of peyote sometimes divided tribes into factions, or set one tribe against the other, with some believing it was good, others considering it evil. The Northern Cheyennes considered peyote treacherous. Flacco, a Cheyenne chief, once said, "It is used to witch people and make them crazy."

Native churches continue to use peyote today. In nighttime ceremonies, worshipers pray, sing, perform rituals, and eat the peyote button.

Red Tomahawk, to arrest the great chief, even though he has done nothing illegal. When Catch the Bear and other supporters of Sitting Bull try to protect their leader, Bull Head and Red Tomahawk shoot Sitting Bull in the chest and the back of his head. His body is wrapped in canvas and buried at Fort Yates, near Standing Rock.

On December 23, Big Foot, leader of the Miniconjou (Mnikowoju) Sioux, accepts the invitation of Red Cloud to travel to Pine Ridge and help work for peace. Although suffering from pneumonia, he sets out for Pine Ridge with 120 men and 230 women and children. At Wounded Knee Creek on December 29, 350 Miniconjou (Mnikowoju) Sioux men, women, and children on their way to a peace conference are attacked by nervous soldiers armed with Hotchkiss cannons that fire fifty rounds per minute. Big Foot and other leaders die. Within an hour, two hundred dead or wounded Sioux men, women, and children lie stretched across the countryside.

1891

Congress passes a law providing for Indian tribes to lease tribal lands to outsiders. The law results in further erosion of tribal control of Indian lands.

Congress passes the Act for the Relief of Mission Indians, which results in Cahuilla and other California Indians losing additional lands. Eleven inadequately small reservations are formed through the act.

> **"They made us many promises, more than I can remember, but they never kept but one; they promised to take our land and they took it."**
> —Sioux elder describing the white man's dealings with Indians, about 1890

After white settlers overrun Indian land in Montana's Bitterroot Valley, Salish Indians are forced to join the Kootenai on the Flathead Reservation in western Montana. They eventually become the Confederated Salish and Kootenai Tribes.

Creek novelist Sophia Alice Callahan publishes *Wynema, a Child of the Forest,* a fictionalized account of the challenges of acculturation.

1892

Reindeer are imported into Alaska from Siberia in an attempt by white bureaucrats to improve economic conditions of Natives. Over the next four decades, the enterprise fails.

1893

Lower Hoh Indian Reservation is established at the mouth of the Hoh River in Washington State as a refuge for the seventy-one surviving Hoh Indians who have not moved in with other tribes. For the next sixty years, it remains accessible only by foot and canoe.

In California, most of the few surviving Serrano Indians settle near the base of the San Bernardino Mountains.

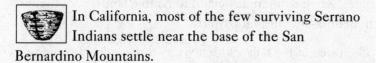

The Quechan (Yuma) people along the Colorado River in Arizona and California lose much of their ancestral land when white officials bully some leaders into signing an unwanted agreement and forge the signatures of others.

1894

 On December 5, Hunkpapa Sioux leader Gall dies of complications from old wounds, a result of a brutal assault by soldiers, during peacetime.

1896

 After waiting more than fifty years for the United States to honor its treaty obligations, the Catawba Indians of South Carolina hire attorneys to plead their case. It takes another half century to achieve federal recognition.

 The rights and freedoms of individual Indians are further jeopardized when the U.S. Supreme Court rules in *Talton v. Mayes* that the U.S. Constitution and the Bill of Rights do not apply to tribal governments.

1897

 Alaska Natives find themselves pushed aside even further as gold is discovered in the Klondike, and thousands of white gold hunters swarm into their territory. The newcomers bring disease and drunkenness. They rape Native women, lay claim to Native lands, and disrupt millennia-old cultural patterns.

The price of fur falls suddenly, creating hardships among those tribes across the U.S. that still rely on furs for income. Hardest hit are Athabaskan groups in Alaska.

> **"*You* tell them."**
> —Quanah Parker, Cherokee leader,
> responding to the order of the
> Commissioner of Indian Affairs to select one of
> his five wives and tell the other four to go away,
> late 1800s

The Indiana branch of the Miami Indians find themselves unilaterally terminated as a tribe when the government decides that the Miami tribespeople it forcibly removed half a century ago are the true Miami people. Economic and cultural upheavals ensue, as the Indiana Miami struggle to maintain their sense of communal identity and heritage.

1900

Across the United States, descendants of the several million Native Americans of 1492 number fewer than 250,000. Of these, approximately 1,000 are reported to live in cities.

Indian tribes hold approximately 80 million acres of land across the United States. Since the turn of the last century, Native Americans have lost more than 95 percent of their remaining land to non-Indians. As one century ends and another begins, they are in the process of losing additional millions of acres through the federal government's destructive allotment policy.

Since 1828, approximately one hundred Indian newspapers have appeared, from Alaska to Florida.

The Office of Indian Affairs has a $7.75-million budget and employs 4,259 people, more than half of them in education. Ten thousand Indian children attend 25 off-reservation boarding schools. Others attend the 81 reservation

WAPAMEEPTO

  By the time Wapameepto (Gives Light As He Walks) was born in 1834, many Shawnee people were living in exile. He was born in Texas, and from there he and his family moved to Oklahoma. As the grandson of Tecumseh, Wapameepto believed deeply in the traditions of his people. When he became chief of the Kispicotha Band of Absentee Shawnee in 1872, he spoke daily on behalf of the goal of preserving tribal traditions.

To him, the earth was his mother, and tilling the soil would wound her, so he consistently refused attempts by non-Indians to turn him into a farmer.

When the Shawnees were being pressured to submit to the allotment policy, which broke up tribal holdings and required the people to farm, he decided to move his band to Mexico. In 1900, he traveled there to search for a place where they would be free from persecution by non-Indians, but while in Mexico, he fell sick with smallpox and died.

boarding schools, 147 day schools, and 32 contract schools. The educational goal in all these schools is to obliterate Indian culture and replace it with white values. Speaking Native languages is forbidden; discipline is rigid and punishments severe.

 After five decades of brutal interactions with non-Indians, entire tribes in California have disappeared. The Patwin and Nomlaki Tribes are typical: 75 percent have died or been murdered. Of sixty Yokuts-speaking tribes, only a few remain, among them the Choinumni, Chuckchansi, Tachi, and Wukchumni. Of the 16,500 surviving California Indians, 11,800 are officially landless.

 Four traumatic decades after the brutal relocation of 2,500 Indians to the Siletz Reservation in Oregon, only 483 Siletz Indians survive.

 Washakie, Shoshone leader, dies in February at about age one hundred and is buried with military honors at the cemetery at Fort Washakie.

1901

 In Oklahoma, the U.S. government unilaterally opens more than 2 million acres of Kiowa land to non-Indian settlement.

 The U.S. Supreme Court rules that the rights of California Indians, guaranteed under Spanish and Mexican rule and protected by treaty with the United States, are void. Cupeños, Kumeyaay (Diegeños), and others are evicted from their land.

In *Indian Boyhood* (1902), Ohiyesa (Charles Alexander Eastman), a Santee Sioux, included this account of his uncle's view of white culture, whom the Santee labeled *wakan,* mysterious.

> They have divided the day into hours, like the moons of the year. In fact, they measure everything. Not one of them would let so much as a turnip go from his field unless he received full value for it. I understand that their great men make a feast and invite many, but when the feast is over the guests are required to pay for what they have eaten before leaving the house. I myself saw at White Cliff [St. Paul, Minnesota] a man who kept a brass drum and a bell to call people to his table; but when he got them in he would make them pay for the food!
>
> I am also informed, but this I hardly believe, that their Great Chief [the U.S. President] compels every man to pay him for the land he lives upon and all his personal goods—even for his own existence—every year! [This was Ohiyesa's uncle's idea of taxation.] I am sure we could not live under such a law.

1902

 Ohiyesa, a Santee Sioux, publishes the story of his childhood, *Indian Boyhood*, under his English name, Charles Alexander Eastman.

  Creek satirist and poet Alexander Posey publishes the first of his famous *Fus Fixico Letters*. Featuring real Creek elders, the letters poke fun at politics in Indian Territory (Oklahoma).

1903

In *Lone Wolf v. Hitchcock*, the U.S. Supreme Court rules that since Congress is the legal guardian of the Kiowa people, it has a right to make decisions without the permission of the Kiowa, including the right to renege on treaty provisions. The ruling allows to stand the government's confiscation of more than 2 million acres of tribal land two years earlier.

1904

Ghost Dance leader Kicking Bear, son of Woodpecker (mother) and Black Fox (father), dies at about age fifty-one.

In what North Dakota Chippewas jestingly call the Ten Cent Treaty, the United States pays the Turtle Mountain Band of Chippewas ten cents an acre for 10 million acres confiscated from the Chippewas decades earlier.

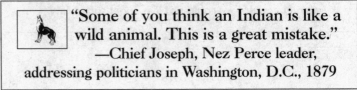
"Some of you think an Indian is like a wild animal. This is a great mistake."
—Chief Joseph, Nez Perce leader, addressing politicians in Washington, D.C., 1879

Exiled Chief Joseph of the Nez Perce dies on the Colville Reservation of Washington State on September 21, never having achieved his dream of returning with his people to live in their ancestral land.

1905

Congress authorizes an investigation of the plight of California's landless Indians, but they continue to suffer.

BLACKFEET

For centuries, the Blackfeet Indians, who are also called Piegan or Pigunni, followed the buffalo across the northern Plains. With the arrival of white explorers, miners, and settlers, the Blackfeet lost much of their traditional hunting lands in northern Montana. In 1877, three tribes of Blackfeet—the Northern Piegan, the Bloods, and the Blackfeet—received reservations in southern Alberta. By 1897, Blackfeet remaining in the United States found themselves restricted to a 3,000-square-mile reservation in northwestern Montana.

There the government forced them to become farmers. But then, with a shift in government policy in 1915, they were required to give up farming and concentrate on raising livestock. Together the two lifestyle changes produced deep poverty. By 1950, one-third of all Blackfeet had left the reservation in search of employment.

Today, of the 13,000 members of the Blackfeet Tribe in the United States, 7,000 live on the reservation. There elders and youth, both mixed-blood and full-blood, work to preserve tribal traditions like singing, dancing, and the opening of sacred medicine bundles, including the Thunder Pipe Bundle. After a century of decline, the Blackfeet language, an Algonquian tongue, is also being revived.

The Pyramid Lake Paiutes find their major source of food, the Lahontan trout, becoming extinct when the Newlands Project dams the Truckee River and diverts water for irrigation of non-Indian farmlands.

As Oklahoma prepares for statehood, Ottawa and other Oklahoma tribes lobby unsuccessfully for creation of a separate Indian state named Sequoyah.

The Indian agent for the Prairie Band of the Potawatomi Tribe of Kansas sets up an Indian fair modeled after farming fairs around the country. Fairgoers ignore the home-made jams and hogs and cluster around a few elders in traditional costumes. The fair continues until the Great Depression and is revived in 1956 as the Potawatomi Powwow.

1906

The Commissioner of Indian Affairs pushes a program to induce young Indian men to leave their reservations and "go out into the world to make a living as white men do." The goal is to further destroy tribal traditions and values by encouraging assimilation into mainstream culture. Few Indians agree to leave.

Among the Hopis, a schism occurs when one group draws a line on the sandstone and forces another group over the line and into exile from their homes. The split focuses attention on the conflict between traditionalists and modernists.

The Taos Indians lose the sacred Blue Lake to the U.S. government and begin a sixty-four-year battle to regain it.

Maidu Indians in California's Sacramento Valley suffer a major cultural loss when hereditary headman Holi Lafonso dies and tribal ceremonial items in his possession are sold to the Brooklyn Museum.

After decades of massacres, epidemics, enforced relocations, and cultural disruptions, the Tolowa people of northern California have shrunk from 4,000 to only a few hundred. Survivors struggle to preserve the traditions and beliefs of their ancestors, including the ancient Naydosh (Feather Dance).

ONEIDA

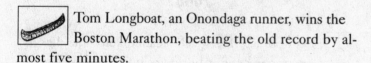 The Oneidas call themselves Onvyo?teaka?, People of the Standing Stone. Members of the original Iroquois Confederacy, they lived in the Oneida Lake area of New York in a complex culture governed by sachems and clan mothers.

By the 1820s, cultural disruptions and pressures from outsiders forced half the tribe to move to Wisconsin. Others fled to Canada. Some of those who remained in New York joined the Onondagas, but a few continued to live in their ancestral homeland.

Today the Oneidas number 11,000, with 3,000 living in Canada and the rest living primarily in Wisconsin and New York. Many still follow the Longhouse religion of Handsome Lake. In this century, some have attempted to reestablish the ancient traditional roles of sachems and clan mothers.

1907

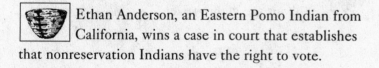 Tom Longboat, an Onondaga runner, wins the Boston Marathon, beating the old record by almost five minutes.

The Chickahominy Tribe of eastern Virginia organizes formally for the first time and establishes its own school.

 Ethan Anderson, an Eastern Pomo Indian from California, wins a case in court that establishes that nonreservation Indians have the right to vote.

 When Oklahoma becomes a state, most Oklahoma Indians automatically become citizens of the United States.

The dispossessed Samish Indians of the San Juan Islands of Washington State begin fighting to regain their lost rights as a tribe, including fishing rights.

1908

In *Winters v. United States*, the U.S. Supreme Court rules that reservation Indians have priority in allocation of water rights, but many tribes continue to find their water rights usurped by non-Indian neighbors.

> "Forty years ago my mother died. She [was] captured by Comanche, [when she was] nine years old. Love Indian and wild life so well no want to go back to white folks. All same people, God say. I love my mother."
> —Quanah Parker, Comanche leader, who reburied the remains of his mother, about 1909

1909

On February 17, Apache leader Geronimo dies of pneumonia and is buried at Fort Sill, Oklahoma, without ever being allowed to return to his native land.

On December 10, Red Cloud, Sioux leader, dies at about age eighty-seven.

By 1910

Although not recognized by either state or federal officials, the Waccamaw-Siouan Indians of North Carolina govern themselves in a council they call the Council of Wide Awake Indians.

ISHI

 Early one morning in August 1911, butchers at a slaughterhouse outside Oroville, California, found a Native American man crouching against the fence of the corral. The man was so emaciated, he looked like a skeleton covered with skin. He wore nothing but a scrap of cloth around his shoulders, deer thongs in his earlobes, and a wooden plug in his nose. He spoke a language that no one understood, including the neighboring Maidu and Wintu Indians.

Finally a scholar armed with lists of vocabularies discovered that the man belonged to a tribe believed to be extinct, the Yahi, from the southern branch of the Yana of northern California. Known simply as Ishi, the Yahi word for man, he was the last surviving member of his people.

Slowly Ishi revealed fragments of his life story. As a child, in the 1860s, he and a dozen other southern Yahis survived a series of attacks by white ranchers. They went into hiding, and for the next forty years lived in well-camouflaged shelters in remote canyons. To avoid leaving footprints, they walked only on stones or in water. In hunting game, they used only silent weapons: snares, bows and arrows, harpoons, and nets.

One by one the others died, until only Ishi survived. For three years, he lived in complete solitude before turning himself over to the white world that August morning in 1911.

During the next four years, Ishi lived and worked at a museum, demonstrating the daily activities of traditional Yahi life, from chipping obsidian to starting fires. He became known across the country as the last Native American in the United States, outside Alaska, to have lived a completely native life.

In March 1916, Ishi journeyed to the Yahi Land of the Dead. His last words, spoken to a friend, were, "You stay, I go."

1910

 Starving and landless, many Kumeyaay (Diegeño) Indians of southern California flee into Baja California to join Kumeyaay bands there.

1911

 Quanah Parker, leader of the Kwahadi Comanches, dies and is buried in the traditional regalia of a Comanche chief.

Omaha writer and ethnographer Francis La Flesche coauthors a classic book on Omaha traditions, *The Omaha Tribe*.

 Native Americans from many different tribes join to establish the Society of American Indians, the first national political organization founded and led by Indians. The SAI encourages Native Americans to maintain strong ties to their own culture and heritage while learning to live in a non-Indian world. Made up largely of Indians trained in off-reservation boarding schools, it lacks appeal for most reservation Indians.

1912

  Chiricahua Apache men, women, and children imprisoned at Fort Sill, Oklahoma, are given the option of remaining in Oklahoma or joining the Mescalero Apaches in southern New Mexico. Of the 258 prisoners, 171 move to a sparse corner of the Mescalero Reservation. The remaining 87 stay in Oklahoma and receive land allotments of eighty-acre tracts near Apache, Oklahoma.

THE ATHABASKAN PEOPLE OF ALASKA

For centuries, a dozen Native groups connected by a common culture and ancestry have lived scattered across Alaska: the Tanaina, Tanana, Ingalik, Koyukon, Holikachuk, Kutchin, Han, Upper Tanana, Tanacross, Ahtna, and Upper Kuskokwim. About half of them lived in the Alaska Plateau. Today they number about 14,000 and live concentrated in fifty-five major villages. But in the past in the Alaska Plateau, in a stark environment of long, brutal winters and insect-clogged summers, the average population density is estimated to have been under two people per hundred square miles.

Complicating cross-cultural contact, the members of these groups spoke many distinct languages. One, Holikachuk, was spoken at a single Ingalik village. Koyukon, by contrast, was spoken in many villages.

For many centuries, the Athabaskan peoples of Alaska, like the peoples of the Northwest Coast, have practiced the potlatch ceremony, an elaborate giveaway that historically helped establish social rank and provide for the well-being of all tribal members, rich and poor. They also continue to perform the ancient stickdance, which honors the dead. When the dance ends, new clothing is left in a sack, waiting for the spirit of the dead to carry it off when the spirit leaves the village for the last time.

People trace their descent through their mothers and the clans of their mothers.

The Athabaskan groups from the Far North are distant, ancient relatives of tribes who migrated southward centuries ago, including two of the most prominent peoples of the U.S. Southwest, Apaches and Navajos.

 The Lower Chinook Indians of western Washington receive compensation for the loss of 213,815 acres of land, but they and other Chinooks remain landless and without official status as a tribe.

The Tulalip Indians of western Washington vow to preserve their traditions and heritage. Their determination is

THE OPINION OF THE U.S. SUPREME COURT

 Anyone who doubts that bias against Native Americans was deeply embedded in official government policy for decades should consider the wording of the decision of the United States Supreme Court in 1913 in United States v. Sandoval:

The people of the Pueblos, although sedentary rather than nomadic in their inclinations and disposed to peace and industry, are nevertheless Indians in race, customs, and domestic government, always living in separate and isolated communities, adhering to primitive modes of life, largely influenced by superstition and fetishism, and chiefly governed according to the crude customs inherited from their ancestors. They are a simple, uninformed, and inferior people.

so strong that they submit to the indignity of asking the U.S. government for permission to build a traditional longhouse in which to perform ancient rituals and dances. Permission is granted, and the longhouse is built.

1913

 Thomas Bishop, Snohomish activist, leads Chinook and other Native Americans in western Washington as they organize a pan-Indian political action group, the Northwestern Federation of American Indians. The group fights for Indian rights and for return of land to landless tribes.

 The U.S. Supreme Court reverses its 1876 decision and decides that Pueblo Indians, like other Native Americans, may not sell their land. This allows the Pueblos to begin reclaiming land from non-Indians and leads to the proposed Bursum Bill of 1922.

 Mohawk writer E. Pauline Johnson publishes *Moccasin Maker*, a collection of short fiction and essays about Indian and mixed-blood women.

1914

 The Indian Bureau decides that all cattle owned by Northern Cheyennes must be combined into a single herd. The Cheyennes protest, but the bureau refuses to reconsider and removes 12,000 cattle forcibly from their owners, promising that within five years the herd will increase to 20,000. The bureau subsequently fences the cattle, which starve to death by the thousands in the winters of 1919 and 1920. Trying to find a break in the fence, the famished cattle wear a deep path in the earth, which

COWLITZ

For many generations, the Cowlitz Indians lived in four separate groups along the Cowlitz River and its tributaries in southwestern Washington. They hewed planks from cedar logs and built communal homes called longhouses, where they spent the cold, wet winters in thirty villages of about two hundred inhabitants each. Although some Cowlitz Indians spoke Sehaptin and others spoke Salish, they could communicate with each other using Chinook jargon, a trade language widely understood by many different peoples of the Northwest Coast and Plateau regions.

The name Cowlitz translates as "seeker of the medicine spirit." Traditionally, the Cowlitz sought visions as a way of encountering a *tomanawa,* a personal spirit guide. They also held spiritual cleansing ceremonies, or sanctification rites, which involved burning sage, cedar, and sweet grass to create a purifying smoke.

In 1855, the Cowlitz refused to sign a treaty that would have deprived them of their ancestral lands and required them to move in with their long-standing enemies, the Quinaults. Their refusal left them legally landless, treatyless, and powerless as a tribe. Nonetheless, they continued to preserve their sense of cultural identity, and in 1919 were described by an Indian agent as "a powerful tribe . . . [who] in the early days constituted the 'blue blood' of western Washington."

Today the Cowlitz number about 1,400. Although they have lost their tribal languages, they continue to use some Chinook jargon, along with English, and they continue to practice ancient rituals, including the search for a personal *tomanawa.* In a meeting of ancient and contemporary ways, they perform traditional cleansing ceremonies to restore the spiritual imbalance at sacred sites that have been disturbed by non-Indian developers.

survives them by·many years. In 1924, the bureau returns the remaining 3,000 cattle to their owners.

The Lower Kalispel (Pend d'Oreille) Indians, homeless since losing their land in 1855, receive a grant of 4,600 acres in eastern Washington. Upper Kalispel/Pend d'Oreille Indians already live on the Flathead Reservation in western Montana.

1915

Athabaskan leaders meet with government officials to address the problem of Native land being taken over by non-Indians. The government offers to establish reservations or provide 160-acre allotments. The chiefs refuse both options, saying neither reflects the Athabaskan way of life. Non-Indians continue to usurp Native lands.

Roe Cloud, a full-blooded Winnebago Indian and Yale graduate, establishes the American Indian Institute in Wichita, Kansas. It is the first college prep school founded by a Native American for Native Americans.

1916

Sioux Indians are required to undergo a citizenship ritual in which they shoot their last arrows, exchange Indian names for white names, place their hands on a plow, and take an oath while touching the U.S. flag.

After three decades of wandering, Little Bear's band of Cree, now under the leadership of Rocky Boy, receives land when the Rocky Boy Chippewa-Cree Reservation is established. Cree belonging to Little Shell's band remain homeless.

The Coquille Indians, led by George Bundy Wasson, begin a thirty-four-year legal battle for compensation for lands lost in an unratified 1855 treaty.

1917

The Chitimacha Tribe of Louisiana receives federal recognition and works to preserve its artisan tradition, including cane basketry and silverwork.

Cocopah leader Frank Tehana helps his people protect a portion of their ancestral lands by petitioning the federal government for formation of a Cocopah reservation. The tribe receives a grant of 446 acres near Yuma, Arizona.

After losing most of their land to white settlers, the Washoes finally acquire small parcels of land near Carson City and Reno, Nevada.

 Creeks and others protest U.S. involvement in World War I in an incident that becomes known as the Green Corn Rebellion.

1917–18

The council of traditional chiefs on the Pine Ridge Sioux Reservation quarrels with the white man serving as Indian agent. In retaliation, the agent dissolves the council.

THE MAN WHO WANTED TO
SEE MA-O-NA

  Among the Winnebago, storytellers tell this tale:

Once a young man fasted, wanting to see a vision of Ma-o-na, the Earthmaker. Again and again, he fasted, and again and again, he saw visions, but never did Ma-o-na appear to him. Finally the young man had seen so many visions that he had seen everything that lived on the earth, beneath the earth, and in the air.

One night a spirit came to him and said, "You have seen everything that Ma-o-na has made. That is the same as seeing Ma-o-na."

Still the young man was unhappy. Still he continued to fast.

Finally one night the voice of Ma-o-na came to him in a vision and said, "You will see me tomorrow. But it is not well. You ask for too much."

The next day the man took an offering of tobacco and went to the place where Ma-o-na had said he would be. A large flag dropped down from the trees, and the young man knew that Ma-o-na was there, but all he could see was Ma-o-na's face and eyes, because the flag covered all the rest. "You should have believed the spirits," said Ma-o-na. "You have dreamed of everything I made. But now you see me here today."

For a long time, the man stared at the face of Ma-o-na. But then the creature shifted, and the man saw that it was only a chicken hawk, a bird sent by an evil spirit. The flag was the chicken hawk's wing.

The man cried and returned to his fasting for another four days. But the spirits came to him on the fourth night and said, "Stop trying to see Ma-o-na. There are many more creatures and birds that the evil spirit could use to deceive you with. There is nothing left for you to dream about, because you have already seen everything."

Only then did the young man finally understand that it is impossible to see Ma-o-na. He stopped fasting and dreaming and went on with his life.

> "I have found you, now open up, show me where the rest of you are; I want to use you to pray for the health of my people."
> —Kiowa prayer, to be said upon encountering the first peyote plant during a peyote hunting expedition

1918

In two decades, use of the bud of the peyote cactus to induce visions in Native American religious rituals has become common in numerous tribes. Non-Indian opponents urge Congress to pass the Hayden Bill, which would outlaw Native American use of peyote. The bill fails. In order to protect their religious rituals, Indians in Oklahoma formally incorporate the Native American Church. Indians in other states incorporate their own churches, too. Peyote use becomes a means of uniting Indians from many different tribes by giving them ceremonies, traditions, and beliefs in common.

The Nisqually Indians of western Washington lose more than two-thirds of their small reservation when the government confiscates their land to build Fort Lewis.

The government issues 400 head of cattle to eighty Apache families at Fort Apache. Over the next twenty-three years, the herds increase to 20,000 head.

1919

The Indian Bureau decides that the Northern Cheyennes have too many horses. It orders one hundred horses shot per month and distributed as meat rations. The bureau also rounds up hundreds of the best

CHEYENNE (TSITSISTA)

Over the eons, the Tsitsista people developed a social order that included six societies of warriors. These were the Bowstrings, the Fox Soldiers, the Red Shields, the Elk Soldiers, the Crazy Dogs, and the Dog Soldiers. Each society had its own traditions. When a Dog Soldier went into battle, he carried a small red stake. If he drove the stake into the ground, that meant he had drawn a line and would not retreat, unless another Dog Soldier came forward and pulled up the stake.

Known to outsiders as Cheyennes, from a Lakota Sioux word meaning "people who talk a foreign language," the Tsitsistas developed strong religious beliefs that survive today. They believe in a supreme being, the Wise One Above, named Maheo. Four spirits serve Maheo, one for each of the four points of the compass. When the Tsitsistas pray to Maheo, they also pray to the four spirits: the spirit of the north, where the cold wind rises; the spirit of the south, where the cold wind goes; the spirit of the east, where the sun comes from; and the spirit of the west, where the sun sets.

Tradition speaks of an ancient prophet known as Sweet Medicine. Once Sweet Medicine went away, and the buffalo and game animals disappeared. In the four years Sweet Medicine was gone, the Tsitsistas nearly starved. When he returned, he sang for four nights, until the buffalo returned, and the people were saved.

According to tribal traditions, Sweet Medicine lived four times longer than the ordinary life span. When it was time for the great prophet to die, he gathered his people and told them to enjoy the life they knew, because someday newcomers would appear, people with white skin, who would overrun the plains, kill the buffalo, and take the Tsitsistas' land away.

At first, the people did not believe the words of Sweet Medicine. Even after they met the first white men, they did not think these could be the people Sweet Medicine spoke of, because there were so few of them. But then, after 1850, thousands of buffalo hunters, prospectors, settlers, and soldiers arrived. For thirty-four years, the Tsitsistas endured ambushes, murder, forced marches, exile, and destruction of their way of life. Northern Cheyennes and Southern Cheyennes became formally separated into two distinct groups. In 1884, the people who had once roamed 350 million acres were given 378,000 acres along the Tongue River. There the Northern Cheyennes began to re-build their culture and their lives. Meanwhile, the Southern Cheyennes were forced to accept reservation life in Okla-homa.

horses and sells them to non-Indians off the reservations. Cheyennes protest, but there is nothing they can do. The number of horses drops from 15,000 to 3,000.

The approximately 10,000 Indian veterans of World War I are allowed to apply for U.S. citizen-ship based on their service as soldiers.

Congress takes away the long-standing power of the U.S. President to establish new reservations and to acknowl-edge Indian groups as tribes.

1920s

The Agua Caliente Band of Cahuilla Indians in California discovers the financial benefits of tourism as tourists flock to Palm Canyon, Murray Canyon, and other picturesque sites on Agua Caliente land.

1920

After enduring generations of cultural disruptions from non-Indians, the Tunica and Biloxi peoples of Louisiana decide to merge.

DAKOTA

 When the first non-Indians arrived, Dakota-speaking groups of Indians lived in Minnesota and Wisconsin, a land they had migrated to from the Southeast sometime around A.D. 1000. In their adopted homeland, they hunted, fished, farmed, and lived in widely dispersed villages spread out across 100 million acres.

Other tribes called them a derogatory name: *nadowesiuh,* meaning "snakes." The word came into English as "Sioux." "Dakota" refers to a dialect of Sioux; those who speak it are sometimes called Dakotas, sometimes Santees, sometimes Sioux. Other branches of the Sioux peoples are Nakotas and Lakotas.

By 1839, only about 4,000 Dakotas survived. Following the Minnesota Sioux War of 1862, the Dakotas were exiled from the homeland they had occupied for so many centuries. Some fled to Canada. Others went to Montana and Nebraska.

Subdivisions among the Dakotas include Mdewakantons, Wahpekutes, Sissetons, and Wahpetons. Today approximately 30,000 people identify themselves as Dakota Sioux. Many live on reservations in North and South Dakota, Nebraska, and Minnesota. In spite of two centuries of cultural disruptions, many Dakotas maintain ancient traditions and beliefs.

 The Mohegan of Connecticut, eager to preserve their language, customs, and tribal identity, found the Mohegan Indian Association.

 Jim Thorpe, a star athlete and member of the Sac and Fox Tribe of Oklahoma, serves as president of the newly formed National Football League.

 In one of the first national shows of Indian art, Native American artists from many tribes find a national showcase for their work at the fourth annual exhibit of the Society of Independent Artists in New York.

1921

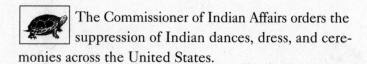

The Commissioner of Indian Affairs orders the suppression of Indian dances, dress, and ceremonies across the United States.

1922

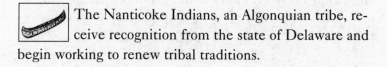

When oil is discovered on the Navajo Reservation, the Secretary of the Interior appoints a council of three Navajos to approve oil leases, even though the treaty of 1868 requires consent of the tribe.

The Bursum Bill, supported by President Warren G. Harding, attempts to settle water and land disputes between non-Indians and New Mexico's Pueblo Indians. But it favors non-Indian claims to ancestral Pueblo lands. To fight the bill, the Pueblos organize the All Pueblo Council and travel to Washington, D.C. With pressure from the APC and other political action groups, the bill is defeated.

The Nanticoke Indians, an Algonquian tribe, receive recognition from the state of Delaware and begin working to renew tribal traditions.

1923

Stephen Knight, a Pomo Indian, goes to court to protest the California segregation laws that prevent his daughter from attending public schools. He wins the case and establishes the right of other Native American children in California to attend public schools.

Native peoples of Alaska face further disruption from outsiders as the Alaska Railroad reaches the interior.

1924

 Congress passes the Indian Citizenship Act, giving all Native Americans United States citizenship, but some states continue to refuse Indians the right to vote.

 The U.S. Supreme Court rules that the Tejon Indians of California, including the Kitanemuk Indians, have lost their right to ancestral lands by not filing claims decades earlier.

 Congress passes the Pueblo Lands Act, which establishes the Pueblo Lands Board to review claims on Pueblo Indian lands.

  Congress authorizes the Wichitas and Affiliated Bands to submit long-standing claims for lost territory to the Court of Claims.

1925

 Although still lacking formal recognition as a tribe, the Chinook Indians of western Washington form a business council. Goals include protecting fishing rights, fighting for a return of traditional lands, and gaining access to Bureau of Indian Affairs services available to other Indians. William Garretson becomes the first Chinook leader chosen in a formal election.

HAIDA

 Like a number of other Native nations, the Haida are an international people. Some live in Canada. About 2,000 reside in the United States.

Traditionally the U.S. Haida lived in small villages in Alaska, including Howkan, Klinquan, Sukkwan, Koinglas, and Kasaan. Today the last major surviving Haida village in Alaska is Hydaburg.

Typical of seesawing government actions related to Native Americans, the Haida received a 7,800-acre reservation in 1912, but in 1926 the government shrank the reservation to consist of nothing more than a 2-acre site for a school. Even after the passage of the Alaska Native Claims Settlement Act in 1971, outsiders have produced upheavals for the Haida people. Today a major focus of the Haida is to restore, preserve, and pass on ancestral traditions.

Tribes of western Washington receive permission from Congress to press claims for traditional lands lost in the mid-1800s.

1927

 A group of Kiowa artists known as the Kiowa Five receive national and international recognition at the American Federation of Arts convention in November and at a European art festival the following year. Their work focuses public attention on the beauties of Indian art. The Kiowa Five are Spencer Asah, James Auchiah, Jack Hokeah, Stephen Mopope, and Monroe Tsatoke.

 Colville novelist Mourning Dove (Christine Quintasket) publishes *Cogewea, the Half-Blood*, the story of an Indian woman coming to terms with her heritage.

Congress passes the Indian Oil Leasing Act, which authorizes the Secretary of the Interior to make long-term oil leases on reservations, without the permission of the tribes involved.

1928

The Meriam Commission issues a report on its year-long survey of social and economic conditions of Native Americans. The Commission, composed of non-Indians from the private sector but working with the cooperation of the Bureau of Indian Affairs, criticizes the allotment policy, advocates protecting Indian rights and traditions, protests the Indian Bureau's education system, and proposes improving access to health care.

Descendants of the ancient Wampanoag Nation of Massachusetts and Rhode Island unite in a confederation of five autonomous bands. They honor the tribal traditions of their ancestors, including leadership by a sachem.

1929

Three generations after losing 1.7 million acres of land, Coos, Lower Umpqua, and Siuslaw Indians receive permission from Congress to petition the Court of Claims. After nine years of testimony and legal work, the court rejects the claim. The tribes remain landless.

"Our power is gone and we are dying, for the power is not in us anymore."
—Black Elk, Oglala Sioux medicine man, 1931

1930s

 The Swinomish (Squinamish) people of western Washington build a ceremonial smokehouse on the pattern of their ancestors and revive the long-forbidden Spirit Dance.

1931

 Tom Smith and María Copa Frías, two Coast Miwok Indians in California worried about the loss of their tribe's traditions and culture, begin passing on information about the Coast Miwok to anthropologists for posterity.

  Cherokee dramatist Lynn Riggs's play *Green Grow the Lilacs* depicts Oklahoma life. Eventually it becomes the hit Broadway musical *Oklahoma!*

 Mohegan medicine woman Gladys Tantaquidgeon and her brother Harold open the Tantaquidgeon Indian Museum in Connecticut.

 In a job placement program based on the policy of assimilation, the Bureau of Indian Affairs places 995 Indian men in off-reservation jobs.

1932

 The number of Indians enrolled as students in colleges and universities around the United States is 385.

HOPI

 For centuries, the Hopi Indians of northeastern Arizona have used dryland farming techniques to grow corn in the parched fields below their mesa-top villages. The westernmost group of Pueblo Indians, the Hopi preserve their ancient culture, traditions, and farming techniques today.

As their ancestors have done for centuries, many Hopi still live in homes made of dried mud and perform corn dances and other traditional rituals in the dance plazas around which their homes cluster. Children still learn that humankind has evolved through several stages, or worlds. In the most recent stage, the Hopi people emerged from the underworld through a supernatural hole, the *sipapu*.

Hopi kivas, the sacred ceremonial structures of the Pueblo Indians, still include a replica of the original *sipapu*. Today when a new village is built, the first elements constructed are the *sipapu* and the kiva.

Like other Pueblo peoples, the Hopi divide the ritual year into summer and winter. Kachina dances, celebrating human links with the supernatural, are among the winter rituals. Hopi artisans also carve kachina figures into wood. To outsiders, the heavily symbolic kachina dolls have become the best-known element of Hopi life.

Since 1900, the Hopi population has increased from 2,200 to about 7,500.

At the Santa Fe Indian School, a formal training program for Indian artists from across the country is launched. Over the years its graduates include Harrison Begay (Navajo), Allan Houser (Apache), Oscar Howe (Sioux), and Pablita Velarde (Santa Clara).

 The Bureau of Indian Affairs takes over control of education of Alaska Natives from the U.S. Office of Education.

Although Chinook Indians are still deprived of their ancestral lands, the U.S. Supreme Court rules that they and other "fish-eating" Indians are entitled to live on the Quinault Reservation. Within the next two years, Chinooks make up 60 percent of the reservation population.

 Osage novelist John Joseph Mathews publishes *Wah'Kon-Tah*, a fictional portrayal of the difficulties Osages have faced in trying to preserve their culture. The novel becomes the first book by an Indian to become a Book-of-the-Month Club selection.

The Pamunkey Indians of Virginia revive their ancient, nearly lost art of making pottery.

1933

Apache cattlemen in Arizona find their herds subject to enforced stock reduction.

President Franklin D. Roosevelt authorizes the Indian Emergency Conservation Work program, a companion to the national Civilian Conservation Corps, designed to offset the economic hardships of the Great Depression. In the nine years of its existence, under various names, the program employs 85,000 Native Americans.

1934

The Indian Reorganization Act (IRA) terminates the General Allotment Act of 1887, provides funds for economic development, allows tribes to expand

OSAGE

 Tribal storytellers among the Osage recall that long ago the Osage moved from the banks of the Ohio River to Missouri, where they settled along the Osage River. Speaking a Siouan language, the Osage divided themselves into numerous clans, which fell into two larger groups: the Sky People, or Tzi-sho, and the Earth People, Hunkah.

In 1825, the Osage were forced to leave their homeland and move to Kansas. In 1871, they moved again, this time to Oklahoma Territory, where they bought land from Cherokees. Throughout these upheavals, the Osage continued to honor ancient traditions, and when they arrived in Oklahoma, they grouped themselves into five villages, based on clans, and continued to think of themselves as Sky People and Earth People.

Only two decades later, their lives changed drastically once more when oil was discovered on Osage land. By the 1920s, they were being called the richest people on earth, but much of the money was lost through the corrupt practices of those appointed by the government to protect Osage interests.

Today only about three hundred people still speak the ancient Osage language, but tribespeople young and old are working to revive and strengthen the traditions and language of their ancestors.

their landholdings, and calls for cultural preservation. For the first time, the government acknowledges the right of Native Americans to freedom of religion. Dubbed the Indian New Deal, the IRA gives tribes the power to negotiate with federal, state, and local governments. It also starts a new era in Indian politics by calling for general elections within each tribe so that tribal members can choose whether to accept or reject the act. But after long years of unhappy dealings with the federal government, many Indians are suspicious of the legislation, which assumes that ultimately Indians will and should be

HOUMA

 With 11,000 members, the Houma (Ouma) are the largest tribe in Louisiana. Like their ancestors, they live in the marshlands in the southeastern part of the state, where they hunt, fish, trap, and practice their traditional culture. Houma weavers still gather the palmetto plant to use in making dolls, baskets, mats, fans, and other items. Houma storytellers still talk about supernatural events and beings which their ancestors honored. Medicine people still use native plants to treat the sick. But after centuries of contact with Europeans, the Houma language has been lost.

assimilated into the mainstream culture. It also pits traditional leaders against nontraditional leaders. Only two-thirds of tribes approve the act, and even fewer reorganize following its guidelines. The country's largest tribe, the Navajo, rejects it. Oklahoma Indians and Alaska Natives are excluded from the act.

The Johnson-O'Malley Act requires states to sign contracts with the Bureau of Indian Affairs for the education of Native American children.

Native Americans from many tribes join to found the American Indian Federation. Joseph Bruner, AIF president, is a wealthy Creek from Oklahoma. Although linked philosophically to non-Indian extremists of the far right, the AIF fights to reverse government policies toward Indians, including the Indian New Deal, and to abolish the Bureau of Indian Affairs.

 Six Navajo agencies are combined into one centralized agency at Window Rock, Arizona.

The Chinook Indians lose their battle to reclaim traditional lands; the Court of Claims rules that since the 1851 Chinook treaty was never ratified, the lands cannot be considered to belong to the Chinooks.

1935

 Congress establishes the Indian Arts and Crafts Board to develop and promote traditional Indian arts.

  Cherokee novelist John Oskison publishes *Brothers Tree*, about a Cherokee family in Oklahoma.

1936

 An amendment to the Indian Reorganization Act of 1934 addresses the unique needs of Alaska Natives, who live in villages, rather than on reservations. The Department of the Interior is instructed to reclassify land already occupied by Alaska Natives as reservations.

The Oklahoma Indian Welfare Act, an outgrowth of the Indian Reorganization Act, attempts to address the special needs of Oklahoma Indians. The Seneca-Cayugas become the first of eighteen Oklahoma tribes to organize under the act.

 Ellison "Tarzan" Brown, a twenty-two-year-old Narragansett runner, wins the Boston Marathon. Three years later, he wins again.

PAIUTE

  Before the arrival of non-Indians, the migratory Paiute peoples drifted in small bands across millions of acres of arid land in the West. They hunted game, large and small, and gathered berries, roots, and nuts. Their territory included central Oregon, southern California, and most of the Great Basin, all the way to southeastern Wyoming. Today the more than 11,000 Paiutes still live widely scattered: in California, Oregon, Arizona, Nevada, Utah, and Idaho.

Outsiders divide Paiutes into three groups: Southern Paiutes, Owens Valley Paiutes, and Northern Paiutes. In Utah, five bands of Southern Paiutes have joined to form the Paiute Tribe of Utah. Other Southern Paiute tribes include the San Juan Paiutes of Arizona and Utah, the Kaibab Paiutes of Arizona, and three southern Nevada tribes: the Pahrump, Maopa, and Las Vegas. Ancient rituals that these groups continue to practice include puberty ceremonies to honor a girl's first menstruation, childbirth rituals, and the Cry, a funeral ceremony that involves singing traditional stories and performing ceremonial giveaways.

The Owens Valley Paiutes live in southern California on the eastern slopes of the Sierra Nevada. Culturally they resemble Northern Paiutes, but they speak the same language as the Mono people on the western side of the mountains. The Owens Valley Paiutes preserve the Cry ceremony, collect native foods such as pine nuts, and are reviving traditional crafts, including hideworking and basketmaking.

In the 1800s, many Northern Paiutes found themselves forced out of their traditional territories by white settlers. Today Northern Paiutes are working to revive ancient songs, stories, and prayers lost during this period of deep cultural disruption.

  Lynn Riggs, Cherokee dramatist, writes *Cherokee Night*, a powerful play about cultural loss.

1937

  Survivors of the dispossessed Cayugas of New York become founding members of the Seneca-Cayuga Tribe of Oklahoma.

 The dispossessed Miami Tribe of Indiana reorganizes itself as a nonprofit corporation, the Miami Nation of Indians of the State of Indiana.

1938

 The White Mountain Apache Tribe is formally acknowledged, under the terms of the Indian Reorganization Act.

 Congress authorizes the Secretary of the Interior to lease tribal lands to mining groups without the permission of the tribes involved.

1939

 Art works by leading Seneca artists, including Sarah Hill, Jesse Cornplanter, and Harrison Ground, are exhibited in the New York State Pavilion of the World's Fair to wide acclaim.

 The Confederated Salish and Kootenai Tribes receive a guarantee from the Federal Power Commission of annual payments of $950,000 from revenues from Kerr Dam on the Flathead River. The figure is later increased to $10 million annually, with transfer of the dam to the tribes set for the year 2015.

O'ODHAM

 Long before the first Europeans arrived in the Southwest, the Hohokam farmed the arid northern reaches of the Sonoran Desert by building an elaborate system of irrigation canals. Their descendants became known as the Papago and the Pima, but they call themselves Tohono O'odham (Desert People) and Akimel O'odham (River People). Today the Tohono O'odham live on reservations in southern Arizona and Northern Mexico, and the Akimel O'odham live along the Gila and Salt Rivers.

To survive in the austere desert climate, the O'odham learned to harvest the fruits of the saguaro and other cacti. They also developed legends about the desert plants, including the belief that saguaros, with their giant forms and upraised arms, are people, too.

Traditional storytellers still refuse to repeat their stories anytime except winter. According to Tohono O'odham belief, if stories are revealed at other times of year, a rattlesnake will bite the storyteller. But year-round it is acceptable to acknowledge that I'itoi, the Creator, made the world and the O'odham people.

Other ancient traditions that survive among the Akimel and Tohono O'odham include basketmaking. The finely crafted baskets of the O'odham feature such ancient patterns as the man in the maze, a representation of Elder Brother beginning his journey through the maze of life. The design is believed to date back to the Hohokam, and for generations the story of the man in the maze has guided the O'odham in their walk through life.

1940

 The total population of Native Americans is listed as 334,000. Of these, only 27,000 live in cities.

Congress passes the Nationality Act, once again confirming citizenship for all Native Americans, but some states continue to refuse Indians the right to vote.

The landless Coos, Lower Umpqua, and Siuslaw Tribes of western Oregon receive a grant of 6.1 acres from a private firm. The land serves as a reservation until Congress confiscates it in 1954, making the tribes homeless again.

1941

Despite a decade of attempts to improve Indian education, 14,000 Indian students still attend boarding schools. An additional 16,000 attend day schools on or near their reservations. The remaining students attend public schools with non-Indians.

1942

Yale University Press publishes *Sun Chief*, by Dan Talayesva, a member of the Hopi Tribe of northeastern Arizona. The first detailed account of Hopi life and customs by a Hopi Indian, the book scandalizes readers with its descriptions of sexual encounters.

  Mojave and Chemehuevi Indians living along the Colorado River face the option of losing tribal land or allowing the government to build an internment camp for Japanese Americans on their land. Tribes acquiesce.

Young Seminole men from Florida, descendants of those who escaped deportation a hundred years earlier, refuse to register for the draft, saying they are not Americans but citizens of the Seminole Nation, a separate sovereign state.

A century after making a treaty with the U.S. government to preserve their tribal status, the Catawba Nation of

South Carolina under Chief Robert Lee Harris achieves
federal recognition as a tribe.

1942–45

 More than 25,000 Native Americans fight alongside other U.S. troops in World War II. At least
40,000 more help on the home front by working in
wartime industries. For many, this is their first experience
of off-reservation life.

 Navajo Marines fighting in the Pacific use the
Navajo language to devise an unbreakable code.
The "code talkers," all Navajos from the Navajo Reservation of Arizona, Utah, and New Mexico, are credited with
making it possible for U.S. forces to take Iwo Jima and
Okinawa. Of the thousands of messages the 420 code talkers send, the enemy fails to decode a single one.

Japanese attack the Aleutian Islands, capture the
Unangan population of Attu, and take the prisoners to Japan. The U.S. government rounds up the remaining Unangan people of the Aleutian Islands and relocates
them to makeshift camps on the mainland. In the camps,
Unangans suffer from hunger, cold, and disease. Many die,
particularly elders, causing a great loss to Unangan culture.

1944

 More than a century after evading forced removal
to Oklahoma, the Mississippi Band of Choctaws
is allowed to protect its traditional lands by forming a
reservation around established Choctaw communities.

HAVASUPAI

The Havasupai of Arizona remain the most physically isolated of all tribes in the United States outside Alaska. Deep in a side canyon of the Grand Canyon, in a location accessible only by pack mule or helicopter, they live surrounded by red rock cliffs and by gardens that their ancestors cultivated before them.

Until recently the Havasupai farmed and hunted in happy isolation from most non-Indians, long after other tribes had lost that option. Today, however, tourism is the main source of income in the hidden canyon village, which is called Supai. In spite of the difficulty of access, tourists arrive year-round, attracted by the dramatic setting, which includes the Southwest's most beautiful waterfalls.

Traditional Havasupai religion focuses on gaining access to supernatural power through dreams. This practice continues. The Havasupai today also focus on the power of the sacred Red Butte, which they have tried unsuccessfully to save from mining activities. To the Havasupai, the Red Butte represents the Earth Navel, the place from which their ancestors emerged into the present world. Violation of the Earth Navel by coal miners is a terrible sacrilege.

Fifty reservations and tribes send delegates to the first convention of the National Congress of American Indians in Denver. A national organization of tribes, the NCAI seeks to preserve Native American cultural values, to foster non-Indian acceptance of Indian values and ways, and to promote the welfare of all Native Americans. In lobbying Congress directly, rather than dealing with the Bureau of Indian Affairs and the Department of the Interior, it becomes the first national organization to give Indians everywhere a national political voice.

Ella Deloria, Sioux writer, completes her classic novel, *Waterlily*, about Sioux life in the 1800s, but it remains unpublished until 1988, exactly a century after her birth and seventeen years after her death.

1945

 Ira Hayes, an Akimel O'odham (Pima) Indian and U.S. marine, helps raise the flag at Iwo Jima and becomes an overnight hero.

Chemehuevi and Mojave Indians living along the Colorado River find themselves forced to share their traditional lands with Hopi and Navajo transplants under a new program known as colonization.

John Joseph Mathews, an Osage Indian, publishes his autobiography, *Talking to the Moon*. Critics praise it for its faithfulness to Osage culture and its literary and philosophical value.

1946

After a century of disagreements with the Cherokee Nation of Oklahoma, the Keetoowah Band of Cherokees receives recognition as a separate tribe. The Keetoowah focus on preserving ancient traditions and cultures.

The National Congress of American Indians lobbies Congress for assistance in settling tribal claims against the United States. Congress establishes the Indian Claims Commission. Tribes no longer have to petition the U.S. Court of Claims, which in sixty-five years has decided only 175 cases.

1947

 Sukulyi Hi-ar (Pete Lambert), last traditional chief of the Fort Mojave Indians, dies.

1948

The Bureau of Indian Affairs starts a job placement program for single Navajo men living on the reservation who are willing to move to Denver, Los Angeles, or Salt Lake City to work. In following years the program is expanded to include other cities and tribes. Because it moves Indians off reservations and into cities, the program becomes known as the relocation policy. It contributes to the further breakdown of cultural traditions and values.

In North Carolina the Eastern Band of Cherokees forms the Cherokee Historical Association to preserve Cherokee history and culture. Among its projects: Oconaluftee, a re-creation of a traditional Cherokee village.

Congress provides for establishment of the Indian Bureau's Higher Education Grant Program. It offers scholarship assistance to Native American college students.

The Ottawa (Odawa) bands of Michigan unite to form the Northern Michigan Ottawa Association. The association works to protect fishing and hunting rights.

1949

In an era when Communists are considered the archenemy and feared to be hiding behind every wall, Indian reservations are billed "natural Socialist environments" and "rural ghettos."

PAWNEE

 To the ancient Pawnee, the universe was ruled by Tirawahut, the greatest supernatural being on earth and in the heavens. The calendar of human activities was rich in rituals marking war, peace, birth, death, illness, healing, and other events. Before the chaos caused by smallpox, white settlers, and the U.S. Army, the Pawnee numbered more than 10,000. By 1906, only 600 Pawnee survived.

Today, five generations after being forcibly removed to Indian Territory from Kansas and Nebraska, the 2,500 Pawnee maintain ancient customs and beliefs in their new homeland in north-central Oklahoma. There the four surviving Pawnee bands perform war dances, round dances, the Young Dog Dance, and others. They also play traditional handgames, and tribal buildings include a ceremonial roundhouse. But some ceremonies, including the Pipe Dance, Doctor Dance, and Bear Dance, ceased early in this century when their owners died without training a spiritual successor.

Two different councils govern the Pawnee: the traditional Nasharo Council of chiefs, who are chosen by their bands, and the Business Council, elected by the tribe at large.

The Hoover Commission on government reorganization urges the U.S. government to transfer responsibility for Indian services to the states and to enforce a policy of assimilation.

The Mississippi Band of Choctaws establishes the annual Choctaw Indian Fair.

1950

 The total Native American population in the United States is listed as 343,000, a mere 2.7 percent increase in ten years. The urban population is 56,000, an increase of 107.4 percent since 1940.

 Congress passes the Navajo-Hopi Rehabilitation Act. It establishes programs to attract industry to the reservations and to relocate Indian families to urban areas.

 In an Associated Press poll, Sac and Fox athlete Jim Thorpe is chosen as the greatest football player of the first half of the twentieth century and the best all-around male athlete.

1951

 The Caddo Tribe of Oklahoma files claims for loss of land in Arkansas and Louisiana that ultimately lead to a settlement of more than $1.5 million.

 The Chickahominy Tribe of eastern Virginia inaugurates an annual autumn festival to help preserve its culture and traditions.

The Chemehuevi people of California and Arizona, close relatives of the Southern Paiutes of Nevada, establish the Chemehuevi Business Committee. The committee arranges for the Chemehuevi to participate in the Indian Claims Commission case brought by Southern Paiutes.

"A new, veteran-led sense of power is everywhere in the Indian country."
—*New York Times,* November 2, 1952

1952

 An earthquake destroys the last traditional homes of the Kitanemuk Indians in Kern County, California.

 The Bureau of Indian Affairs spends half a million dollars in its effort to move Indians, one person at a time, or one family at a time, away from reservations by placing men in jobs in urban areas. This same year, it spends $1.5 million to help create jobs in industry and agriculture on reservations. The National Congress of American Indians attacks relocation as a form of cultural destruction.

  Chemehuevi and Mojave Indians on the Colorado River Indian Reservation vote to rescind the government's policy of colonizing their land with other Indians. The Department of the Interior ignores the vote and continues to move the culturally unrelated Navajos and Hopis to the Colorado River reservation.

1953

 In a policy that becomes known as termination, Congress decides to dismantle the reservation system. It grants states the right to assume civil and criminal jurisdiction on Indian reservations. It provides for the transfer of Indian health and education services from the Bureau of Indian Affairs to other federal agencies and to the states. It opens the possibility of states being allowed to tax Indian lands. Approval of Native Americans involved is not required. The cruel, disruptive policy, aimed

MIWOK

 At one time, the Miwok, or Mewuk, people were numerous. Although they lived in many small bands scattered across central California from the Pacific coast to the Sierra Nevada, they kept in close contact with one another. Those of central California, for instance, traveled to the sea to gather clams, shellfish, and seaweed among their coastal relatives.

Today the Miwok live primarily in three pockets: along the coast, where they are known as the Coast Miwok; in central California, where they are known as Lake Miwok; and in the foothills of the Sierra Nevada, where they call themselves the Sierra Mewuk. Miwok and Mewuk mean simply "People."

All three groups have worked to preserve their cultural heritage. Today, among the Sierra Mewuk, people young and old are struggling to resurrect nearly forgotten traditional dances and to rebuild roundhouses, the ceremonial dance sites. Acorns were once a Mewuk/Miwok staple, and at the Tuolumne Rancheria each September, the Sierra Mewuk celebrate the Acorn Festival with traditional dances and ceremonial food, including acorn soup (*nupa*).

at eliminating a sense of tribal unity and tribal identity, does enormous cultural and economic damage to tribes across the country.

 The Otoe-Missouria Tribe of Oklahoma becomes the first group to receive a favorable settlement from the Indian Claims Commission regarding lost tribal lands. Congress approves a $1.5-million payment, which is divided among tribe members.

In spite of protests from the National Congress of American Indians and the Three Affiliated Tribes of North Dakota's Fort Berthold Reservation, construction of Garrison Dam begins on the Missouri River. This forces the

Native peoples living below the dam to give up the fertile riverlands that they have farmed for seven hundred years.

 Chippewa athlete Charles A. "Chief" Bender is elected to the Baseball Hall of Fame.

Indians in Maine receive the right to vote when Maine becomes the last state in the Union to accept the 1924 Indian Citizenship Act.

1954

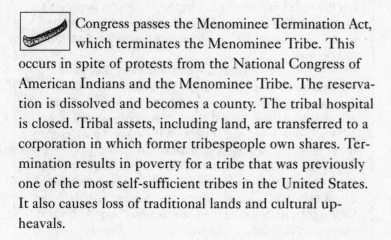 Congress passes the Menominee Termination Act, which terminates the Menominee Tribe. This occurs in spite of protests from the National Congress of American Indians and the Menominee Tribe. The reservation is dissolved and becomes a county. The tribal hospital is closed. Tribal assets, including land, are transferred to a corporation in which former tribespeople own shares. Termination results in poverty for a tribe that was previously one of the most self-sufficient tribes in the United States. It also causes loss of traditional lands and cultural upheavals.

The construction of the St. Lawrence Seaway combines with pollution to ruin two major sources of income for the Akwesasne Mohawks of upstate New York: dairy farming and sport fishing.

The Klamath Tribe of south-central Oregon, another highly self-sufficient tribe, is terminated by an act of Congress. Termination leads to the loss of 862,000 acres of land and decades of financial and cultural hardships.

POTAWATOMI

 The Potawatomi call themselves Neshnabek, Genuine Human Beings. About the time Columbus sailed from Spain, the nomadic Neshnabek migrated southward to the lower shores of eastern Lake Michigan. There, according to tribal legend, they taught the Sac, Fox, and Kickapoo to make birch-bark canoes. Their new neighbors showed the Neshnabek how to grow corn, beans, squash, and other crops. Now men hunted and women farmed.

But they preserved ancient beliefs and customs, including the belief in Nampizha, a horned creature, part human, part panther, who lurked beneath the water. To appease Nampizha, boaters sprinkled tobacco on the water before setting out.

In 1634, Jean Nicolet, a French explorer, met some Neshnabek travelers. He asked a Huron guide, "Who are these people?" Misunderstanding, the guide said, "They are making a fire." Nicolet wrote this Huron phrase down as "Pouutouatami," and it became the name by which other people called the Neshnabek.

In the 1650s, as the Five Nations of the Iroquois Confederacy swept westward, about 2,500 Potawatomi fled across Lake Michigan to present-day Wisconsin. There they built a fortified village called Mitchigami (Large Lake) and defeated the invaders. The tribe grew, establishing clan-based villages from the Mississippi River eastward through Ohio. In 1763, the Neshnabek joined Pontiac, an Ottowa chief, in trying to overthrow the British.

Today the Potawatomi live primarily in four states—Michigan, Wisconsin, Kansas, and Oklahoma.

The Coquille Indians and forty-two other tribes from western Oregon are terminated as tribes and must fight for decades to regain lost status and rights.

 Congress orders the Bureau of Indian Affairs to turn over Native American health care to the

Public Health Service, which establishes the Indian Health Service. At this point, tuberculosis is still endemic among many Native Americans. The IHS begins a massive program to eliminate the disease.

1955

When the Bureau of Indian Affairs attempts to terminate the Spokan (Spokane) Indians as a tribe, they fight back. Unlike many other tribes who have tried to avoid termination, the Spokan are successful; the victory increases their solidarity as a tribe.

1956

The first Workshop in American Indian Affairs is held in Colorado Springs. The six-week summer workshops give young Native Americans an intensive look at Indian issues across the United States. The workshops contribute to the growing pan-Indian movement, in which tribes across the country put their common concerns and needs ahead of their numerous cultural and political differences.

The Indian Vocational Training Act establishes vocational training programs for Indians. Graduates of the programs can typically find work in urban areas, but not on their reservations.

The Coos, Lower Umpqua, and Siuslaw Tribes of western Oregon petition the United Nations for return of land taken from them by Congress in 1954. The petition brings the tribes publicity, but they remain landless for twenty-eight more years.

Charles Edward Ned, the last full-blooded Coquille Indian, dies.

HUPA

 When Athabaskan-speaking peoples migrated southward from Alaska and Canada many centuries ago, some of them followed the coast and ended up in California. Among them were the Hupa, who settled along the Trinity River of northwestern California. They harvested acorns and fished for salmon, steelhead trout, and lamprey eels.

At the village of Takimildin, they developed a spiritual center. There they danced the White Deerskin Dance, which ensures the continued vitality of human beings and the earth. It also wards off illnesses and disasters such as famine. At Takimildin, they also celebrated the Jump Dance, which expresses the gratitude of the Hupa people for their beautiful valley, its dense forests, and the bounty of the rivers.

Like other tribes, the Hupa have endured enormous cultural upheavals, beginning with the arrival of Jedediah Smith in 1828 and continuing into the twentieth century. But the more than 3,000 Hupa who survive have preserved many of their traditions and beliefs. Although they lost much of their ancestral land to non-Indians, their 89,000-acre reservation, in northwest California, encompasses part of their traditional homeland. It is the largest reservation in California today.

 The Lumbee Indians of North Carolina receive congressional recognition as a tribe but are denied federal services extended to other tribes.

1957

 Mohawk Indians from the St. Regis Reservation announce that New York State has no political sovereignty over them. They refuse to pay state taxes and tear up summonses issued because of nonpayment.

For the first time in tribal memory, Shoshone women in Wyoming break with tradition and perform their own version of the formerly all-male War Dance.

The Seminole Tribe of Florida receives federal recognition as a tribe.

Two thousand Native American students are enrolled in colleges and universities around the United States, five times more than a quarter century earlier.

Ten years after the death of the last traditional Mojave chief, a Mojave woman, Malyika Chupek (Frances Wilbur Stillman), becomes the first tribal chairperson of the Fort Mojave people.

1958

The New York State Power Authority tries to confiscate more than one-fifth of the Tuscarora Indian Reservation for a reservoir. Tuscarora officials order Power Authority officials and surveyors off their land. When one hundred armed county deputies and state troopers arrive the next day to escort the surveyors onto Indian land, the Tuscaroras lie on the ground to prevent government vehicles from entering.

After the Ku Klux Klan harasses Lumbee Indians in Robeson County, North Carolina, the Lumbee arm themselves with guns, break up a Klan rally, and drive the Klan out of the county.

The Bureau of Indian Affairs approves a project to encourage non-Indians to adopt Indian children. Tribes protest but find themselves powerless to stop the adoptions. Over the next decade, at least 1,000 Indian children are removed from tribal settings and adopted by non-Indian families.

 Prominent Sioux artist Oscar Howe protests when the Philbrook Museum in Tulsa, Oklahoma, rejects his work on the grounds that it does not represent traditional Indian art. His protest results in a lifting of the unwritten dictum that Indian artists may create only certain types of art approved by the non-Indian art community.

 Navajos and Hopis ask for and receive permission from Congress to sue each other over land disputes. It is the first time that one tribe in the United States has sued another.

 Following Alaska statehood, Native groups find their traditional territories transferred from federal landholding to the state of Alaska. Natives form political action groups to fight for their land.

1959

 In order to protest the government's termination policy, several hundred Indians march to the Bureau of Indian Affairs headquarters in Washington, D.C. Although they fail in their attempt to arrest the Indian Commissioner, they succeed in reminding the public of the cruelty of the termination policy.

The Indian Claims Commission determines that the 102,000 acres taken from the Muckleshoot Tribe in Washington State in the 1800s is worth $86,000. The Muckleshoots use the funds to begin buying back ancestral lands.

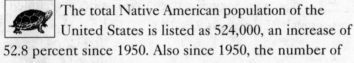 The last fluent speaker of the Catawba language dies, but other members of the Catawba Nation of South Carolina work to preserve and resurrect the language, which belongs to the Sioux family of languages.

1960

 The total Native American population of the United States is listed as 524,000, an increase of 52.8 percent since 1950. Also since 1950, the number of Indians living in urban areas has climbed by 161 percent, to 146,000. By comparison, the urban population of the country in general has increased by only 29 percent.

Opposition from Native Americans and state governments forces the U.S. government to stop implementing the termination policy adopted in 1953.

1961

About five hundred Indians from seventy tribes attend the American Indian Chicago Conference to protest the termination program and other destructive government policies. They draft the Declaration of Indian Purpose. It calls for a reversal of the termination policy, for reduction in the influence of the Bureau of Indian Affairs, and for the protection of Indian water rights. The conference leads to a strengthening of intertribal solidarity.

Following the American Indian Chicago Conference, young Indian activists establish the National Indian Youth Council. It becomes a leading activist organization, enrolling 5,000 members within the next two years.

1962

Traditionalists in the Seminole Tribe in Florida break away from the main tribe. They form the separate Miccosukee Tribe as a way of protecting and conserving ancient values and traditions.

Along Healy Lake in Alaska, the last Natives desert an ancient village that has been occupied continuously since about 9,000 B.C.

After fifty-six years of petitioning the U.S. government unsuccessfully for payment for lands lost to white settlers in the 1800s, the Confederated Tribes of the Chehalis Reservation vote to accept $754,380 for 838,000 acres of stolen land.

The Institute of American Indian Arts is established with the goal of training talented young Native American artists and promoting Native arts.

In a land dispute that has simmered for centuries, a federal district court rules in *Healing v. Jones* that Hopis and Navajos have joint rights to Hopi lands. Both sides are unhappy with the decision and continue their legal battles.

PUEBLO INDIANS

 The Pueblo peoples of New Mexico trace their ancestry back to the Anasazi and to the ancestors of the Anasazi, the Basket Makers. Noted for their fine pottery, elaborate dance rituals, and picturesque villages, the Pueblos have been able to preserve their ancient traditions, beliefs, clan systems, and worldviews uninterruptedly, in spite of more than four and a half centuries of buffeting by non-Indians. Today they still live in the villages of their ancestors, in twenty separate Pueblo groups, speaking six separate languages.

The westernmost Pueblo Indians are the Hopis of Arizona, but most Pueblo Indians live in New Mexico, near the Rio Grande and its tributaries. Farthest north is Taos Pueblo, a 650-year-old multistory village. Like Anasazi villages before it, Taos Pueblo is laid out in the traditional pattern around a central plaza that marks the division between Summer People and Winter People.

Each Pueblo is distinctive. For centuries, the people of Acoma Pueblo protected themselves from unexpected invasion by living high on a mesa top in western New Mexico. Religious leaders known as *caciques* ruled the village, and traditional ceremonies marked the passing of the months and years. Today the old mesa-top village survives as a ceremonial site to which the Acoma people return throughout the year to celebrate ancient dances and rituals. Although Acomas elect political leaders, the *caciques* still rule, and elected officials must report to them.

Laguna Pueblo is said by non-Indian historians to have been established in 1699 by refugees from the Rio Grande villages in the aftermath of the Pueblo Revolt, but the Laguna people themselves recall that they have lived on the same site since long before that.

After centuries of interference from outsiders, the Pueblo peoples prefer not to share their worldview with non-Indians. When a San Juan Pueblo Indian, Alfonso Ortiz, who had been trained as an anthropologist, published *The Tewa World: Space, Time, Being, and Becoming in a Pueblo Society* in 1969, many labeled him a traitor.

Although some ceremonies are open to the public, many Pueblos forbid photography, and certain rituals and dances are closed to outsiders. Taos Pueblo shuts the world out completely each winter by closing the Pueblo from the beginning of Lent until Easter.

KICKAPOO

  For centuries, the Kickapoo Indians lived around the Great Lakes. But when Europeans arrived and began dislocating tribes farther east, the Kickapoo migrated westward and southward. They settled in small bands in Indiana, Illinois, Missouri, Texas, and Mexico, and tried to maintain their traditional customs and way of life.

In the 1830s, the Kickapoo in Illinois were forcibly removed to northeast Kansas. There, as the decades passed, whites tore away chunks of their 768,000-acre reservation, until only 7,000 acres remained.

Today Kickapoo live primarily in Kansas, Oklahoma, and Texas. Many of the descendants of those who fled to Mexico in the 1830s still live part of the year in Mexico, in the state of Coahuila, and part of the year in the United States. In Coahuila, they continue to reside in traditional Kickapoo houses made of reed mats.

Among the Oklahoma Kickapoo, the language remains strong. Nearly half of the 1,900 Oklahoma Kickapoo speak only Kickapoo.

Although scattered far from one another today, Kickapoo in all regions are working to preserve and resurrect the cultural patterns and beliefs of their ancestors.

1963

 Leery of losing their traditional style of governing themselves, the Winnebago of Wisconsin reluctantly reorganize according to the guidelines of the 1934 Indian Reorganization Act. But they also preserve their chief-clan structure, based on four Sky clans and eight Earth clans. Elders continue to guide young people through vision quests.

 The Association of American Indian Affairs establishes the New York City American Indian

Arts Center, which exhibits and sells art by leading Native American artists.

1964

  Mojave and Chemehuevi Indians win a twenty-year battle when Congress rescinds the policy of colonizing the Colorado River Indian Tribes with Indians from outside the area. Congress also turns over title of the Colorado River Indian Reservation to the tribes, allowing them freedom to develop land for commercial, recreational, business, agricultural, and residential use.

  All known Chemehuevi Indians meet and agree to settle their land claims with the U.S. government for $1 million, or slightly less than $1,000 per person.

 Passamaquoddy and other Maine Indians stage a protest against three centuries of land seizures by whites.

Puyallup activist Robert Satiacum and others are arrested during a "fish-in" that protests the government's failure to honor the treaty-guaranteed fishing rights of the Puyallups and other Northwest peoples.

Cahuilla Indians and others establish the Malki Museum on California's Morongo Reservation. It displays items from traditional culture and establishes a publishing program focusing on southern California Indians.

In March, a devastating earthquake produces a tidal wave that destroys the Alutiiq (Aleut) villages of Old Harbor, Kaguyak, Afognak, and Chenega.

Fifteen Native Americans found the American Indian Historical Society, with Rupert Costo, a full-blooded Cahuilla Indian, as president. Over the next twenty-two years, the society publishes books and periodicals on Indian history and campaigns for Indian issues around the country.

In a lawsuit, the Haliwa-Saponi Tribe successfully forces the state of North Carolina to change birth certificates of tribe members to identify them as Indians.

1965

The last surviving speakers of the Tillamook Salishan language begin a five-year project to record and preserve the tongue of their ancestors.

  Watt Sam, the last fluent speaker of the ancient language of the mound-building Natchez Indians, dies.

The Bureau of Indian Affairs spends $11.5 million relocating Indians from the reservation to areas with job opportunities. Approximately half of those relocated abandon the city and return to their reservations within one year. In the same year, the Bureau spends approximately $6.5 million to develop jobs on reservations in agriculture and industry. The National Congress of American Indians continues to attack relocation as another form of termination.

1966

 A survey finds that Native Americans from more than seventy tribes live in Los Angeles.

> "We are not free. We do not make choices. Our choices are made for us."
> —Clyde Warrior, Ponca Indian and president of the National Indian Youth Council, 1967

1967

ABC television broadcasts a series on General George Armstrong Custer. Native Americans complain to the network, without success. Yakima tribal attorney James Hovis suggests tribes across the country petition local stations for equal time to show their side of the story. The ploy works. After nine episodes, ABC cancels the series.

The American Indian Law Center is founded at the University of New Mexico Law School. At this time, there are only twenty-five Native Americans with law degrees in the United States. The center offers courses in Indian law, provides assistance to tribal governments, and institutes a summer program to prepare Native American students for law school.

Twelve regional associations of Alaska Natives unite to form a single statewide group, the Alaska Federation of Natives. The federation pushes for Native rights to ancestral lands.

The Haliwa-Saponi Tribe of North Carolina inaugurates the annual Haliwa-Saponi Powwow. It evolves into one of the most popular powwows in the Southeast.

SHOSHONE

   Before the arrival of non-Indians, the people known today as Shoshone Indians lived scattered across the Great Basin, the Plateau, and the western edge of the Great Plains. In the Plateau, they hunted bison, fished, and gathered wild foods. Their descendants are called Northern Shoshone. In the Great Basin, they, like the Paiute peoples, followed game and harvested wild foods. Their descendants are called Western Shoshone. At the edge of the Great Plains, the Shoshone lived like other Plains peoples, moving their tepee villages as they followed the buffalo herds. The descendants of these hunters are called Eastern Shoshone.

In the 1800s, all groups of Shoshone suffered the devastation of the white man's diseases, especially measles and smallpox. And they all suffered the cultural upheavals caused by the advancing hordes of non-Indians.

Today the Eastern Shoshone live in Wyoming, where they are reviving the Shoshone language. They continue to be wary of their ancient enemies, the Arapaho, and of whites. They perform traditional dances, including the ancient Naraya (Shuffle Dance). They also play an ancient team guessing game, the handgame, and they listen to storytellers and singers recount the legends of their people.

The Northern Shoshone live in southern Idaho on a reservation that includes the Bannock people, who speak Northern Paiute. The two groups have combined their cultural traditions and typically perform rituals like the Sun Dance and the Great Basin Round Dance together, as if they were all one tribe.

The Western Shoshone call their Great Basin homeland Pia Sokopia (Earth Mother), and they call themselves Newe, meaning "the People." Today they and the related Goshutes live primarily in Nevada and Utah. Besides preserving and reviving ancient dances, prayers, and songs, they are working to revive traditional arts and crafts, including basket weaving and the construction of fine cradleboards.

1968

Congress passes the Indian Civil Rights Act. It provides for freedom of speech, press, assembly, and religion but allows tribal governments to determine the official tribal religion. It fails to provide for enforcement.

The Mohawk Nation begins publishing *Akwesasne Notes*. It becomes a leading voice in pan-Indian political activism and gains a readership of 100,000 nationwide.

Dennis Banks, Mary Jane Wilson, and other Chippewas found the American Indian Movement in Minneapolis. Its original mission is to curtail police harassment of Indians living in Minneapolis's Native American ghetto. In the first year, AIM succeeds in reducing unprosecuted arrests of Indians in Minneapolis by 50 percent. AIM goes on to become a leading national activist organization. Within the next two years, it organizes Native Americans on reservations and in cities around the United States.

In upstate New York, two concerned Mohawk parents, Chief John Cook and Minerva White, lead the Mohawk Parents Committee in a boycott to protest failures in the educational system. The boycott focuses national attention on the difficulties faced by Native American students across the country.

Akwesasne Mohawks from the United States and Canada blockade the Cornwall International Bridge on the U.S.-Canada border to protest Canada's failure to honor treaty obligations that allow them unrestricted travel back and forth across the border.

THE OCCUPATION OF ALCATRAZ

 When the federal government closed the prison on Alcatraz Island in 1963, the island automatically fell into a special category: unused federal land that had originally been occupied by Indians. The 1868 Treaty of Fort Laramie provided that Indians could reclaim such land.

In March 1964, four Sioux captured the island and held it symbolically for three hours, demanding that they be allowed to found an all-Indian university on the island. The U.S. Attorney General ruled the treaty provision no longer valid.

Five years later, the island remained abandoned and unused. On November 11, 1969, fourteen college students seized the island for nineteen hours, then gave in to government pressure and left.

On November 20, about one hundred Native Americans from many different tribal backgrounds disembarked on the island and claimed it as Indian land. Calling themselves Indians of All Tribes, they incorporated and settled in to live on the island. They established schools for the children, started a newspaper, and arranged for food and health care for residents. They also established Radio Free Alcatraz and broadcast reports on Native American problems in the areas of health, education, and cultural preservation. To maintain law and order, they formed a security force called the Bureau of Caucasian Affairs. The tribal background of the leaders of the occupation included Mohawk, Shoshone-Bannock, and Chippewa.

When the government realized the occupiers intended to stay permanently, it cut off food and water to the island in late May 1970. Then a fire destroyed several buildings, and many residents and leaders left. With only fifteen occupiers remaining, federal marshals stormed the island in June 1971 and ended the occupation.

KIOWA

Kiowa call themselves Ga'igwu, which in their language means "Principal People" or "Most Important People." But after centuries of disruptions by outsiders, fewer than 400 of the 10,000 enrolled members of the Kiowa Tribe speak the ancient language of the Ga'igwu fluently.

Most Kiowa today live in Oklahoma, with the seat of Kiowa government based at Carnegie. Cultural preservation focuses on traditional customs, songs, and stories. Warrior societies that survive include the Ohomah Lodge, the Kiowa Gourd Clan, and the Kiowa Blacklegs. Kiowa children belong to the Rabbit Society and learn traditional dances and songs.

Kiowa also cherish and practice traditional arts, including beadwork and buckskin paintings. In the twentieth century, many Kiowa artists have become well known for their fine art, the most famous being T. C. Cannon. Three Kiowa artists—Parker Boyiddle, Mirac Creepingbear, and Sherman Chaddleston—have painted ten vast murals with a record of Kiowa history, which begins with tales of the sea. The murals can be seen at the Kiowa Tribal Museum in Carnegie, Oklahoma.

Among a remote group of Esselen Indians in California, an eight-year-old named Tom Little Bear begins having visions about reclaiming the ancient powers of the Esselen Tribe. Over time, the visions lead to resurrection of the language and many nearly forgotten elements of the culture.

The Navajo Nation founds Navajo Community College. The first reservation-based community college run by Native Americans, it becomes a model for other tribes.

Kiowa writer N. Scott Momaday publishes *House Made of Dawn*, a novel about an Indian veteran. The following spring the novel is awarded the Pulitzer Prize.

 "During my three years as Executive Director of the National Congress of American Indians it was a rare day when some white didn't visit my office and proudly proclaim that he or she was of Indian descent."
—Vine Deloria, Jr., Standing Rock (Yankton) Sioux, in *Custer Died for Your Sins,* 1969

1969

 Vine Deloria, Jr., a Yankton Sioux, publishes *Custer Died for Your Sins: An Indian Manifesto*. The book challenges Americans to look at Native Americans and Native American history in a new way. No longer can historians hide behind the doctrine of Manifest Destiny or the genocidal assumption that Indians deserved to lose their lands, cultural identities, and lives.

 The Marine Corps declassifies information about the Navajo "code talkers" of World War II. The Navajo Code Talkers Association is born.

 To protest government policies, Native Americans invade and occupy Alcatraz Island on November 20.

 Kiowa writer N. Scott Momaday publishes *The Way to Rainy Mountain*, recounting the origins of the Kiowa people.

The Edisto Indians of South Carolina reorganize a century after disbanding.

1970

The total number of Indians in the United States is listed as 792,000, an increase of 51 percent in ten years. Since 1960, the number of Indians living in urban areas has risen by 144 percent, to 356,000.

President Richard Nixon declares self-determination for Indian tribes, giving tribal governments more power. This formally ends the termination policy.

The Bureau of Indian Affairs' budget includes a record $10 million for funding economic development on individual reservations, and economic development becomes the new focus of the federal government's policy toward Native Americans. Native American opponents point out that this is one more way of dissipating traditional values and pressuring Native Americans to assimilate to mainstream culture.

Judges from tribal courts across the country organize to provide judicial training to tribal judges.

The American Indian Press Association is founded. It operates a news service out of Washington, D.C., and distributes news of interest to Native Americans to more than 150 Indian newspapers.

The Indian Historian Press, publishing division of the American Indian Historical Society, publishes its first book, *Textbooks and the American Indian*.

The National Indian Education Association is established, with the goal of improving the quality of education for Native American students at all levels.

The Native American Rights Fund is established to provide legal representation to Native Americans and address their legal problems.

Defiant Menominees try to counter the horrendous effects of tribal termination by establishing DRUMS, the Determination of Rights and Unity for Menominee Shareholders. DRUMS lobbies for restoration of tribal status and federal recognition.

A storm along the Pacific coast exposes an ancient Makah village, buried centuries earlier at Ozette, Washington. Excavation of the village and its more than 55,000 artifacts reveals to Makahs and anthropologists much about the customs and daily life of the Makahs' Nootka ancestors.

Congress approves payment to the Chinook tribe of western Washington for land seized from it in the 1800s, but the Bureau of Indian Affairs refuses to pay the money because the Chinooks are not a federally recognized tribe.

The Maliseet, Micmac, and other dispossessed Indian tribes in Maine form the Association of Aroostook Indians. The association's goal is to campaign for Native rights and to improve living conditions.

Chickasaws, long dispossessed of tribal lands and tribal power, receive congressional permission to choose their own leaders for the first time in more than half a century.

Taos Pueblo wins the battle to regain possession of its sacred Blue Lake and surrounding lands from the federal government. Assisting the fight are Americans for Indian Opportunity, the Association on American Indian Affairs, and other political action groups. The Taos Indians receive title to 48,000 acres of land in Carson National Forest and waive all future claims to the nearby town of Taos.

1971

 Three Indian attorneys, Vine Deloria, Jr., Kirke Kickingbird, and Franklin D. Ducheneaux, found the Institute for the Development of Indian Law.

On June 11, federal marshals evict the remaining fifteen Native Americans who occupy Alcatraz Island. This ends one of the most high-profile Indian protests in decades.

On July 4, members of AIM, the American Indian Movement, stage a countercelebration at Mount Rushmore. On Thanksgiving Day, at Plymouth, Massachusetts, other AIM members paint Plymouth Rock red and board the *Mayflower* replica. The events focus public attention on the issues of Native peoples.

 Tukemas (Hawk Pope), grandson of Reva Pope, deceased leader of traditionalist Shawnees, forms the United Remnant Band of Shawnee and moves from Indiana to Ohio, back to Tecumseh's homeland.

In one of the first ceremonies of its kind in the country, the Narragansett people of Rhode Island rebury skeletal remains of their ancestors which have been removed from a Narragansett cemetery by an anthropologist.

MARIA MARTINEZ

 Since about A.D. 500, the Pueblo Indians of New Mexico have been curling ropes of clay between their hands and forming them into pots. In 1908, anthropologists digging in a canyon in New Mexico uncovered some unusual black pot shards and showed them to a young Pueblo Indian potter from San Ildefonso named Maria Martinez. She studied the shards, began to experiment, and by 1918 had re-created the pottery of her ancestors. Called black-on-black, the pottery has a lustrous black surface, with matte-black designs. These designs depict images from Pueblo cosmology, like avanyu, the horned water serpent, which represents the first flow of water hurrying through an arroyo (a dry streambed) after a thunderstorm.

Over the next six decades, Maria Martinez became the most widely known Pueblo potter of all times. She produced hundreds of pieces of her trademark pottery, which sell today for thousands of dollars. Before she died, in July 1980, she passed on her pottery making techniques to her grandchildren and great-grandchildren. Today many potters from San Ildefonso and nearby Santa Clara Pueblo produce fine black-on-black pottery.

LAKOTA

  Oceti Sakowin, Seven Fireplaces, is what the people who became known as Sioux called themselves. Eventually the western branch also called themselves Lakotas, or Titunwan. That term, which means "prairie dwellers," came into English as "Teton"; the Lakotas are also called Teton Sioux.

By the mid-1700s, the Lakotas left the lake region of Minnesota and moved westward across the Plains, following the buffalo herds. Soon after that, they discovered the Black Hills and made it their spiritual center. Also about this time, they divided into seven tribes: the Oglala, Sicangu, Hunkpapa, Mnikowoju, Itazipco, Oohenunpa, and Sihasapa.

It was from the Lakotas more than any other group that non-Indians developed their ideas about the Indians of the Great Plains. They lived on horseback, moved their tepee villages often, and were superb buffalo hunters. They also routinely bested the U.S. Army, most notably in battles that led up to the Treaty of Fort Laramie in 1868, which has been described as the only time Indians won a war against the U.S. government. Later, they defeated General George Armstrong Custer.

But after gold seekers swarmed through the sacred Black Hills, the Lakotas, like other Native Americans across the continent, found they had no choice but to give in to the one-sided demands of the U.S. government.

Today's Lakotas are best known to outsiders for their participation in the American Indian Movement in the 1970s and for their outstanding silverwork and fine quilts, called star quilts.

Each August, the Oglala Sioux hold the Oglala Nation Powwow, which draws thousands of visitors from around the world.

 After enduring a twenty-year legal battle for compensation for lost lands, the Samish Indians of the San Juan Islands of Washington State refuse a government offer of $5,800 as compensation.

Under the Alaska Native Claims Settlement Act, Alaska Natives relinquish their general claims to most of the land in Alaska. In exchange they receive the right to select 40 million acres of public land in the state for themselves and to collect $962 million in reparations.

In an attempt to provide employment and keep Blackfeet at home on their traditional lands, the Blackfeet establish the Blackfeet Writing Company, which manufactures pens and pencils.

1972

In February, Russell Means, an Oglala Sioux and AIM leader, leads 1,000 people into Gordon, Nebraska. The caravan protests failure to arrest the two white murderers of Raymond Yellowthunder, an Oglala. Following the protest, the murderers are tried, convicted, and sent to prison. This is the first time in Nebraska history that whites have been sentenced to prison for murdering an Indian.

Hyemeyohsts Storm, part Cherokee, part Sioux author, publishes *Seven Arrows*. The controversial novel focuses on Native American spirituality, but many Native American readers protest that Storm has passed off his own ideas as traditional religion. The book becomes popular among non-Indians.

Through the efforts of Earl Old Person and other Blackfeet leaders, members of the Blackfeet Tribe receive $500 each in compensation for land grabs of Blackfeet territory by whites in the late 1800s.

At the age of twenty-two, Kiowa artist T. C. Cannon wins national and international recognition when his work is

WOUNDED KNEE II

In the early 1970s, on the Pine Ridge Reservation of South Dakota, a corrupt tribal government collaborated with U.S. government efforts to take mineral-rich land away from the Sioux. Sioux elders and traditionalists who protested were harassed and banned from meeting.

On February 26, 1973, the banned protesters met secretly and requested help from the American Indian Movement. The next night, a caravan of fifty-four cars of AIM activists arrived in Wounded Knee, a tiny village on the reservation. At dawn, the two hundred people inside Wounded Knee found themselves sealed off by roadblocks and surrounded by government agents. The siege had begun.

On March 11, the government opened the roadblocks to allow non-AIM members to leave the village. Instead, traditionalists led by Oglala head chief Frank Fools Crow poured into Wounded Knee.

During the seventy-one-day ordeal, government troops harassed the besieged occupants by firing half a million rounds of ammunition into the village. Frank Clearwater, an Eastern Cherokee, and Buddy Lamont, an Oglala, were killed; fifteen others were seriously wounded.

On May 3, the siege ended, but 563 people were arrested. Of these, 185 were indicted, but only 15 were convicted—all on such charges as interfering with a postal inspector and trespassing. AIM leader Russell Means faced thirty-seven felony charges; it took three years of trials and more than a million dollars to clear him of the charges.

Following the siege, repression on the reservation increased. Over the next three years, 342 AIM supporters were physically assaulted, and 69 resistance members were murdered. In 1975, Oglala tribal president Richard Wilson transferred 76,200 acres of Sioux land to the federal government.

shown at the National Collection of Fine Arts in Washington, D.C.

 The Yakima Indians receive title to a portion of the Mount Adams Wilderness Area adjoining the reservation.

 On November 3, more than 1,000 Indians from one hundred reservations arrive in Washington, D.C., in the Trail of Broken Treaties caravan. In their Twenty Points petition, they ask the federal government to abolish the Bureau of Indian Affairs, allow Indian governments to deal directly with the White House, and restore treaty-making powers to U.S. tribes. Four hundred AIM members storm the Bureau of Indian Affairs and occupy the headquarters building for six days. Before leaving, they seize confidential Indian Bureau files that show government abuses related to mineral rights on Indian lands.

Wassaja, a national newspaper about Native Americans, publishes its first issue. It continues to publish until 1984.

Lloyd Kiva New, a Cherokee, becomes chairman of the federal Indian Arts and Crafts Board and pushes for development of Indian-controlled cultural institutions, such as museums.

The General Revenue Sharing program begins, allotting tribes access to federal funds, with few restrictions on spending.

The Native American Rights Fund establishes the National Indian Law Library, devoted entirely to Indian law.

 The Penobscot and Passamaquoddy Indians sue the state of Maine for hundreds of thousands of

IOWAY

After decades of being pushed from their home-lands by the westward advance of whites, the Iowa Indians, or Ioway, ended up in three states—Kansas, Nebraska, and Oklahoma. The Iowa Tribe of Kansas and Nebraska, about 2,000 strong, operates on a 1,500-acre reservation in a checkerboard of Indian and non-Indian land. The Oklahoma Ioway lack a reservation and occupy 1,300 acres of individually owned land.

The Ioway language, a Siouan language, is similar to Winnebago. Few people speak Ioway today, but among the Ioway in all three states, people are working to resur-rect the language, along with ancient cultural practices and beliefs.

acres of lost land, encompassing much of Maine. The suit leads to the Maine Indian Land Claims Settlement Act of 1980.

1973

 John Echohawk, a Pawnee attorney, becomes the first Indian director of the Native American Rights Fund.

 On February 6, two hundred American Indian Movement members gather in the town of Custer, South Dakota, to protest the brutal murder of Wes-ley Bad Heart Bull, an Oglala, by a white man. The pro-testers demand that his killer be charged with murder. Local officials refuse, and an altercation follows. Bad Heart Bull's mother and several AIM members are sent to prison. The murderer remains free.

On February 28, at the Pine Ridge Reservation in South Dakota, a seventy-one-day siege begins. Federal agents pummel AIM members and traditional Oglalas inside Wounded Knee with half a million rounds of ammunition. It is the longest and most serious armed conflict between Native Americans and the government since the end of the Indian wars in the 1800s.

Recalling ancient warnings of the prophet Sweet Medicine, the Northern Cheyenne tribal council votes eleven to zero to cancel all coal leases and exploration permits on tribal lands, which cover part of the vast Fort Union coal formation, site of 40 percent of the country's known coal reserves. The next year, the Secretary of the Interior agrees that no mining can occur until the tribe allows it, but he doesn't cancel the permits.

Congress restores tribal status to the Menominee Indians, nineteen years after terminating it without their consent. The Menominee vow to protect and restore Menominee traditions, such as clan structures, creation stories, and the Menominee language.

Fourteen years after having its tribal status unilaterally terminated by the Bureau of Indian Affairs, the Catawba Nation reorganizes itself as a nonprofit organization under Chief Gilbert B. Blue.

Congress passes the Comprehensive Employment and Training Act (CETA), which provides jobs for unemployed Native Americans, both on and off the reservation.

NAKOTA

 Less well known to non-Indians than the Lakota and Dakota Sioux, the Nakota Sioux survive in the Yankton, Yanktonai, and Assiniboine peoples of the United States, along with the Stoneys (Hohes) of Canada. Like other Sioux, the Nakotas found themselves bullied into accepting unfavorable treaties again and again, only to see whites breaking their promises in a spiral of increasing selfishness and greed for Nakota land. In 1830, the Nakotas gave up more than 2 million acres. In 1858, they were forced to sign over another 11 million acres. The land grabs weren't over; they continued for decades.

Among the best-known Nakota Sioux today is a Yankton attorney and writer from South Dakota, Vine Deloria, Jr. His family has worked for generations to honor ancient traditions. They have also tried to make non-Indians face and acknowledge the brutality and genocidal policies to which Native Americans have been subjected since the day the first non-Indians arrived on Indian shores.

Native Americans win the right to be given preference for Bureau of Indian Affairs jobs when the U.S. Supreme Court rules in *Morton v. Mancari et al.* that this allows Indians an opportunity to govern themselves. In the next seven years, the number of Indian Bureau employees of Indian descent rises from under 50 percent to nearly 80 percent.

Administrators from Native American colleges across the United States form the American Indian Higher Education Consortium and begin lobbying for more funds for Native American colleges. Their efforts lead to the Tribally Controlled Community College Assistance Act of 1978.

 Nearly 120 years after being deprived of their land and tribal status by the Point Elliott Treaty of

1855, the Nooksack Indians of western Washington receive federal recognition as a tribe.

1974

One of seven bands of Kutenai (Kootenai), the Bonners Ferry Band of northern Idaho, declares war on the United States in an attempt to gain attention for a century and a half of injustices. Congress grants the band a 12.5-acre reservation.

Tribes concerned about protecting themselves from mining companies form the intertribal Native American Natural Resources Development Federation, forerunner of the Council of Energy Resource Tribes.

More than two hundred Indian newspapers and newsletters are being published around the United States, and more than one hundred intertribal organizations offer social, political, professional, cultural, and economic benefits to Native Americans.

AIM leader Russell Means forms the International Indian Treaty Council to bring charges to the United Nations that the U.S. government is violating provisions of the 1868 Fort Laramie Treaty. The council later expands to include issues of all indigenous peoples of the Americas.

The Native American Programs Act includes Native Hawaiians among groups eligible for federal services.

Russell Means, AIM activist, runs for president of the Pine Ridge Reservation and loses in an election that is said to be rigged. The Civil Rights Commission calls for a new, supervised election, but the Department of the Interior allows the vote to stand.

YAKIMA

 Anthropologists believe that by about 12,000 B.C. the ancestors of today's Yakima Indians had already moved into the plateau area east of the Cascade Mountains in Washington State. Yakima legends say the People have always lived there, ever since the Creator planted the first man and first woman on the earth, as if planting a garden.

Through the long, cold winters, the Yakima lived in numerous small villages. During the spring, summer, and fall, they drifted from one seasonal camp to the next, collecting food. Using harpoons, gaffs, and nets, they fished for salmon, sturgeon, and steelhead trout. They hunted elk, mountain sheep, bears, and deer. They dug roots with a special tool made of hardwood and antlers, and they wove fine baskets in which to cook and store foods.

They made cradleboards from wood and buckskin and protected a baby from physical and spiritual danger by placing a hoop made from rosebushes above its head. Onto the hoop they tied a medicine bag with the baby's umbilical cord inside, to ensure good health and long life.

For money, the Yakima used dentalium shells from the west coast of Vancouver Island.

When a woman reached puberty, she began the equivalent of a lifelong diary, a counting-the-days ball made of handwoven string. When something important happened to her, she tied a bead or a shell to her string to remind her of that day. After her death, her family buried this record with her.

In 1855, the Yakimas were required to merge with thirteen other tribes and bands from the Plateau region. Although many ancient traditions have been lost, the Yakima still weave fine baskets, and the Dreamer religion of Smohalla remains strong. The Confederated Tribes and Bands of the Yakima Nation have approximately 8,000 members and a reservation that covers more than 1 million acres in south-central Washington State.

Through the Indian Culture Development Project, the Yuki people of northern California begin to recover and preserve nearly forgotten elements of their ancient lifeways.

In the Hopi-Navajo Land Settlement Act, Congress formally grants the Navajos title to half of the Hopi Reservation and establishes procedures for relocating Hopis and Navajos living on each other's land. The act results in a massive relocation program to move Navajo families from land claimed by Hopis. Many refuse to leave, but over the next two decades, 2,600 families are relocated, at a cost of $330 million. Both Hopis and Navajos protest loss of sacred sites and traditional lifestyle.

In a major victory for Indian rights, Judge George Boldt of federal district court rules that treaties allot Native Americans of western Washington up to 50 percent of the commercial harvest of salmon. The U.S. Supreme Court later upholds the Boldt decision.

1975

Tribes in western Washington establish the Northwest Indian Fisheries Commission to coordinate fishing policies and responsibilities.

With only three speakers of the Twana language of western Washington surviving, the Twana people inaugurate the Twana Language and Culture Project. Over the next five years, the spoken language is recorded, dictionaries are developed, and a cultural renaissance begins. Ceremonies unperformed for seven decades are revived, including salmon ceremonies, spirit dancing, naming ceremonies, and secret society initiations.

NAVAJO

 Perhaps as much as a millennium ago, as groups of Athabaskan speakers drifted south from Alaska and Canada, the ancestors of today's Navajos migrated toward the Southwest. When they reached the mountains and upland plains of the Four Corners area of Arizona and New Mexico, they decided they had found their new home. They named the four sacred mountains, one for each of the four compass directions, and settled into a seminomadic life, following game and harvesting wild foods.

Combining the traditions of their ancestors with customs borrowed from other tribes, they developed a rich ritual life that flourishes still. Ceremonies like the Blessingway and the Enemyway nurture and protect the Dineh, the People, as they call themselves. These rituals maintain and restore harmony, balance, and beauty to the world. They also involve hours and hours of singing the ancient stories of the Navajos, which tell of legendary, archetypal beings like Monster Slayer and Changing Woman.

After the brutal years of exile and imprisonment at the Bosque Redondo in the 1860s, the Navajos returned to their beloved homeland. Once again, they farmed corn and herded sheep and goats as they began rebuilding their culture and lives.

In 1868, only 9,000 Navajos survived. Today the tribe is estimated to be between 150,000 and 200,000 strong. At 29,000 square miles, the Navajo Reservation is more than twice as large as the states of Massachusetts and Connecticut combined. It is the largest reservation in the country.

Navajo weavers, silversmiths, and other artists and artisans produce fine works treasured by collectors worldwide.

 The Indian Self-Determination and Education Assistance Act establishes the right of tribes to provide tribal members with programs and services previously provided through the Bureau of Indian Affairs.

 The education act leads to establishment of a test school, the Rough Rock Demonstration School,

NEZ PERCE: CHUTE-PA-LU

When the French arrived in the Plateau region, they found a group of people wearing rings in their noses for ornaments. The people called themselves Chute-pa-lu, but the French named them Nez Perce, meaning "pierced nose."

The Nez Perce were once the most populous and powerful tribe in the Plateau region and lived spread across vast portions of the northern Great Plains and Plateau. But the U.S. government forced the Nez Perce to agree to shrink their territory and live on an 8-million-acre reservation. Then the government took away even more Nez Perce land. Ultimately that led to the Nez Perce War of 1877 and Chief Joseph's surrender.

Today the Nez Perce own fewer than 100,000 acres and number about 3,000. Although the people have largely given up their tradition of wearing nose rings, they continue to honor and pass on other ancient customs and beliefs to their children. These include E-peh-tas dances, spring celebrations, and the Talmaks festivities of early summer.

on the Navajo Reservation. The school includes Navajo traditions in the curriculum and allows community members to help make decisions.

Ohlone (Costanoan) Indians arm themselves and barricade a construction site in Watsonville, California, to prevent destruction of an ancient burial ground. In the aftermath of the incident, the Pajaro Valley Ohlone Indian Council is founded.

The Jamul Band of Kumeyaay (Diegeño) Indians of southern California, landless and unprotected since before the turn of the century, receive federal recognition.

At the Pine Ridge Reservation of South Dakota, government agents open fire on an encampment of AIM members on June 26. Two FBI agents and a Coeur d'Alene Indian, Joe Stuntz Killsright, die. Bob Robideau, Ojibway (Anishinabe), and Darrell Butler, a Tuni, are charged with murdering the two agents, but an all-white jury in Cedar Rapids, Iowa, finds them innocent by reason of self-defense. Leonard Peltier, Sioux-Ojibwa, is then charged with murder, extradited illegally from Canada, and tried for the agents' murder. He is not allowed to plead self-defense and is convicted of murder, even though prosecutors later admit no one knows who killed the agents. Over the next two decades, the Leonard Peltier Defense Committee works unsuccessfully to free him.

On the Pine Ridge Reservation, 250 FBI agents terrorize residents with warrantless searches and air assaults during July and August. In September, tribal president Dick Wilson signs over 76,200 acres of mineral-rich Sioux land to the federal government.

The Cherokee Nation of Oklahoma adopts a new constitution and elects Ross Swimmer as principal chief.

Novelist James Welch, of Blackfeet/Gros Ventre heritage, publishes *Winter in the Blood*.

1976

The Indian Health Care Improvement Act provides for improved health services to Native Americans.

Leaders of twenty-five tribes create the Council of Energy Resource Tribes (CERT). The organization's goal is to gain control of energy resources on tribal lands.

UTE

Before the coming of non-Indians, the Utes were one of three major groups who hunted and gathered wild crops among the sparsely vegetated mesas, valleys, mountains, and canyon lands of the Great Basin. The other groups were Shoshones and Paiutes. For the Utes as for the others, environment dictated lifestyle. After they had collected food resources and killed the game available near any one campsite, it was time to move on.

This concept was beyond the understanding of the non-Indians who moved into the Great Basin in the mid-1800s. The non-Indians were ranchers and farmers, and they demanded that the Utes become ranchers and farmers like them. The Utes saw their 79 million acres of traditional lands shrink to 23 million acres of reservation, then down to 4.5 million, before the allotment policy of the late 1800s further decimated their holdings.

Although some land has been reclaimed in this century, all together the three main groups of Utes—Southern Utes, Ute Mountain Utes, and Northern Utes—now hold only 2 million acres of land, less than 3 percent of their original homeland.

In this area, today's Utes struggle to retain and reclaim ancient traditions while dealing with the realities of contemporary American life. They still perform the ancient Bear Dance and other traditional ceremonies. Ute artisans still weave baskets, work in leather, and create intricate beadwork designs. Many still speak the Ute language. And they still feel linked in ways that few non-Indians can understand to the mesas, canyons, and vistas of their ancestors.

The Blackfeet establish Blackfeet Community College to provide Blackfeet young people with a chance to earn a college education while remaining at home on their traditional lands.

After six years of legal fights, the Winnebago Tribe of Nebraska wins a battle to stop an Army Corps of Engineers project that would have flooded much of the Winnebagos' land.

In the Catawba Nation of South Carolina, the only eastern tribe to retain an unbroken tradition of pottery making, the Catawba Pottery Association begins formal classes to pass on the ancient art, which has survived nearly unchanged for at least seven centuries.

The Eastern Band of Cherokees receive a grant of 3.6 acres of sacred land from the city of Kingsport, Tennessee.

Eleven bands of Pit River (Achumawi and Atsugewi) Indians in California receive federal recognition as the Pit River Tribe.

Maidu Indians in Placer County, California, seeking to preserve their cultural heritage, build a ceremonial roundhouse. Because the roundhouse doesn't meet county building codes, government officials require it to be torn down.

1977

The American Indian Science and Engineering Society is founded to provide financial assistance to Native Americans who wish to study in the sciences.

The American Indian Policy Review Commission reports that in the forty years since passage of the Indian Reorganization Act, the government has seized 1.8 million acres of Indian land. By contrast, Native Americans have been able to purchase only 600,000 acres to add to their holdings.

Novelist Leslie Marmon Silko, a Laguna Indian, publishes *Ceremony*. Reviewers praise the novel's depiction of the healing power of traditional stories.

The Nanticoke Indians of Delaware intensify their efforts to revive and preserve their ancient Algonquian traditions by establishing the Nanticoke Indian Heritage Project.

1978

Dennis Banks, AIM leader, organizes "The Longest Walk," a march on Washington, D.C., that begins in California. Participants walk across the United States promoting Indian rights and educating the public on Indian issues. In late July, several hundred marchers, representing about eighty Indian nations, arrive in Washington, and several thousand people stage a rally in their support.

The American Indian Religious Freedom Act acknowledges the right of Native Americans not merely to preserve their traditional religious practices but also to have access to sacred sites outside the reservations. But no judicial recourse is provided to prevent government destruction of such sites.

> **"Indians always have been politically savvy. What's changed is their resources."**
> **—Vine Deloria, Jr., Standing Rock (Yankton) Sioux, 1978**

The approximately 165 Native American groups who have not yet achieved the legal status of tribe gain new hope when the Department of the Interior establishes new guidelines for recognition as a tribe. Tribes must document their existence from first contact with whites to the present. They must also prove they are already a separate and active community with a governing structure in place.

Congress passes the Indian Child Welfare Act. It protects Indian children from being removed from their people and

LENAPE (DELAWARE)

  By 1700, the Lenape people who lived along the Delaware River and the Atlantic coast found themselves driven from their homes by European settlers. For the next century and a half, the Lenape, or Delawares, as whites called them, wandered. Unhappily they traveled farther and farther from their homeland, moving from Pennsylvania to Ohio to Indiana to Missouri to Kansas, and finally to Oklahoma.

Throughout generations of disruptions, the Lenape people clung to their culture and traditions. A single clan—the wolf clan, turkey clan, or turtle clan—usually dominated the life of any given village. Puberty ceremonies and other ancient rituals remained strong. But by the twentieth century, many traditions had died. In the last half of this century, three Delaware women—Lucy Parks Blalock, Linda Poolaw, and Nora Thompson Dean—have devoted themselves to preserving Lenape customs and language.

Today the only officially recognized Delaware community is in Oklahoma. Other Delaware communities are in Wisconsin and Kansas.

being adopted by non-Indians. But it cannot undo the damage that thousands of children and their families and tribes have suffered in the past two decades.

Indian tribes are declared to be immune from being sued in federal (non-tribal) courts when the U.S. Supreme Court rules seven to one in *Santa Clara Pueblo v. Martinez* that the Indian Civil Rights Act of 1968 does not waive sovereign immunity of tribes. Subsequent rulings restrict tribal sovereignty to internal tribal affairs.

Congress passes the Tribally Controlled Community College Assistance Act. Funding from this act makes it easier for Indian students to receive college training at community colleges located on their home reservations.

The Indian Claims Commission ceases operation. In its three-decade existence, the ICC has decided 546 cases and awarded more than $800 million in claims. Remaining unresolved cases are turned over to the U.S. Court of Claims.

Congress authorizes the Department of the Interior to establish the Branch of Acknowledgment and Research. Its role: to determine tribal status for Native American groups still not acknowledged as tribes. Over the next ten years, more than one hundred groups apply for recognition.

 A century after forcibly moving 153 Modocs to Indian Territory from their homeland near the Oregon-California border, the U.S. government finally recognizes their descendants as the Modoc Tribe of Oklahoma. The Oklahoma Modoc continue to maintain close cultural ties with their Oregon relatives.

 The Ottawa, Wyandotte, and Peoria peoples, all victims of the brutal termination policies of the 1950s, are restored to tribal status.

The O'odham (Pima and Papago) peoples of Arizona win the right to increase their water use to irrigate and farm their land. The victory reflects a centuries-old Native American tradition of irrigating crops in the desert.

The Pascua Yaqui Indians near Tucson, formerly of Mexico, receive federal recognition as a tribe.

The Quechan (Yuma) people regain 25,000 acres of land stolen from them by the government in the late 1800s, but the arid land is returned to them without accompanying water rights.

"AIM never died. It only changed form. Anywhere Indians are standing up for themselves, whether they are struggling as individuals whose basic civil rights are being denied, as peoples whose human rights are being denied, as nations whose sovereign rights are being denied, or any combination of these factors, that's where you'll find the American Indian Movement. In that spirit of resistance to oppression, that's where you'll find AIM. In other words, AIM is now in every single Indian community, and it always will be."

—Russell Means, former AIM leader, after the national AIM organization was formally dissolved to protect its members, following the deaths of the family of AIM Chairman John Trudell in 1979

1979

 After decades of effort, the Karuk Tribe of northwestern California receives federal recognition. This coincides with a revival of cultural traditions, including the ancient Irahiv ("fix the world") ceremonies.

 The Makah Indians of western Washington open the Makah Cultural and Research Center, a museum displaying the rich artifacts of their ancestors. The museum becomes a leading tourist attraction and a source of employment for tribal members.

The U.S. Supreme Court rules that Indian tribes do not have criminal jurisdiction over non-Indians who are present on Indian lands.

John Trudell, AIM chairman and spokesperson for the Leonard Peltier Defense Committee, gives an antigovernment speech in Washington, D.C., on February 11. That night, his wife, their three children, and his wife's mother die in an unexplained fire on the Duck Valley Reservation in Nevada. To prevent further persecution of AIM leaders, the national AIM movement is dissolved. AIM survives only in autonomous, anonymous local units.

Tribes involved in timber sales create the Intertribal Timber Council to promote the wise use of tribal forest resources.

1980s

 The Quileute people along the Pacific coast of Washington State revive the canoe building and ocean voyaging of their ancestors, together with ancient potlatch traditions.

LUMBEE

The Lumbee Tribe of Cheraw Indians is about 40,000 strong. Most reside in Robeson County, North Carolina. Once neighbors of the Cherokees, they lived deep in the marshlands and escaped being deported with the Cherokees and other tribes.

During the Civil War, the Lumbees, led by Henry Berry Lowerie, rebelled against the Rebels to protest being forced to serve as Confederate soldiers. Although the Lumbees continued fighting for a decade after the war ended, most of the ringleaders were killed or captured. Lowerie disappeared, to survive in Lumbee memory as a cultural hero.

Eight decades later, in 1958, the Lumbees rallied against a group of whites again, this time successfully, when they drove the Ku Klux Klan out of Robeson County.

Lumbee settlements today include Union Chapel, Saddletree, Pembroke, Moss Neck, and Prospect. Lumbees in Robeson County attend more than 120 different churches, all Indian, all Protestant, and the churches have become a focal point for tribal events and cultural continuity.

In the 1980s, greedy collectors illegally destroyed hundreds of ancient burial sites across the Southwest in their search for thousand-year-old Mimbres and Anasazi pottery, valued at as much as $60,000 a pot.

1980

The total Native American population is listed as 1.364 million, an increase of 72 percent since 1970. The five states with the highest ratio of Native Americans to non-Indians: Alaska (16 percent), New Mexico (8.1 percent), South Dakota (6.5 percent), Arizona (5.6 percent), and Oklahoma (5.6 percent). Across the United States, only ten counties have populations of 50 percent Native Americans or higher. Since 1970, the number of Indians living in urban areas across the United States has doubled. For the first time, more than half of the nation's Native Americans live in cities, away from their tribal roots. Los Angeles County holds more Indians than any reservation except the nation's largest, the Navajo.

 Western Shoshones, unable to find a forum in the United States, file a case with the Russell Tribunal on Rights of the Indians of the Americas in Rotterdam, Netherlands. Shoshones complain that land stolen from them in 1868 is being used as a site for construction of the MX missile. Publicity resulting from the case prompts the U.S. government to postpone MX construction and reconsider sites.

The Washoe Nation of Nevada wins a victory when the court grants it the right to manage hunting, fishing, and deer herds in traditional Washoe territory.

 The Jamestown Band of Klallam Indians receives federal recognition. This ensures them the right to participate in the salmon harvest, along with the Elwha and Port Gamble Bands of Klallam.

 After a seven-year struggle between coal interests and the Northern Cheyennes, Congress passes a law canceling coal leases and permits on Northern Cheyenne land.

The U.S. Supreme Court awards the Sioux more than $100 million as compensation for U.S. seizure of the Black Hills a century earlier, in direct defiance of the Fort Laramie Treaty of 1868.

 The dispossessed Cayuga Indians of New York sue for return of 64,000 acres of territorial land taken from them in the late 1700s and early 1800s.

SHAWNEE

  Long before Europeans arrived, the Shawnee lived along the Ohio River. Pressure from other tribes and from white settlers caused them to move away. For generations, they drifted across the Northeast and Southeast before returning to Ohio. In the 1800s, their enforced wanderings resumed. Some Shawnees ended up in Oklahoma, where they clustered into three groups: the Absentee Shawnee, the Eastern Shawnee, and the Loyal or Cherokee Shawnee. Others stayed in Ohio and adjacent states.

The Loyal Shawnee, numbering about 8,000, are descendants of Shawnees who sided with the Union during the Civil War. After the war, whites ignored the Shawnees' loyalty, and they were uprooted again, this time from Kansas to Oklahoma, where they settled among the Cherokee. Although the Loyal Shawnee have nearly lost their traditional language, they retain ancient rituals, including the Bread Dance, the Buffalo Dance, and the Green Corn Dance.

The Shawnee language survives among the Absentee Shawnee, but for years tribe members have struggled with the five-century-old conflict, present to some degree in all tribes of the Americas, of assimilation vs. retention of traditional culture and values.

The Maine Indian Land Claims Settlement Act attempts to compensate for centuries of suffering and loss on the part of Maine's Native peoples, but both Indians and non-Indians find the provisions of the complex settlement frustrating.

The Ramapough Mountain Indians of New York and New Jersey receive tribal recognition from the state of New Jersey but still lack federal recognition.

1981

A Linowes Commission report shows that corrupt management and auditing practices on the part of the Department of the Interior and oil companies cost energy-resource tribes hundreds of thousands of dollars annually.

The Powhatan-Renápe Nation of the Delaware Valley, descendants of the Powhatan people of Virginia and other tribes, receive a grant of 350 acres from the state of New Jersey.

In the Black Hills, Sioux activists Russell and Bill Means establish Yellow Thunder Camp on an 880-acre parcel. The occupation lasts for four years and precipitates a landmark federal court decision that the Sioux have religious rights to the entire Black Hills area.

1982

Through the work of Earl Old Person and other Blackfeet leaders, the Blackfeet are awarded $29 million in compensation for unsound federal accounting practices over the previous decades.

In an important victory for energy-resource tribes, the U.S. Supreme Court rules that the Jicarilla Apache Tribe has the right to tax mining companies operating on their reservation.

The Indian Tribal Governmental Tax Status Act acknowledges the right of tribes to raise money by issuing tribal bonds.

MICMAC

For many generations, the Micmac people have lived on both sides of the U.S.-Canada border. Traditionally they have hunted, fished, and collected wild foods, moving with the game they hunted and the ripening of berries and other staples. As part of the Wabanaki (Abenaki) Confederacy, they were allied historically with the Passamaquoddy, Maliseet, and Penobscot Indians.

Today Micmacs live in twenty-eight bands on both sides of the border, with a total population of 25,000. The best-known band in the United States is the Aroostook, headquartered in Presque Isle, Maine. When it found itself excluded from the Maine Indian Claims Settlement Act of 1980 for failure to comply with paperwork demands, the tribe went to court and fought for more than a decade. In 1991, Congress passed the Aroostook Band of Micmacs Settlement Act, which provided the 482-member band with funds to buy 5,000 acres of trust lands and gave it the same status and recognition as other Maine tribes.

Jaune Quick-to-See Smith, a Flathead artist, prepares a traveling photography exhibit that features the works of Native American photographers.

The Council of Energy Resource Tribes wins two victories when Congress passes the Indian Mineral Development Act and the Federal Oil and Gas Royalty Management Act. The bills give Native Americans a say in development of energy resources on tribal lands.

After sixty-one years of fighting in the courts and Congress, the Cow Creek Band of Umpqua Indians in Oregon receives recognition as a tribe.

ORAL TRADITIONS

 For millennia, the Indian peoples of the Americas have passed on their history to their children and grandchildren in the form of unwritten stories and songs, recounted and sung around campfires for hundreds of generations. Following the European invasion, missionaries and others began writing Indian languages down in translations of the Bible, but the oral tradition continues today.

Besides legends and myths, the oral literature preserves ancient prayers. These ritual incantations sometimes last for hours, and must be repeated in precisely a certain order, precisely a certain way, or harm might befall. Young people interested in learning them must study with elder singers for years before being allowed to chant these ancient, sacred prayers. Today the tradition of repeating ancient prayer songs remains strong among Navajos and other peoples.

1983

 Exactly three hundred years after being forced onto their first reservation in Connecticut, the Mashantucket Pequot Indians receive federal recognition as a tribe and a settlement for lost lands. This allows them to expand tribal holdings from 214 acres to 1,800 acres.

In a move that is centuries overdue, the Rappahannocks of Virginia receive recognition from Virginia as a tribe but still lack federal recognition.

 In Oklahoma, the Chickasaws approve a tribal constitution. Government officials include a governor and lieutenant governor, a three-judge judiciary, and a thirteen-member judiciary.

 Paula Gunn Allen, a novelist and poet of mixed Laguna Pueblo and Sioux heritage, publishes *The Woman Who Owned the Shadows*, a novel about an Indian woman's quest to reclaim her inner power, guided by stories of spirit women.

 In Oklahoma, the Ponca Indian Women's Society resurrects the Scalp Dance, which was last performed four decades earlier.

1984

 The Quinault Indians of western Washington celebrate their first potlatch in half a century when Oliver Mason, great-great-grandson of Quinault chief Taholah, is named hereditary chief of the Quinault Tribe.

The Cow Creek Band of Umpqua Indians in Oregon selects Susan Crispen Shaffer as their tribal chairperson.

Three decades after losing their 6.1-acre reservation, the Confederated Tribes of Coos, Lower Umpqua, and Siuslaw regain their land by an act of Congress.

  Cherokees from North Carolina and Oklahoma attend the first joint council of Eastern and Western Cherokees in nearly a century and a half.

 The Eastern Band of Cherokees receives three tracts of ancient Cherokee land in the Little Tennessee Valley from the Tennessee Valley Authority. On the largest, on Fort Loudoun Island, they build Sequoyah's Birthplace Museum. Another is the site of the Cherokee capital from 1753 to 1788, Chota Townhouse.

 In a move reminiscent of the absolutism of the previous century, the U.S. government ignores the wishes of the Wintu people of California. It bulldozes away buildings located at the Toyon-Wintu site in Wintu territory and removes the people living there.

 Descendants of the Nansemond Indians in Virginia receive state recognition as the Nansemond Indian Tribal Association.

 The Zuni people finally regain title to their ancient sacred site, Kolhu/wala:wa, or Zuni Heaven, where Zunis who have died are believed to reside. It takes another six years to obtain the right to cross private land to reach the land.

TRIBAL NAMES

 For centuries there has been a wide range in names assigned to Native groups and in the spellings and plurals of those names. Most tribal names come into English from Native languages or from French or Spanish.

In the Northeast, an Algonquian group living along the upper Hudson River has been variously called Agotsaganes, Hikanagi, Loups, Ourages, Pohegan, Uragees, Muhhekanew, Mehihammers, Morargans, Mahican, Mohican, Mohegan, and dozens of other names. Today's Mohegans consider themselves to be the descendants of that group, but they acknowledge that non-Indian scholars believe the Mohegans and Mahicans were once two separate peoples.

In the twentieth century many tribes have chosen to modify or standardize their names. The Nez Perce, Zuni, and Brule Sioux, for instance, have all dropped the diacritical markings from European languages which formerly made them known as the Nez Percé, Zuñi, and Brûlé. Similarly, the Sac and Fox people have dropped Sauk, a common alternate spelling of their name.

For many names, plurals in English may be formed with or without an "s." However, some names, like Iñupiat, never add a final "s."

1985

 Cherokee leader Ross Swimmer is appointed Assistant Secretary of the Interior for Indian Affairs. Wilma Mankiller replaces him as principal chief of the Cherokee Nation of Oklahoma, making her the first woman chief of a major tribe in more than a century.

The Texas Band of Traditional Kickapoos receives federal recognition as a tribe.

 In a victory for all tribes, the U.S. Supreme Court rules that the Navajo tribe has a right to impose business and property taxes without the permission of the Secretary of the Interior.

 The Upper Skagit people of western Washington begin manufacturing replicas of their ancestors' bentwood boxes as a way of improving the tribal economy.

1986

 After twenty-two years, the American Indian Historical Society dissolves. The University of California at Riverside establishes the Rupert Costo Chair in American Indian History, named for the society's long-time president, a full-blooded Cahuilla Indian.

 Ojibway novelist Louise Erdrich publishes *Beet Queen*.

 Blackfeet/Gros Ventre writer James Welch publishes *Fools Crow*, a historical novel about the efforts of Blackfeet Indians to cope with white settlers in the 1870s.

OJIBWA / CHIPPEWA

  Today there are twenty-five different tribes of Ojibwas (Ojibways), or Chippewas, as they are also called. They call themselves Anishinabe, which in the Algonquian language of the Ojibwa means "the People." They live in Michigan, Wisconsin, Minnesota, North Dakota, and Montana, with the largest landholdings in Minnesota, home to approximately 40,000 Ojibwas/Chippewas.

Each group works to maintain tribal traditions. These include the Midewiwin Society, the Big Drum Society, sweat lodges, and ancient stories. The Ojibwa language, once in danger of becoming extinct, is now spoken widely in some Ojibwa groups and being revived in others.

Western Ojibwas migrated to Montana sometime before contact with whites. More arrived in the 1800s, pushed westward by the upheavals farther east and the scarcity of game animals, due to the fur trade. There they were joined by Cree refugees from Canada, and after repeated intermarrying, a new amalgamated tribe emerged which is both Cree and Chippewa.

The North Dakota Chippewas migrated westward in the 1600s and suffered land loss and cultural disruption at the end of the 1800s. The U.S. government reduced the North Dakota Chippewas' already badly shrunken lands from twenty townships to two, then proceeded with the destructive allotment program, further dispossessing the people.

In Wisconsin, six Anishinabe bands number more than 16,000 people. After surviving the threat of removal to Indian Territory in the mid-1800s and the disruptions that followed, they are currently working to reclaim their lost language, arts, and cultural practices.

The Minnesota Ojibways have produced many writers, beginning with William Warren in the middle of the last century and continuing with such contemporary award-winning writers as Ignatia Broker and Maude Kegg, two tribal elders. Other talented Ojibway artists are Frank Big Bear, Robert Rose Bear, and Florian Fairbanks.

The Chippewas of Michigan have spent much of this century trying to recover from such disasters as loss of their land and enforced detribalization.

 "Now they want the vote. What next?"
—Montana rancher, in reference to Indian protests against being excluded from local government, 1986

The Cocopah Indians near Yuma, Arizona, receive an additional 615 acres of land, giving them 6,000 recognized acres.

The federal government reinstates the Klamath Tribe of southern Oregon, which suffered termination in the 1950s.

1987

In *California v. Cabazon Band of Mission Indians,* the U.S. Supreme Court opens the way for casino-style gambling on Indian reservations. The Cabazon Band uses gaming revenues to provide health and dental benefits, homes, jobs, and scholarships to tribal members.

1988

Congress passes the Indian Gaming Regulatory Act. It allows federally recognized tribes to negotiate with states regarding casino operations. Native Americans split on benefits of gaming. Proponents cite increased tribal revenues and increased job opportunities. Opponents warn of further deterioration of tribal values and of the danger of organized crime becoming involved.

In a blow to tribal traditions across the country, the U.S. Supreme Court rules in *Lyng v. Northwest Indian Cemetery Protective Association* that the Forest Service may desecrate sacred land in California by building roads across it, even if that prevents further practice of ancient rituals and beliefs.

The Tubatulabal people of California, under tribal chairman Ron Wermuth, vow to resurrect lost traditions. They establish a three-day Monache Gathering. The annual event includes traditional dances, singing, stories, and ceremonies.

 The Coquille Indians of Oregon resurrect their ancient salmon ceremony.

In factionalism that dates back a century and a half, the Snoqualmie Tribe of western Washington splits in two. The new band, the Snoqualmoo, petitions for federal recognition as a separate tribe.

1989

 After years of negotiations, the Onondaga Indians reclaim twelve traditional wampum belts from the state of New York. This restores the Onondagas to their centuries-old position as wampum keepers of the Iroquois Confederacy.

Akwesasne Mohawks in upstate New York lose a major source of revenue and employment overnight when the FBI raids Mohawk casinos on the grounds that they are operating illegally. The raid divides the community into pro- and antigambling factions, who skirmish violently for months.

 Omaha tribal historian Dennis Hastings and chairman Doran Morris succeed in gaining the return of the sacred *Umon'hon'ti*, the traditional emblem of the Omaha Tribe, from the Peabody Museum.

Northern and Southern Arapaho join to fight for preservation and accessibility of a traditional medicine wheel located in the Bighorn National Forest.

Rock Baby

The Kawaiisu people of California believe that petroglyphs, ancient images pecked into rocks, are not the work of earlier peoples, as non-Indians imagine, but of a malevolent supernatural being, Rock Baby. Rock Baby is said to live among the rocks and to create petroglyphs when the mood hits him. Anyone who sees Rock Baby, or touches or photographs a petroglyph, is asking to die.

Earthen Homes

 For centuries, the Indians of the Southwest used the soil around them as a component in their homes. Sometimes they wet the earth and made layers of mud, called puddled adobe. After the Spanish arrived, Indians began to make adobe bricks from the mud. Today adobe bricks remain the leading component of older homes in traditional Pueblo villages.

Kiowa artist Vanessa Paukeigope Morgan of Oklahoma receives a National Heritage Fellowship from the National Endowment for the Arts in honor of her talents in beadwork and other traditional Kiowa art forms.

 In March, the Exxon *Valdez* oil tanker runs aground near the Alutiiq (Aleut) village of Tatitlek. The oil ruins beaches near all Alutiiq settlements and destroys the sea life on which Alutiiqs depend for survival.

In *State of Alaska v. Native Village of Venetie*, a federal appeals court decrees that the rules regarding tribal status that apply in other states also apply to the villages of Alaska Natives.

 Colorado River Indian Tribes win a suit against the town of Parker regarding use of Indian-owned land within the city limits. The town is forbidden to impose building codes on tribal land, even those born off the reservation.

 Tribes across the country win a victory when the U.S. Supreme Court reaffirms in *Mississippi Indian Band v. Holyfield* that tribes, not states, have jurisdiction in determining who can adopt Indian children, even those born off the reservation.

 The Coquille Indian Tribe of western Oregon, six hundred strong, wins a thirty-five-year legal battle and regains its status as a tribe.

Twenty tribes participate in a "Paddle to Seattle" event celebrating and reenacting the oceangoing canoe voyages of their ancestors.

 Gary Kimble, a Gros Ventre Indian from Montana, becomes the first Native American director of the Association of American Indian Affairs in the organization's seventy-seven-year history.

 Centuries after the first contact between Monacan Indians and whites, the state of Virginia recognizes the Monacan Indian Association, which consists of descendants of the Monacans and other tribes.

1990

 The census places Native American population of the United States at just under 2 million. For the first time in five hundred years, the Native American population is beginning to approach its numbers before the arrival of Europeans. Slightly less than 40 percent of Native Americans still live on reservations.

States with the highest Indian populations are Oklahoma (252,000), California (236,000), Arizona (203,000), New Mexico (134,000), and North Carolina (80,000).

The most populous tribes are Cherokee (308,000), Navajo (219,000), Chippewa (104,000), Sioux (103,000), and Choctaw (82,000).

To date, the federal government has recognized 321 tribes outside Alaska and 210 Alaska Native governments.

The Native American Graves Protection and Repatriation Act requires museums to inventory all human remains, funeral objects, sacred artifacts, and cultural items. Objects of importance to tribes must be repatriated to them.

Native Americans learn how vulnerable their religious practices are when the U.S. Supreme Court decides, in *Employment Division v. Smith*, that Indian employees can legally be fired for using peyote during religious rituals.

Enemies

The Ahtna, an Athabaskan-speaking group in southern Alaska, still tell stories about raids made against them in the 1800s by their traditional enemies, the Chugach Alutiit.

According to Ahtna storytellers, the Chugach waited until Ahtna men went hunting in the mountains, then swarmed into Ahtna villages. The raiders departed with snowshoes, copper bracelets, wooden dishes, and Ahtna women.

Costanoan (Ohlone) Indians of California win a battle with Stanford University over ownership of skeletons of their ancestors, which the university holds as artifacts. The Costanoans rebury their ancestors on traditional Costanoan soil.

 Fifty-four years after the death of Colville novelist Mourning Dove (Christine Quintasket), her life story is published in *Mourning Dove: A Salishan Autobiography.*

 St. Regis Akwesasne Indians of upstate New York continue to fight about the role of gaming. The Warrior Society supports casinos; traditionalists oppose them.

1991

 The Omaha Indians of Nebraska regain possession of their Sacred White Buffalo Hide from the Museum of the American Indian. They also reclaim and rebury remains of their ancestors who once lived in the village of Ton'wontonga.

  After months of lobbying, members of the Native American Church and other Native Americans in Idaho convince state legislators to allow peyote to be transported legally on nonreservation lands.

 Alutiiq (Aleuts) rebury 756 skeletons of their ancestors which have been locked away in museums for more than half a century.

The Nipmuc Tribe of Massachusetts, 1,400 strong, formally reconstitutes itself as a tribe, in spite of its failure to receive federal recognition.

The Aroostook Micmac Tribe of Maine, formerly of Canada, receives recognition as a tribe.

 Leslie Marmon Silko, a Laguna novelist, publishes *Almanac of the Dead*. The epic novel looks at cultural conflicts between Indians and non-Indians.

1992

In the four years between 1988 and 1992, 60 percent of the Shoalwater people of western Washington have died, many as a result of inadequate health care.

The California Tribal Status Act creates a commission to make recommendations regarding federal acknowledgment of unrecognized tribes, including those that were subjected to genocide by white settlers in the last half of the 1800s. The commission consists of sixteen Native American members from acknowledged, unacknowledged, and terminated tribes, plus two nonvoting non-Indian members.

The Lower Brule Sioux Tribe buys ninety-one acres in central South Dakota near Interstate 90 to place in trust. State and local governments object, since Indian trust lands are not subject to state and local taxes and thus cost non-Indian taxpayers money by causing taxes on non-Indian land to rise. The governor of South Dakota warns that Indians plan to buy up all of western

Basketmaking

 For thousands of years, in areas as diverse as the Great Plains, the Great Basin, the Plateau, the Southeast, and the Northwest Coast, Native Americans have used grasses, reeds, and other natural materials to weave baskets. The oldest method of creating baskets was to twine a soft material such as grass around a firmer material, like twigs. Before the introduction of pottery, watertight baskets were used in cooking. Today the millennia-old basketmaking tradition is still strong among the Shoshone, Ute, Paiute, Tohono O'odham, and Hopi peoples, among others.

Beadwork

 For thousands of years, Native groups in many parts of the continent created beads from stones, shells, horn, bones, clay, copper, and other materials. When Europeans arrived, Native craftspeople began using the newcomers' manufactured glass beads. Today thousands of bead artists pursue this ancient craft, using both traditional and contemporary materials and designs.

MOTHER EARTH, FATHER SKY

 In the 1990s non-Indian scholars have become agitated about the question of exactly what role Mother Earth and Father Sky played in the worldview of the Native peoples of North America before the arrival of Europeans. These scholars worry that non-Indians have erroneously assumed that Native Americans considered the earth a goddess.

With so many diverse cultural and linguistic groups sharing the continent for millennia, there was, in all probability, a wide range in the ways in which people viewed the earth. For some Native peoples, the idea of the earth as the mother of human beings was probably no more than a convenient metaphor. For others, the concept may not have existed at all. Probably few peoples, if any, worshiped the earth as a literal goddess in the European understanding of that word. The worldviews of the Native peoples were so different from those of the invading Europeans that no matter how carefully one might try to reconstruct ancient beliefs, nuances cannot be known with certainty.

South Dakota. A lengthy lawsuit that could affect Indian trust lands across the United States begins.

 The Mohegan Indians of Connecticut revive their annual wigwam festival and rename it the Wigwam Powwow. Activities include building a traditional brush arbor and serving traditional foods.

Women among the Shinnecock Indians of New York receive the right to vote on matters relating to tribal business but are still not allowed to vote in the election of tribal trustees.

 Five hundred years after Europeans invaded the Americas, more than one hundred Indian groups wait for federal recognition as Indian tribes. These include the Chicora-Waccamaw people of South Carolina, the Lumbees of North Carolina, and the Piscataway Conoy Confederacy of Maryland.

1993

The Indian Treaty Room, on the fourth floor of the Executive Office Building next door to the White House, becomes a symbol for the misappropriation of the name Indian when it is discovered that no Indian treaties were ever signed there.

Across the United States, there are now 1,000 Native Americans holding law degrees, up from 25 in 1967. Many are graduates of the American Indian Law Center's Pre-Law Summer Institute.

After decades of promoting traditional Miami culture and values, Frances Shoemaker, principal chief of the Indiana Miami Tribe for the past forty-four years, retires and becomes chief of the Elders Council.

> "The Indian heads on bridges, the devoid-of-substance Indian Treaty Room in the White House complex—they are indicative of a Manifest Destiny mentality where you can just slap the name 'Indian' on anything to adorn or to enhance or to romanticize. And somehow that takes you off the hook about doing anything that would even acknowledge actual living Indians."
> —Suzan Harjo, president of Morning Star Foundation, dedicated to promoting Indian cultural rights, 1995

Ada Deer, Menominee activist and former tribal chairperson, becomes Assistant Secretary for Indian Affairs in the Department of the Interior.

Nineteen canoes of Quileute Indians resurrect the traditions of their ancestors and paddle from the west coast of Washington State all the way up to the 'Qátamas festival among the Heiltsuk people of British Columbia.

Janet Campbell Hale, of Coeur d'Alene and Kootenai heritage, publishes the memoir *Bloodlines*, to critical acclaim.

> **"The white people's historians are wrong. The Spanish didn't give the Navajos horses and sheep. The Navajos have always had horses and sheep."**
> —Navajo medicine woman at a puberty ceremony, 1993

The Catawba Nation of South Carolina regains tribal status thirty-four years after losing it under the federal termination policy.

1994

Mescalero Apache leaders agree to allow construction of a nuclear waste storage facility on Apache land. Traditionalists protest that this is a desecration.

After more than three centuries of unhappy interactions with whites, the Mohegans of Connecticut receive federal recognition as a tribe.

1995

Jane Mt. Pleasant, an Iroquois Indian trained in agronomy at Cornell, introduces ancient techniques of Native American agronomy to non-Indian farmers. Like her ancestors, she advocates planting corn, beans, and squash together. The cornstalks serve as beanpoles. The squash leaves discourage weeds. Bacteria growing among the bean roots transform atmospheric nitrogen into natural fertilizer.

> **"If a tribe never declared war on the United States, and if a tribe never had anything the United States wanted, then the United States just ignored them."**
> **—Arlinda Locklear, attorney, regarding the plight of unrecognized tribes, including her own people, the Lumbee of North Carolina, 1995**

The Nottawaseppi Band of Huron Potawatomi in Michigan gains federal recognition as a tribe after a sixty-one-year struggle. Two hundred people are registered as members of the tribe.

Ojibway writer David Treuer publishes *Little*, a moving and widely acclaimed first novel about an Indian town called Poverty and the people who live there.

A federal appeals court rules that the practice of tribes buying land outside the reservation and placing it in trust is illegal. The decision puts the status of thousands of acres of Indian trust land around the U.S. in question.

After more than a century of disputes with their Navajo neighbors, Hopis agree to allow 2,000 Navajos to remain on land previously claimed by Hopis.

THE GREAT SPIRIT SPEAKS

 "The earth is getting old, and I will make it new for my chosen people, the Indians, who are to inhabit it, and among them will be all those of their ancestors who have died, their fathers, mothers, brothers, cousins, and wives—all those who hear my voice and my words through the tongues of my children.

"I will cover the earth with new soil to a depth of five times the height of a man, and under this new soil will be buried all the whites, and all the holes and the rotten places will be filled up. The new lands will be covered with sweet-grass and running water and trees, and herds of buffalo and ponies will stray over it, that my red children may eat and drink, hunt and rejoice. And the sea to the west I will fill up so that no ships may pass over it, and the other seas will I make impassable."

—Kicking Bear, Sioux leader of the Ghost Dance religion, reporting the words of the Great Spirit, 1890

Bitterness between the two tribes continues. Each family will be permitted a three-acre homesite and ten acres for grazing.

 "Much of what we are collectively facing as a tribal people stems from opening up our sacred ceremonies to include non-Indians."

—Statement by Zuni tribal council, on banning non-Indian spectators at religious ceremonies, December 1995

At the request of religious leaders at Zuni Pueblo, the Zuni tribal council bars all non-Indians from sacred ceremonies for a trial period of one year. Previously, thousands of visitors have traveled to Zuni each year to see Shalako and other ceremonies. The council cites rudeness and disruptiveness of outsiders and failure to honor tribal prohibition against photography. The ruling causes dissension among Zunis; opponents label Zuni a theocracy and a dictatorship and call for separation of church and state.

 Sioux and other Native groups argue that using the name of famous Sioux leader Crazy Horse on alcoholic beverages is offensive. The state of Minnesota agrees and bans the sale of Crazy Horse malt liquor. Brewing companies appeal.

1996

 Pueblo Indians and other opponents succeed in stopping the New Mexico Department of Game and Fish from allowing hunters to thin the state herd of sixty buffalo.

 Southern Utes tussle with state and county officials over the question of whether land they buy is subject to state and local taxes.

 Crow Indians vow to fight a federal appeals court decision that rights granted in the 1868 Fort Laramie Treaty are no longer valid. At issue: whether Crows can hunt in uninhabited federal lands off the reservation, as granted by the treaty.

1997

 A federal judge rules Native Americans may file a class-action suit against the Interior Department regarding mismanagement of $450 million in 300,000 Indian trust accounts.

"ALONE IN MY TEPEE"

 "Alone in my tepee, I dreamed and saw visions, and communed with the spirits. And I went forth and taught the people and told them of the Father's word and of the help that should come to the Indians. . . . In this world the Great Father has given to the white man everything and to the Indian nothing. But it will not always be thus. In another world the Indian shall be as the white man and the white man as the Indian. To the Indian will be given wisdom and power, and the white man shall be helpless and unknowing with only the bow and arrow."
—Short Bull, Dakota Sioux, speaks of the future, about 1900

2000 *and Beyond*

Medicine people among the San Carlos Apaches predict that the Anasazi Indians will return from their home in the Big Dipper and create a renaissance of Native American beliefs and life.

According to ancient legends among the Okanogan Indians of Washington, the lakes and rivers of the world will bring about the end of earth as we know it. The lakes will dissolve the foundations of the earth, and the rivers will set it free. Then it will float away.

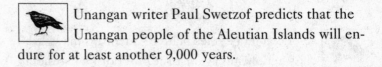

"I will take from the white man the secret of making gunpowder."
—Kicking Bear, Sioux visionary, reporting the words of the Great Spirit, 1890

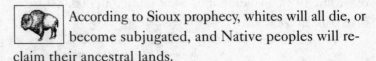

Unangan writer Paul Swetzof predicts that the Unangan people of the Aleutian Islands will endure for at least another 9,000 years.

According to Sioux prophecy, whites will all die, or become subjugated, and Native peoples will reclaim their ancestral lands.

ACKNOWLEDGMENTS

———◆———

Without the fine scholarship and hard work of hundreds of other scholars and writers, a book like this could not be born. I am grateful for the careful and thoughtful scholarship of the many Indian and non-Indian writers, anthologizers, and editors whose works I consulted in preparing to write this book. I would especially like to acknowledge the fine work of the following: Paula Gunn Allen, Margot Astrov, Stephen Cornell, Natalie Curtis and her informants, Mary B. Davis and the writers under her direction, Vine Deloria, Jr., Frederick J. Dockstader, Stuart J. Fiedel, Frederick Webb Hodge, Alvin M. Josephy, Jr., N. Scott Momaday, Peter Nabokov, Alfonso Ortiz, Francis Paul Prucha, Joe Sando, Leslie Marmon Silko, Edward Spicer, William Sturtevant and the writers under his direction, Robert M. Utley, W. C. Vanderwerth, David Weber, and Paul Zolbrod.

Thanks, too, to librarians Eleanore Voutselas and Laura Holt for their patience and help with the research.

In addition, I would like to offer special thanks to the following Native Americans who have made important personal contributions to my thinking and my life: Mary Yazzie Sampson, Anita and Joseph Suazo, Larry Yazzie, Ruth Roessel, Monty Roessel, Stella Tucker, Edith Franklin, Harold Kenton, and Evelyn Martine.

Finally, deepest thanks to Irene Prokop, now editor-in-chief at Jeremy P. Tarcher, for offering me the opportunity to write this book, and to Sheila M. Curry, my editor at Perigee, for her encouragement, support, and fine editing. Special thanks to Schia Muterperl for his wise input into my life. And warmest thanks to Henry R. Mandel for his constant interest, support, and nurturing.

RECOMMENDED READING

―――――◆―――――

The following list offers a brief sampling of authors and points of view. It is designed to help readers begin to travel deeper into the many-layered past.

To obtain the full list of references consulted by the author in preparing *Timelines of Native American History*, write to PO Box 8400, Santa Fe, NM 87504-8400. Enclose a self-addressed 9″-x-12″ manila envelope stamped with $3.00 postage, plus $2.00 to cover copying costs.

To learn more about the ways in which contemporary events are linked with the near and distant past, read the independent, Indian-owned weekly newspaper *Indian Country Today*, published by Native American Publishing, 1920 Lombardy Drive, Rapid City, SD 57701. (http://www.indiancountry.com)

Allen, Paula Gunn. *Grandmothers of the Light: A Medicine Woman's Sourcebook*. Boston: Beacon, 1991.

―――. *The Sacred Hoop: Recovering the Feminine in American Indian Traditions*. Boston: Beacon, 1992.

―――, ed. *Song of the Turtle: American Indian Literature, 1974–1994*. New York: Ballantine, 1996.

―――. *Spider Woman's Granddaughters: Traditional Tales and Contemporary Writing by Native American Women*. Boston: Beacon, 1989.

―――. *Voice of the Turtle: American Indian Literature, 1900–1970*. New York: Ballantine, 1994.

Ambler, Marjane. *Breaking the Iron Bonds: Indian Control of Energy Development.* Lawrence: University of Kansas Press, 1990.

Andrist, Ralph K. *The Long Death: The Last Days of the Plains Indian.* New York: Collier, 1993.

Berger, Thomas R. *A Long and Terrible Shadow: White Values, Native Rights in the Americas: 1492–1992.* Seattle: University of Washington Press, 1992.

Black Elk, Wallace, and William S. Lyon. *Black Elk: The Sacred Ways of a Lakota.* San Francisco: HarperCollins, 1991.

Boyer, Ruth McDonald, and Narcissus Duffy Gayton. *Apache Mothers and Daughters: Four Generations of a Family.* Norman: University of Oklahoma Press, 1992.

Brown, Dee Alexander. *Bury My Heart at Wounded Knee: An Indian History of the American West,* reprint edition. New York: Henry Holt, 1991.

Brown, Joseph Epes. *The North American Indians: A Selection of Photographs by Edward S. Curtis.* New York: Aperture, 1972.

Bruchac, Joseph. *The Native American Sweat Lodge: History and Legends.* Freedom, California: Crossing Press, 1993.

Brugge, David M. *The Navajo-Hopi Land Dispute: An American Tragedy.* Albuquerque: University of New Mexico Press, 1994.

Buchanan, Kimberly Moore. *Apache Women Warriors.* El Paso: Texas Western Press, 1986.

Canfield, Gae Whitney. *Sarah Winnemucca of the Northern Paiutes.* Norman: University of Oklahoma Press, 1983.

Clifton, James A., ed. *The Invented Indian: Cultural Fictions and Government Policies.* New Brunswick, NJ: Transaction, 1990.

Cohen, Felix S. *Handbook of Federal Indian Law,* 1982 edition. Charlottesville, Virginia: Michie Company, 1982.

Copway, George. *Indian Life and Indian History,* reprint edition. New York: AMS Press, 1976.

Cornell, Stephen. *The Return of the Native: American Indian Political Resurgence.* New York and Oxford: Oxford University Press, 1988.

Crow Dog, Leonard, and Richard Erdoes. *Crow Dog: Four Generations of Sioux Medicine Men.* New York: HarperCollins, 1995.

Davis, Mary B., ed. *Native America in the Twentieth Century: An Encyclopedia.* New York: Garland, 1994.

Debo, Angie. *The Rise and Fall of the Choctaw Republic.* Norman: University of Oklahoma Press, 1961.

DeJong, David H. *Promises of the Past: A History of Indian Education in the United States.* Golden: North American Press, 1993.

Deloria, Philip J., et al. *The Native Americans: An Illustrated History.* Atlanta: Turner Publishing, 1993.

Deloria, Vine, Jr. *Behind the Trail of Broken Treaties: An Indian Declaration of Independence.* Austin: University of Texas Press, 1985.

———. *Custer Died for Your Sins.* Norman: University of Oklahoma Press, 1988.

———. *God Is Red: A Native View of Religion,* 2nd edition. Golden, Colorado: Fulcrum Press, 1992.

———. *Indians of the Pacific Northwest: From the Coming of the White Man to the Present Day.* New York: Doubleday, 1977.

———. *Red Earth, White Lies: Native Americans and the Myth of Scientific Fact.* New York: Scribner, 1995.

———. *We Talk, You Listen: New Tribes, New Turf.* New York: Macmillan, 1970.

Deloria, Vine, Jr., and Clifford M. Lytle. *American Indians, American Justice.* Austin: University of Texas Press, 1983.

———. *The Nations Within: The Past and Future of American Indian Sovereignty.* New York: Pantheon, 1984.

Dockstader, Frederick. *Indian Art in America: The Arts and Crafts of the North American Indian.* Greenwich, Conn.: New York Graphic Society, 1961.

Dowd, Gregory Evans. *A Spirited Resistance: The North American Indian Struggle for Unity 1745–1815.* Baltimore: Johns Hopkins University Press, 1992.

Eastman, Charles Alexander. *Indian Boyhood,* reprint edition. Lincoln: University of Nebraska Press, 1991.

Ehle, John. *Trail of Tears: The Rise and Fall of the Cherokee Nation.* New York: Doubleday, 1988.

Erdoes, Richard, and Alfonso Ortiz. *American Indian Myths and Legends.* New York: Pantheon, 1984.

Fiedel, Stuart J. *Prehistory of the Americas.* Cambridge: Cambridge University Press, 1987.

Folsom, Franklin. *Indian Uprising on the Rio Grande: The Pueblo Revolt of 1680.* Albuquerque: University of New Mexico Press, 1996.

Folsom, Franklin, and Mary Elting Folsom. *America's Ancient Treasures: A Guide to Archeological Sites and Museums in the United States and Canada,* 4th edition. Albuquerque: University of New Mexico, 1993.

Foster, Morris W. *Being Comanche: A Social History of an American Indian Community.* Tucson: University of Arizona Press, 1991.

Francis, Lee. *Native Time: A Historical Time Line of Native America.* New York: St. Martin's, 1996.

Gill, Sam D., and Irene F. Sullivan. *Dictionary of Native American Mythology.* New York: Oxford University Press, 1992.

Hampton, Bruce. *Children of Grace: The Nez Perce War of 1877.* New York: Henry Holt, 1994.

Hathaway, Nancy. *Native American Portraits: 1862–1918.* San Francisco: Chronicle, 1990.

Hauptman, Laurence M. *Tribes and Tribulations: Misconceptions about American Indians and Their Histories.* Albuquerque: University of New Mexico Press, 1995.

Heizer, Robert F., ed. *The Destruction of California Indians: A Collection of Documents from the Period 1847 to 1865 in which Are Described Some of the Things that Happened to Some of the Indians of California.* Salt Lake: Peregrine Smith, 1974.

Hirschfelder, Arlene, and Paulette Molin. *The Encyclopedia of Native American Religions.* New York: Facts on File, 1992.

Jackson, Donald, ed. *Black Hawk: An Autobiography.* Urbana: University of Illinois Press, 1964.

Johansen, Bruce E. *Life and Death in Mohawk Country.* Golden, Colorado: North American Press, 1993.

Josephy, Alvin M., Jr., ed. *America in 1492: The World of the Indian Peoples Before the Arrival of Columbus.* New York: Vintage, 1991.

Josephy, Alvin M., Jr. *The Patriot Chiefs: A Chronicle of American Indian Resistance.* New York: Penguin, 1977.

Klein, Laura F., and Lillian A. Ackerman. *Women and Power in Native North America.* Norman: University of Oklahoma Press, 1995.

Kroeber, Theodora. *Ishi in Two Worlds: A Biography of the Last Wild Indian in North America.* Berkeley: University of California Press, 1969.

Krupat, Arnold, ed. *Native American Autobiography: An Anthology.* Madison: University of Wisconsin Press, 1994.

Linderman, Frank. *Plenty Coups, Chief of the Crows.* Lincoln: University of Nebraska Press, 1962.

Lippard, Lucy R., ed. *Partial Recall: With Essays on Photographs of Native North Americans.* New York: The New Press, 1992.

Lurie, Nancy Oestreich, ed. *Mountain Wolf Woman, Sister of Crashing Thunder: The Autobiography of a Winnebago Indian.* Ann Arbor: University of Michigan Press, 1966.

Mankiller, Wilma Pearl, and Michael Wallis. *Mankiller: A Chief and Her People.* New York: St. Martin's, 1993.

Marquis, Thomas B. *Wooden Leg: A Warrior Who Fought Custer.* Lincoln: University of Nebraska, 1931.

Matthiessen, Peter. *In the Spirit of Crazy Horse: The Story of Leonard Peltier and the FBI's War on the American Indian Movement.* New York: Penguin, 1992.

McNitt, Frank. *Navajo Wars: Military Campaigns, Slave Raids, and Reprisals.* Albuquerque: University of New Mexico Press, 1990.

McWhorter, Lucullus V., ed. *Yellow Wolf: His Own Story.* Caldwell, Idaho: Caxton, 1984.

Miller, Lee, ed. *From the Heart: Voices of the American Indian.* New York: Random House, 1995.

Momaday, N. Scott. *The Names,* reprint edition. Tucson: University of Arizona Press, 1987.

Mooney, James. *The Ghost Dance Religion and the Sioux Outbreak of 1890,* reprint of 1896 edition. Lincoln: University of Nebraska Press, 1991.

Moses, L.G., and Raymond Wilson, eds. *Indian Lives: Essays on Nineteenth and Twentieth Century Native American Leaders.* Albuquerque: University of New Mexico Press, 1993.

Mourning Dove. *Mourning Dove: A Salishan Autobiography,* edited by Jay Miller. Lincoln: University of Nebraska Press, 1990.

Nabokov, Peter., ed. *Native American Testimony: A Chronicle of Indian-White Relations from Prophecy to the Present, 1492–1992.* New York: Viking, 1991.

———. *Two Leggings: The Making of a Crow Warrior.* New York: Thomas Crowell, 1967.

Nabokov, Peter, and Robert Easton. *Native American Architecture.* New York: Oxford University Press, 1989.

Native American Directory. San Carlos, Arizona: National Native American Cooperative, 1996.

Neeley, Bill. *Last Comanche Chief: The Life and Times of Quanah Parker.* New York: Wiley, 1996.

Neihardt, John G. *Black Elk Speaks: Being the Life Story of a Holy Man of the Oglala Sioux,* reprint of 1932 edition. Lincoln: University of Nebraska Press, 1979.

Nerburn, Kent, ed. *The Soul of an Indian and Other Writings from Ohiyesa (Charles Alexander Eastman).* San Rafael, California: New World Library, 1993.

Norman, Howard, ed. *Northern Tales: Traditional Stories of Eskimo and Indian Peoples.* New York: Pantheon, 1990.

Ortiz, Alfonso. *The Tewa World: Space, Time, Being, and Becoming in a Pueblo Society.* Chicago: University of Chicago Press, 1969.

Paterek, Josephine. *Encyclopedia of American Indian Costume.* New York: Norton, 1994.

Peterson, Scott. *Native American Prophecies.* New York: Paragon, 1990.

Prucha, Francis Paul. *The Great Father: The United States Government and the American Indians,* 2 vols. Lincoln: University of Nebraska Press, 1984.

Quam, Alvina, trans. *The Zunis: Self-Portrayals by the Zuni People.* Albuquerque: University of New Mexico Press, 1972.

Reddy, Marlita A., ed. *Statistical Record of Native North Americans.* Detroit: Gale Research, 1993.

Roessel, Robert A., Jr. *Dinétah: Navajo History*, v. 2. Rough Rock, Navajo Nation, Arizona: Navajo Curriculum Center, 1983.

Roessel, Ruth. *Women in Navajo Society*. Rough Rock, Navajo Nation, Arizona: Navajo Resource Center, 1981.

Sams, Jamie. *The Thirteen Original Clan Mothers*. San Francisco: HarperCollins, 1993.

Sando, Joe S. *Nee Hemish: A History of Jemez Pueblo*. Albuquerque: University of New Mexico Press, 1982.

———. *Pueblo Nations: Eight Centuries of Pueblo Indian History*. Santa Fe: Clear Light, 1992.

Silko, Leslie Marmon. *Yellow Woman and a Beauty of the Spirit: Essays on Native American Life Today*. New York: Simon and Schuster, 1996.

Simmons, Leo W., ed. *Sun Chief: The Autobiography of a Hopi Indian*. New Haven and London: Yale University Press, 1942.

Standing Bear, Luther. *Land of the Spotted Eagle*. Lincoln: University of Nebraska Press, 1978.

Stands In Timber, John, and Margot Liberty. *Cheyenne Memories*. New Haven: Yale University Press, 1967.

Steiner, Stan. *The New Indians*. New York: Harper, 1970.

Stewart, Hilary. *Stone, Bone, Antler, and Shell: Artifacts of the Northwest Coast*, 2nd edition. Seattle: University of Washington Press, 1996.

Sturtevant, William C., series ed. *Handbook of Native American Indians*, 10 volumes to date. Washington, D.C.: Smithsonian Institution, various dates.

Suzuki, David, and Peter Knudtson. *Wisdom of the Elders: Sacred Native Stories of Nature*. New York: Bantam, 1993.

Turner, Frederick W., III, ed. *Geronimo, His Own Story: The Autobiography of a Great Patriot Warrior, As Told to S.M. Barrett*. New York: Penguin, 1996.

Utley, Robert M., and Wilcomb E. Washburn. *The American Heritage History of the Indian Wars*. Boston: Houghton Mifflin, 1987.

Vanderwerth, W.C., comp. *Indian Oratory: Famous Speeches by Noted Indian Chieftains*. Norman: University of Oklahoma Press, 1971.

Vizenor, Gerald Robert. *The People Named the Chippewa: Narrative Histories*. Minneapolis: University of Minnesota Press, 1984.

Walker, James R. *Lakota Belief and Ritual*, edited by Raymond J. DeMallie and Elaine A. Jahner. Lincoln: University of Nebraska Press, 1991.

Welch, James, with Paul Stekler. *Killing Custer: The Battle of the Little Bighorn and the Fate of the Plains Indians*. New York: Norton, 1994.

Williamson, Ray A., and Claire R. Farrer, eds. *Earth and Sky: Visions of the Cosmos in Native American Folklore*. Albuquerque: University of New Mexico Press, 1992.

Willis, Velma. *Two Old Women: An Alaska Legend of Betrayal, Courage, and Survival*. New York: HarperCollins, 1994.

Yava, Albert. *Big Falling Snow: A Tewa-Hopi's Life and Times and the History and Traditions of His People*, edited by Harold Courlander. New York: Crown, 1978.

Yazzie, Ethelou, ed. *Navajo History*, v. 1. Many Farms, Navajo Nation, Arizona: Navajo Community College Press, 1971.

Young Bear, Severt, and R.D. Thiesz. *Standing in the Light: A Lakota Way of Seeing*. Lincoln: University of Nebraska Press, 1994.

Young, M. Jane. *Signs from the Ancestors: Zuni Cultural Symbolism and Perceptions of Rock Art*. Albuquerque: University of New Mexico Press, 1988.

Zolbrod, Paul G. *Diné Bahane': The Navajo Creation Story*. Albuquerque: University of New Mexico Press, 1984.

INDEX

———— ◈ ————